High Yella

High Yella

A Modern Family Memoir

STEVE MAJORS

The University of Georgia Press
Athens

Published by the University of Georgia Press
Athens, Georgia 30602
www.ugapress.org
© 2021 by Steve Majors
All rights reserved
Designed by Rebecca A. Norton
Set in 10.5/14 Adobe Jenson Pro
Printed and bound by Sheridan Books, Inc.
The paper in this book meets the guidelines for
permanence and durability of the Committee on
Production Guidelines for Book Longevity of the
Council on Library Resources.

Most University of Georgia Press titles are
available from popular e-book vendors.

Printed in the United States of America
25 24 23 22 21 C 5 4 3 2 1

Library of Congress Cataloging-in-Publication Data
Names: Majors, Stephen, 1966– author.
Title: High yella : a modern family memoir / Steve Majors.
Description: Athens, Georgia : The University of Georgia Press, [2021] |
Series: Crux: the Georgia series in literary nonfiction
Identifiers: LCCN 2021013965 | ISBN 9780820360317 (hardback ; alk. paper) |
ISBN 9780820360324 (ebook)
Subjects: LCSH: Majors, Stephen, 1966– | African American gay
men—Biography. | African American families—Biography. | African
Americans—Social conditions. | African Americans—Race identity. |
African Americans—Color. | Gays—Identity. | Gay parents—United
States—Biography.
Classification: LCC E185.97.M225 A3 2021 | DDC 306.76/6208996073—dc23
LC record available at https://lccn.loc.gov/2021013965

To Todd and our daughters,
   Thank you for being my forever family.

Contents

High Yella

CHAPTER I

The Music Man

In 1971 Pops took me for a drive in his beat-up Ford station wagon. We were at the head of a long line of cars on Main Street, and it felt like I was riding in a parade. As we sailed through the yellow light, I could hear horns give out polite toots, annoyed honks, and a few blind-rage blares. Pops loved the attention, but for all the wrong reasons.

"Goddamn palefaces," he laughed.

I kneeled on the bench seat in the front of the car to peek in the rearview mirror. Behind us, I could just make out the rusted muffler that had dropped off our car a half block away. It sat there like a turd in the heart of our small town of Batavia, New York. Pops might have been too crocked to notice, or he could have just looked back and re-minded himself, as he often told us kids, *he didn't give a damn what whitey thought.*

Pops had also told me that whitey couldn't be trusted. I glanced over at his brown face glistening with sweat and then back at my own pale reflection in the mirror. Was I a whitey?

I let the strange thought go when I felt my bare knees scorching on the sunbaked plastic upholstery. I plopped back down on my butt and scrambled over to the passenger window to hang my head out and catch a breeze. Before I leaned against it, I made sure the creaky door was latched shut. Even at five years old, I knew Pops might take a wild turn that could fling me out onto the street. He might leave me behind like the muffler.

The whoosh of the wind felt good on my face and brought some relief from the sweet stink of the exhaust that now came from the back of the station wagon. Hanging half out the window, I could also see the sights. We only visited town when we had money to spend, overdue bills to pay, or trouble to resolve with the police. On this day, Pops was headed to the liquor store. I was excited. A trip to the liquor store meant I'd get free candy from the owner. But I also knew that he might look at my face and crack a joke: "What, you the mailman's kid?"

As Pops guided our station wagon down Main Street, I looked out at Batavia. There were big two-story department stores, old brick banks, and a single-screen movie theater. To us, living out in the country, "town" seemed like a big place. Later as an adult, I'd realize that Batavia was just a small ugly dot on the map exactly halfway between Buffalo and Rochester. It was built around cornfields, dairy farms, and a few factories. Bought (or stolen) by Dutch investors from Native Americans, it was settled by the English and then populated in waves by Irish, Italian, and Polish immigrants who had come looking for work.

But back then, the people in town all appeared the same to my five-year-old eyes. They just looked white.

I looked at the places where my Black family was familiar to those white folks, if maybe not always welcome. There were the dry cleaners where, when he was sober, Pops had a job working for the white owner. It sat a three-minute walk from the jail where he landed when he was two sheets to the wind. Both were in direct sight of the department store where Ma and Grandma were sometimes allowed to buy a few things on credit. Grandma was trusted there because for years she had cleaned the owners' big homes, scrubbing their floors on her hands and knees. And then there were the elm-, maple-, and birch-shaded neighborhoods that sprouted off in both directions from Main Street. I knew that's where the white people lived—families with Italian and Polish names that I couldn't pronounce.

Maybe one or two Black families lived somewhere in those tree-lined middle-class neighborhoods. The rest, a few hundred, could only afford to buy older, cheaper homes or rent neglected apartments on the south side of town. My family was even more isolated, way out in the country among the cornfields.

"Boy, hand me the rest of my grape juice," Pops bellowed over the now unmuffled engine.

I reached onto the trash-strewn floor, where a small bottle sat in a wrinkled paper bag, and handed it over. Pops expertly grabbed it with one hand, slid it between his bony thighs, unscrewed the top, and emptied what was left in it. He smacked his lips at me, and I laughed.

I wasn't completely afraid of Pops at times like these. He was fun and silly. I knew all it took to keep him in a good mood was just a little of his grape juice. Earlier that summer, he was liquored up just a little when he loaded my three older brothers, my sister, and me into the car and drove for miles in search of illegal fireworks. After he found them and brought the stash home, he set them off in our backyard, eliciting quick popping noises. Pops said the white people down the road only called the police on him because he was Black, even though Ma tried to explain it was because the fireworks sounded like gunshots. You couldn't blame the neighbors. The Fourth of July was still weeks away, and he'd set them off at midnight.

A few weeks later, he pitched tents for all us kids in the backyard, then built a huge bonfire. Pops danced around it wildly without his shirt, until the fire got out of control and threatened a farmer's hayfield. That time the neighbors called the county fire department.

While Pops railed against the white man for always killing his dreams, there was one area where he thought they had no power over him. That was his music. Pops had a used electric guitar and a few dented amps that he hauled around town for drunken, out-of-tune jam sessions with his regular drinking buddies. He said that one day he might be as big as James Brown, and he hoped us kids could learn to be his backup band.

In pursuit of that dream one summer, he temporarily put aside his resentments against the white man and signed up my older siblings for a free youth band in town. All the rest of the kids there were white, but Pops said we just had to beat the white man at his game—whatever that meant. He'd show up during rehearsals and try to jam along. During competitions, he gave pointers from the sidelines. But his greatest performance was during a gathering of the entire group and their parents one muggy Saturday night for a band cookout.

That's when he grabbed the fuzzy hat off the drum major, stuck it on his head and tried to lead a sing-along by plucking the strings on his unplugged guitar. Soon he was leading a mini-parade around the picnic tables, the white kids and their parents clapping, laughing, and following along. We looked on in disbelief. Pops had once again used his slick talk, mediocre guitar playing, and false-teeth grin to trick these white people into thinking he was harmless. It didn't take long for him to knock a kid's trombone to the ground and accidentally stumble into the campfire. As the parents slowly headed to their freshly washed station wagons and drove away, we were left behind, struggling to help Pops to the car so he could drunkenly drive us home. There, we knew, he would drink a little more grape juice, get his second wind, and be ready for his next act.

As we passed into the south side of town, Pops careened over the railroad tracks. I looked behind, wondering if we'd left behind another part of the car, but Pops looked straight ahead as he pulled up to a rotting rooming house. I recognized it as the place where Pops's family lived, alongside some of the other families who looked like mine.

"Gotta take a quick piss," Pops announced.

My stomach tightened. I feared these visits to his family. Normally, if Ma was here, I'd stick to her side or try to hold on tight to one of my brothers' belt loops. Today I was on my own. I worried Pops might forget me and leave me behind.

"Open the goddamn door. I'm thirsty," Pops yelled as we neared the top of the stairs of the rooming house.

His father, a shriveled dark-skinned man we called Grandpappy, met us at the door. Behind him, slumped on raggedy furniture, were the rest of the Majors clan—Pops's brother Clarence and his two sisters.

As we walked in, I shrank into a nearby corner. The dim room smelled like fresh pee and old throw-up.

"What this bright yellow boy scairt of?" Grandpappy asked. Purple gums showed through his rubbery lips because he'd taken out his dentures again.

"I said, what you 'fraid of, boy?"

He looked at me and laughed until he began to cough up brown phlegm into a dirty handkerchief. Then he looked around for his bottle of booze to clear his throat. I could see it had fallen off a table and rolled underneath. When I pointed it out, Grandpappy got down on his ancient knees to retrieve it and let out a string of curses. The bottle was empty. He'd apparently taken the last swig and been too drunk to notice. As he lay half under the table to mourn his lost liquor, his grown kids staggered to their own feet to watch him. Like half-crocked blackbirds they crowed with laughter.

"Get your tired ole ass off the floor," one of my aunties yelled.

Grandpappy dragged himself up. It seemed to take forever, but once up, he moved like a cat. Before anyone could run for cover, he stretched back a wrinkled arm and hurled the empty bottle toward us. It missed. I had learned what to expect next. Fists and furniture were about to fly, like they often did at home, but here I couldn't tell the difference between the good guys and the bad guys. Pops pushed me behind the couch. I closed my eyes and prayed God would keep him safe. If he did, I thought I could at least depend on Pops to take me home to Ma.

I listened to the sound of crashes and cusses moving from one side of the room to the next. I squirmed around and pressed my face to the wall, hoping to stay out of harm's way, but even here I could feel the ratty couch bucking and sliding against my back when the fight moved closer to me. It seemed at any time the breath might be squeezed out of me. Finally the wild wrestling stopped. After a few minutes I opened my eyes and came out from my hiding place. Grandpappy and his kids lay sprawled across the floor or slumped back in their chairs. I didn't know if they were knocked out or just passed out. Pops was still standing, and I felt relieved. He grabbed me by the hand and yanked me along. As he slammed out the door, I heard him mutter, "Stupid cocksuckers." I knew God wouldn't like it, but in my head I agreed with him.

Years later I'd realize they weren't stupid. Just ignorant. A long line of trauma had passed through their blood. I couldn't trace it back to the original wound, but I could guess. They'd been trapped in this small town for at least forty years. Generations of poor education, a lack of jobs and housing discrimination kept them in this poor neighborhood, where their wounds just festered and their sins multiplied.

As Pops and I climbed back into the station wagon, I thought about our big adventure. I'd have a lot to tell Ma when we got home. What I wouldn't be able to explain is how I felt about Pops in that moment. There was hate for what he'd put me through and some fear, because I saw what he was capable of doing, but I also felt grateful. For once he'd looked out for me. I looked up at Pops and realized he wasn't giving it a second thought. His bloodshot eyes were already staring straight ahead as he steered the rumbling station wagon down the block toward the liquor store. He ignored me and the glares of the drivers who were caught behind us in a trail of smoky exhaust.

While we spent years talking about the ways Pops embarrassed us in public, it took much longer for us to talk as a family about the things Pops did to us when he didn't have an audience—things he did behind closed doors and not in the light of day. It took a lifetime for some of us to admit them, or even to allow ourselves to remember them.

As Ma used to say, you have to give the devil his due. Pops managed to convince everyone around us that he was just a harmless wino, a hard-drinking musician, or a mean drunk, but we all knew he was far more dangerous than that.

CHAPTER 2

Ole Cat Eyes

It seemed like Pops was present from my earliest memory. In truth, he wasn't always there. Before I was born, he regularly moved between our tiny house, stints in the county jail, and a few boardinghouses in the nearby city of Rochester. There we heard rumors that he lived with other women. Despite his wandering, we were always keenly aware of his presence. Even his worn chair that reeked of stale wine was off limits while he was gone.

When I was old enough, I asked Ma how she and Pops had first met. She avoided my eyes and murmured, "I can't remember. It was a long time ago." Looking at my mother, it was hard to imagine her choosing to live her life with him. My grandma and my aunt didn't understand her decision either, yet they had seen it for themselves. When I asked them to tell me the story, they both sucked their teeth and shook their heads in regret.

"Virginia was purty when she met that bastard," Grandma said.

"And smart as a whip, too," Aunt Bonnie added. They both bobbed their heads in agreement.

Then they told me how, one day around 1954, my mother left school in the afternoon and, instead of coming straight home, decided to walk the five miles into town. In the tiny farm community where we lived, she was among the few Black children who went to the county school alongside the whites. Maybe that day she'd grown tired of her classmates' constant stares and slurs and wanted to clear her head. Or maybe she didn't want to go straight home and face the constant hectoring from my grandmother.

Either way, when she finally made it to what passed for a downtown in Batavia, there was no way Pops could have missed noticing her. The few photos of Ma from back then show an almond-complexioned girl with a shy smile. She also had what Grandma called "ole cat eyes"— gray-green irises swimming in a sea of white. Pops was a few years older, with brown-sugar skin, a slim build, and conked hair. Grandma said he looked like an "ole black rooster," strutting around in his slick city clothes. I suppose to Ma he must have simply looked sophisticated and so different from the white farmers' sons she had to go to school with each day.

That first meeting led to a quick courtship, and within a couple of months she had married Pops and moved away from her family to Rochester. With that decision, just months from graduation, my mother gave up a high school diploma for a husband and a new baby.

I've always wondered what Pops said that convinced her to choose a future with him. Her willingness to take a chance on him may have been rooted in her own deprived childhood. In the early 1950s when the growing American middle class dreamed of a house, a white picket fence, and the latest model from Detroit, Ma still lived in an old farmhouse and walked to school wearing her older brothers' shoes and carrying a tin pail lunch of cornbread and molasses. The country was changing, but not fast enough for a poor Black girl living in the backwoods.

My mother was too quiet and shy to tell anyone what she really wanted out of life, but apparently she was willing to take a calculated risk to get it. A story from her childhood hints at how that drive was formed. Her brothers, my uncles Raymond and Bunny, could barely contain their laughter when they told me about the day my mother pulled off a major heist.

"Your grandmama had this sack of fifty-cent pieces she was saving," Uncle Raymond told me. "She had it in the back of her closet, tucked in one of them glass mason jars. We weren't allowed to touch it. But one day your mama snuck in, took the coins, and divided them equally among all five kids."

"And let me tell you, we took that money straight to the candy store and had ourselves a good ole time," Uncle Bunny continued, wiping tears of laughter from his round face. "And listen to this, when your grandmama found the empty coin sack, Virginia stood there and fessed up. She took all the blame, and she took the beatin' of her life!"

"Jenya always did watch out for us," Raymond said, suddenly looking serious.

That Ma would gladly take the beating of her life from her mother to give her siblings a chance to buy dime-store candy also taught me something else about her. As a young girl she wasn't just deprived of food, clothes, and some of the things that kids want. She was starved for love. Growing up, my mother endured many beatings and quite a bit of verbal abuse from my grandmother. A high school diploma might or might not have helped her escape that life. She took a gamble on Pops.

The few Kodak photos that survived from their early years together showed a hopeful look on my mother's face. Meanwhile Pops would smirk in almost every picture, a cigarette dangling out of the corner of his mouth.

I'll never know how Ma felt going from the quiet of the country to the inner city as a young married woman. But certainly it must have been freeing in some ways. For the first time in her life, she wasn't the only black face around for miles. She was in the middle of a large Black community in Rochester. But if she was expecting that she might be joining the small but growing Black middle class in that city, she was badly mistaken. Pops's friends from the city were the men who stood on the neighborhood corner with bottles in paper sacks or his buddies from the barroom down the block.

I'd like to think that Ma was smart enough to see the danger early on. The older man she must have thought was fun-loving and good-looking was just a jobless drunk. Worse than that, he was a serial cheater. As Grandma told it, Pops was often gone for days from their small apartment. And when he returned, there were always a few drunken men and women stumbling in behind him. Ma would never share the stories of what happened those days, but Aunt Bonnie reveled in retelling them.

"That drunkard would parade these black-assed hussies right in front of her," she said. "And then he'd pull these women into a side room and dare your mother to come in. Now, can you imagine?"

No one is sure when the beatings started. My grandmother and aunt could only say with certainty that Ma must have quietly endured them for some time before she finally called them for help one day in the spring of 1956. Ma was pregnant with her second child at the time. She overcame the humiliation and shame, not to save herself, but to save her unborn child.

As the story goes, Pops came home in a drunken rage, acting paranoid and delusional. He accused her of becoming pregnant by another man. The fact that she knew no one in this new city and rarely left their dim apartment didn't matter. He'd become convinced the child in her swelling belly was not his. And that had to change. So Pops hauled off and punched Ma in her stomach. The blow brought her to her knees and put her into labor, two months early. She was rushed to the hospital, where she gave birth to their second child, my brother Rick. His survival was considered miraculous. Photos from months later show my mother changing him, using a small handkerchief instead of a diaper to cover his tiny body.

Around this time my mother called her family and headed back to the country and her childhood home. Not even my grandmother and aunt can explain what happened next. Pops pursued her and begged for forgiveness. I suppose Ma must have taken him at his word that things would be different, because five months after Rick's premature birth she was pregnant again, this time with my sister, Denise.

"I don't know why Vir-jen-ya didn't leave that black bastard right then and there," my grandmother complained.

As a kid, I couldn't understand either. It wasn't until I was much older that I understood that Ma was like many women who struggle for years to work up the courage to leave abusive partners and spouses. She was trapped in a cycle of abuse, paralysis, and just plain fear.

She also must have felt some measure of shame. She had gone in search of a bigger world and better life. Now every morning all she had to do was look out the window to see my grandmother next door, standing on her porch, scrubbing clothes in a plastic basin. Seeing that must have been a constant reminder of how far my mother had once traveled in life and a reminder of how far she still had to go.

But I'd like to believe that my mother returned home with one thing she'd gone in search of—love. She now had her own children, and even during her most desperate times she let us know we were what sustained her. Over the next decade, Ma kept her focus and attention on us, even as Pops came and went as he pleased. I suppose it was bearable because he was gone for long stretches—sometimes months at a time—sleeping in jail cells or other women's beds.

The off-and-on status of their relationship gets fuzzy in 1966. But he was apparently gone long enough for my mother to find another relationship, at least for a short time. And when Pops stumbled back into our lives that summer, it was clear to him he'd been gone far too long. While he was away, she had her fifth baby—a pale, curly-haired little boy with eyes that sometimes looked brown, and other times gray-green.

Perhaps the years of drinking and recent drug use had begun to take a toll on Pops, because he didn't immediately lash out at her or at the light, bright boy, who looked nothing like him but who shared his last name. That didn't mean all the fight was out of him. Now that he was back home, he was determined to stay and stake his claim.

If there was ever any doubt, he wanted Ma to know she was his property, to do with as he pleased.

And that meant we kids were, too.

At a young age, I understood that to be truly free of someone like Pops or even my grandmother, I might have to one day find a new family, a better one.

That meant I'd have to leave home.

But unlike my mother, I had to be sure to never come back.

CHAPTER 3

This Is How Things
Get Out of Hand

As a kid, I lived in 760 square feet of hell. Three broken-down bedrooms, a crammed kitchen, and a tiny bathroom left few places for my mother and us kids to hide from Pops. Our house was a pressure cooker where alcoholism and abuse raised everyone's temperature until things would blow up.

That's why in the years that followed, I looked for some quiet place to retreat from those awful memories. I bought and sold three spectacular houses. I rented a pricey Manhattan apartment, a trendy Brooklyn co-op, two waterfront condos, and a series of huge apartments where I rattled around with a few pieces of furniture. Now I was in a place that was supposed to feel like home.

The house that I lived in with my husband and two daughters squatted on a small hill next to a stand of woods. It also offered a panoramic view of the cookie-cutter brick Colonials in our suburban Maryland neighborhood. Normally I could peer directly into the neighbors' living rooms. But on this night, my glasses lay somewhere inside the house, probably shattered. Still, if I squinted hard enough, I could see light and dark shapes in their windows. I noticed that the middle-aged lesbian couple across the street had finally turned off their TV and gone to sleep. A few doors away, the immigrant family from El Salvador were still awake. I knew their lights would go out soon. They ran a neighborhood daycare and had to be up early. My only concern was the South Korean couple right next door. They'd rise in a few hours, before the sun, to head to work in their flower shop. I imagined what they might think, seeing me shoeless and without a coat sitting on my doorstep on a chilly March night. I had to get indoors to avoid their sympathetic looks.

But as I tried to work up the courage to open the front door, a sudden and unpleasant thought made me wonder: Would the door even open? Or had my family chosen to lock me out?

A few hours earlier, I sat in my bedroom listening to my daughters' screams echo throughout the house. I wondered, was it loud enough to draw our neighbors to their windows?

"It's nothing, probably," I imagined them murmuring to themselves. "Just kids playing."

I knew differently.

The girls ran through the house, shouting, shoving, and playing keep-away from one another. It would have been one thing if they were still toddlers. Now they were nearly teens, and when they chased one another, it wasn't for fun. They no longer played games anymore. They played for keeps.

My mother would have said of their horseplay, "This is how things get out of hand." And they had.

At the time, my shoulders hunched as I stared at the closed bedroom door. When they were younger, having their rooms just steps away from ours reassured me they were safe. Lately, it felt like I couldn't get far away enough from their childhood spats. I willed myself not to go over and check on them. I told myself that Todd would deal with it. I'd come to learn my husband had the kind of patience that parents often need. I knew it was something I lacked.

Suddenly he called out from the kitchen at the front of the house, "What the heck is going on?"

I waited, listening for the bangs of their bedroom doors, which would signal they had retreated to their rooms and, for now, there was a truce. Instead our younger daughter, Rachel, cried out, startled.

"She slapped me!"

A second later Todd's steps echoed as he came toward the bedrooms. I pictured him stopping a few feet away from where I was sitting, to stand between our kids.

"Stop crying. What happened?" he asked.

"I didn't hurt her." It was the voice of our older daughter, Mariah.

"You . . . you *slapped* me," Rachel insisted.

"You always get me in trouble!"

Mariah's voice drifted away as she spoke. She was retreating to her room. Yet I could still hear her unmistakable afterthought.

"Little bitch," she muttered.

Later I would wonder whether she intentionally wanted to have the last word in the argument or just meant to whisper to herself. At that moment, it didn't matter to me. I stomped out of the room and cut her off midstride. I stood like an awakened giant, hovering above her. When I replayed the scene in my head, I would recall the sharp contrast of our skin as my winter-white hands pushed her deep brown shoulders against the wall. The impact was so hard, the series of framed family photographs on the wall behind us rattled. One fell, shattering the glass. It was the photo of my side of the family.

"What. Did. You. Say?" I asked through gritted teeth

"Let go of me."

My daughter wrenched her hard-angled body, trying to release my grip. On another day, a good day for me, I might have been able to stop myself and use the rehearsed phrase our daughter's therapist said in a singsong voice: "You seem angry, let's talk." Instead I heard the familiar voices of my family members in my head and then heard their words tumble out of my mouth.

"You think that hurts? Do you? You'd better take your black ass to bed right now before I give you something to cry about."

Mariah struggled harder. This time, when she spoke, I was sure she wanted me to hear her.

"You're not even my real family," she hissed. "I don't want gay people as my parents. Why did you two ever adopt me, anyway?"

It was as though my chest burst into flames. I knew I couldn't make her take back the words or change how she felt, but I wanted to know she could feel hurt, like me. I squeezed her upper arms harder until tears rushed down her face.

"Stop it!" Todd yelled. "What the hell are you doing?"

Todd tried to wedge his body between us and then pulled at my hands trying to break my grip on Mariah. As we wrestled for control of her, I heard my glasses clatter to the floor. But still I refused to let her go.

Finally, in desperation, Todd stepped back. Out of the corner of my eye, I saw him draw back a clenched fist and aim at my face.

"*Let her go!*"

Seeing Todd raise his hands toward me shocked me out of my blind fury. I stood looking at him, mouth agape.

"You're going to fucking hit me?" I managed to spit out.

Todd didn't move. My hands trailed down the length of Mariah's arms and I stumbled back away from her and slumped against the opposite wall. I could taste blood in my mouth from where I'd bitten through my bottom lip. Salty sweat trailed into my right eye, stinging it closed. I rubbed it clear and looked up to see my daughters. Mariah massaged the spots where my fingers had dug into her upper arms. She stood quietly, glancing back and forth between me and Todd. Rachel hugged herself. Now that it was quiet, I noticed her soft sobs.

For a moment, no one moved. Todd and I stood in opposite corners of that tight hallway. The kids stood framed in the doorways of their bedrooms. Our family photos watched over us all. Todd's chest, heaving as he tried to catch his breath, slowed enough for him to choke out a single word.

"Enough."

I looked at him for a minute, then shook my head.

At first light I slipped back into the house, through what turned out to be an unlocked front door, and down into the basement. I tucked my body into a small green love seat. The custom velour upholstery smelled faintly of mildew. Once it had been among my mother's most cherished possessions, and then a reminder of her that I prized as well. It had been tossed down here into the cellar, just another piece of cast-off furniture. It was like the memories of my childhood—always close by, but best kept tucked away.

It was more than fifteen years since I met my husband. Now I sat in our dank basement, hiding from him, our kids, and the life we had built together. As I looked up through the cobwebs and listened to my family's hushed voices and muffled steps, I half imagined a pounding on the front door. It would be child welfare coming to remove the kids from our home. The police might show up, too, ready to write up a report on the "abusive gay father." A story might make it into the paper.

I imagined our neighbors would shake their heads and say, "See, I told you so. White gay men have no business trying to raise Black kids." People at our superprogressive synagogue would find out and sigh to each other, "Kids need a mother." Then there were my old work colleagues from CNBC, MSNBC, and NBC from long ago. Maybe they would learn about me from a scrolling headline at the bottom of the TV screen that would blare: *Gay Parents Gone Bad!*

The wild scenarios raced through my head all morning.

Todd's soft tap on the cellar door interrupted my thoughts. He must have realized I'd be there. After all, where else could I go? Like a chastened child, I flipped over and hid my face in the cushions, pretending to sleep. I expected to hear him pad down the steps. Instead, he called out from the top of the stairs.

"The kids left for the school bus," he said in a flat tone. "I'm going to work."

I waited for him to ask me to leave the house again or at least ask how long I was staying. Instead, he closed the door lightly behind him. We both knew I had nowhere to go—no real family, no true friends. The only person who would take me in was that nice Jewish boy, the Boy Scout I'd first met all those years ago in the coffee shop. I often wondered what good thing he'd seen in me all those years ago and whether he still saw it. For now, apparently, he was willing to at least pretend that he did.

It seemed like only one of us had changed since then. I'd decided to move to Manhattan in late 1999 and taken a new job as a producer at the rapidly growing cable news channel CNBC. It was a big break for my career after years working in smaller local TV news stations. For the first few months, I spent long hours trying to prove to my bosses, and myself, that this small-town boy deserved to be there. On my days off, I was trying to prove myself elsewhere. I went to every gay dance bar, piano bar, and leather bar in the city, hoping to find where I fit in as a gay man.

AOL chat rooms were another destination. The chat rooms were the pre-Tinder and pre-Grindr online dating alternatives. There an attractive online profile was just as good as any pickup line. So on a mild Sunday afternoon in January of 2000, I sat alone inside my overpriced and underfurnished Midtown apartment and threw a hook into the water. Gym rat, masculine, I typed into my computer. I included a photo of me flexing my biceps. I'd spent hours lifting weights in the gym and hundreds of dollars a month on a personal trainer. Now I was the perfect bait, I thought. After a few hours of sifting through instant messages, I found a reply from someone with the screen name HeartofBklyn. His picture caught my eye. He stood shirtless and smiling beneath a waterfall.

"It's me, on a pilgrimage to Israel," he typed in reply to me.

I'd been raised Catholic and by a family who allowed their ignorance about the wider world to make them suspicious of Jewish people, if not slightly anti-Semitic. But by then I'd met and befriended many different types of people in my life. And after some back and forth, I recognized what I had in front of me—someone who was sincere, cute, and smart. Here was a nice Jewish boy.

Later I'd lie and tell people I was first attracted to his smile or the fact our slow dial-up connections couldn't keep pace with our good conversation. Truthfully, I liked the way the water rippled off his smooth chest. He must have at least appreciated my biceps, because he accepted my invitation to meet in person.

Walking into a Union Square cafe, I recognized his wavy black hair and warm brown eyes from his profile photo, but not the physique. He didn't look as muscular. I thought about turning around, or making up a sudden excuse so I could leave, but his smile drew me in closer to the small table where he sat.

He stood up and offered me a handshake. His hand felt warm, dry, and steady in mine. As we slid into seats across from one another, I looked him over again.

"My name's Todd," he said. I remembered then that we'd only known each other's screen names.

"That's also my middle name," I said.

"Well, if we ever dated, that might be weird," he replied with a crooked grin.

I wondered how serious he was being. Our profiles said we wanted to date. But the truth was, AOL was generally used for quick hook-ups. I realized it felt odd for me to be looking for that in a crowded coffee shop during the day and not in a dark corner of a bar or on the internet, but I willed myself to hear him out.

Todd struck me as a real Boy Scout type, clean cut, trustworthy. Then he volunteered to me that he was an actual Eagle Scout. I wondered whether opposites could attract. I had my doubts. He peppered me with questions, easy ones at first. We discovered we'd been born just three weeks apart. We were both the youngest in our families. Our sisters shared the same birthday. Listening to him, I found out quickly that his life as a gay man until this point had been very different from mine. Todd had put in more than a decade's worth of time visiting bars and online profiles. He'd been in long-term relationships before. He knew what he wanted at this stage of his life, and it was becoming clear to me that it wasn't quick sex. Barely an hour into our conversation, he popped the question.

"You ever want kids?"

I banged down my mug hard enough to slosh the coffee around and then wiped some imaginary lint from the front of my sweater. I remember him looking at me, so damned puppy-dog-eyed and earnest. When I spoke, I noticed how I'd come to sound like one of those gay guys I kept coming across in bars, snarky and skeptical.

"What is this, some kind of interview?"

But Todd didn't seem offended. He offered me another sincere and crooked grin.

"Yeah, I guess it is."

Gay parenting wasn't exactly a new thing in the late 1990s, but it was becoming trendy. The "gayby boom" is what some media called it. They didn't realize there had always been LGBTQ parents. Many were divorced parents who later came out of the closet. What had recently changed was that "out" gay and lesbian couples were now forming their own families through fostering, adoption, and surrogacy.

At age thirty-three, having children wasn't something I'd ever considered. I'd never had a boyfriend, let alone a vision of what it would be like to have a partner and kids. I didn't tell Todd, but I'd only recently come out. Before then, I'd spent my twenties trying to fit into an all-white world of college, grad school, and then a series of ever bigger jobs across the country. Now I was facing a question of whether I wanted to be out and proud, and a parent.

Todd stirred his mug of green tea and waited. It gave me time to think about where I'd come from and where I wanted to go in life. Given what I'd been through as a kid, maybe I should have stood up, headed back to my apartment, and sorted through more headless, shirtless photos of men on the prowl. It would have been safer that way. But maybe because of my childhood, I decided to stay.

"So, kids?" Todd asked again.

"Sure," I said, matching his smile. "Maybe. With the right guy."

From the very beginning, Todd had taken a chance on me. He'd grown up in an upper-middle-class family. Later in the date when he asked me to tell him about my own upbringing, I remember pausing again—staring down into my extra-light coffee, trying to decide how to answer.

Had he noticed the fullness of my bottom lip or the way my nose turned up at the end? I looked at our hands cupped around our mugs. His olive-colored skin looked darker than mine. New York City was a rich stew of people with different races, nationalities, and ethnicities. You might be anything. Or you might be a little bit of everything. But you had to be something. Did he look at me and guess Italian, Puerto Rican, or Mediterranean? Truthfully, I might be half of any one of those things, but I didn't know for sure. All I could tell him was that I probably looked like something I was not. That was just plain white.

In the past, when I attempted to tell people I was Black, I heard the doubt in my own voice. And I saw the confusion on their faces. By the time I met Todd, I was trying to head off the uncomfortable reactions with humor.

"Remember the movie *The Jerk*?" I'd usually say at some point on a date. "That line by Steve Martin where he says, 'I was born a poor black child'?"

Guys usually laughed or at least shook their head in confusion when I used that line. But that afternoon, when I decided to try it on Todd, he didn't laugh or look befuddled. He nodded to himself as if to say, it makes perfect sense. It was enough of an explanation for him. He accepted me at face value.

I remember looking out the window at the rush of people and traffic. Outside was a world of possibilities. Thinking about who I could be out there and all the different people I could be with was exciting. But it also gave me the same wild, dizzy feeling I felt at the top of a roller coaster. I didn't want to fall or get flung off. I pulled my gaze back inside and locked my eyes on a spot straight ahead, on Todd, and tried to breathe slowly. Here, I thought, I could be safe. Here I could feel grounded.

Two hours later when we got up to leave together, I remember telling myself I would need to explain much more to Todd about who I really was. The fact that I was born a poor Black child was just part of my past. The full story of how that poor Black child grew up and escaped his past was wilder and crazier than any screenplay Steve Martin could ever dream up.

CHAPTER 4

Pops's Blood

Pops liked to dress in Ma's underwear, but only when he was drunk. One night in 1972 when I was six years old, he smeared her crimson lipstick across his mouth and staggered around in her underthings and high heels for a show in our living room. I squirmed, but not at the sight of Pops. I was used to that by now. It was that damned raggedy couch. Rusty springs sprouted from holes beneath the cushion. I wanted to leave, but Pops had other ideas. He leaned over, breathing Mogen David Concord wine in my face.

"Boy, go pick up your mother's wig."

I crawled out of the sinking pit of the sofa and dashed across the living room. There, in a coiled heap, sat the late-sixties-style wig, looking like it belonged to Diana Ross. It had slipped off Pops's sweaty head. As I handed it over, he smacked his lips, leaving red lipstick on his yellowed dentures. Then he hiked up Ma's slip, revealing her girdle underneath.

"This girdle is a motherfucker. Virginia! How do you wear this shit every day?"

I didn't even cringe at his words—my family cussed all the time— but my mother still cried out from the kitchen, around the corner, telling him to quit that cursing in front of us kids. If she leaned back from where she stood at the dirty stove, frying fatty pork chops and onions, she could also see Pops in the living room. If it disturbed her that her husband danced around in her bra, slip, girdle, and heels, she never let it show. It didn't shock us kids anymore, either.

My older brothers and sister and I had front-row seats for Pops's latest performance. We sat wedged together, butt cheek to butt cheek, on our worn couch. I poked my fingers through the rips in the upholstery and played with the rusty springs. It was just another thing inside our house that we couldn't afford to repair or replace. As I settled in, I edged closer to my big sister Denise. I called her Neecie. She was fifteen and took care of me when Ma was working. I hoped she could keep me safe from the sharp edges of the springs, and hopefully from Pops.

I glanced over at my chubby brother Mike. He was closest in age to me, only eight years older. He nervously plucked the stuffing out of the ripped fabric, avoiding Pops's eyes. Out of all of us, he seemed most scared of Pops. In the meantime Jim, or "Jim-Jim," stared at Pops with a look of scorn. At sixteen he was the oldest of us kids. His football-player-sized frame took up most of the cushions, squeezing everyone else toward the sides. Rickie, slimmer and a year younger than Jim-Jim, was gone that night. If I had to guess where, I'd say he had snuck out with his friends again. Ma yelled at Rick for "running the streets"— smoking cigarettes, guzzling beer, and getting into trouble—but he didn't care, and we didn't blame him. He had managed to escape.

Past midnight, Pops continued shouting along to the music from our used hi-fi. After the Supremes, he mimicked James Brown, doing the famous shuffle and a few more dance moves. The song "Hot Pants" ended on the turntable, and all of us looked forward to what we hoped would be the finale to this long night. Pops bent over, apparently to curtsy or bow, but as he rose to straighten up, he lost his balance and toppled head over high heels. He landed on top of the couch, pinning us in our places. As I sat there struggling beneath him, I noticed he smelled of his sweat and a good dousing of Ma's perfume.

Jim-Jim didn't bother to struggle like the rest of us. With one giant shove, he pushed Pops onto the floor. There Pops rocked back and forth like an overturned turtle. I closed my eyes and said a quick prayer, hoping that God would make Pops pass out there and leave us alone for the rest of the night. But it didn't work. Pops tried to stand up, and Jim-Jim jumped to his feet and stood over him.

"Stay down, ya goddamn drunk," he ordered.

That challenge was enough of a trigger for Pops. He lurched to his feet and exploded with a giant cuss of "motherfucker."

I then heard Ma shove the frying pan to the rear burner. A moment later, all five-feet-two of her stood in the path of Jim-Jim, trying to protect him from Pops with her short, nut-brown arms. Jim-Jim nudged Ma aside. His meaty paws flew up, and he crouched, swaying from side to side.

"Think you can take me?" Jim-Jim taunted. "Come on."

Ma only came up to their shoulders, but she pressed at both of their chests, crying, "Stop it." The rest of us jumped up onto the furniture. Our family circus had been converted into a boxing ring, and we needed to get out of the way while also finding a way to see clearly in case Jim prevailed this time. Pops ditched the heels and the wig.

"Get him, Jim. Kick his ass!" Neecie yelled.

I slid beneath Neecie's arm to avoid getting hit. Mike grabbed Ma by the back of her nurse's-aide smock and pulled her out of the way. Soon we saw fists, chairs, ashtrays, and an empty wine bottle fly in front of our faces. Watching Neecie and Mike cheer on Jim-Jim, I knew I should be proud of my big brother for standing up for us. After all, Pops had used his fists and belt for years to terrify us. Yet I also couldn't help feeling embarrassed. I knew this wasn't how other families acted.

Within a few minutes, Pops fell flat on his ass. This time, he stayed down. He had a black eye, and lipstick was smudged across his whole face. Jim-Jim stood over him again, wiping the blood off his own top lip. Now I was sure the show was over, but I also knew Pops would be back on his feet in the morning. That meant we'd once again be forced to be his captive audience.

Jim's attempted coup to overthrow Pops was not only retaliation for the years of abuse he had suffered at our father's hands, but it was also a calculated effort to protect the rest of us for when he was no longer around. Jim knew he'd be old enough to leave our troubled house in just a year or two. I suppose he understood that, in his absence, no one could stand in the way of Pops doing whatever the hell he wanted to us.

Before I was born, there had been years of ruthless beatings of my mother and violent attacks on my siblings. The scars of long-ago battles lingered around our house. Once when my fingers traced over the badly patched walls in the house, Mike laughed and shook his head.

"Oh yeah, that's from when Pops put his fist through the wall during that one fight," he said. I also learned that our empty TV stand once held a television that Pops had smashed during another tirade.

But while Jim and my other siblings were old enough to be able to protect me from the worst types of abuse they themselves had endured, we all shared the same emotional trauma.

One of my earliest memories is of my three-year-old self looking over my shoulder at my mother standing in the kitchen. The door to the cellar, which hung at the edge of our tiny kitchen, was wide open. I stood on the top step with the cold, fluorescent kitchen light and presence of my mother at my back. Beneath me, down the stairs was another world, cold, wet, and dark. I was on the threshold.

Crack!

I heard Pops's leather belt echo across the basement. Then I heard cries and the sound of feet running here and there on the concrete floor. It was too dim to make out the faces of my brothers and sister, but I knew they were down there, running from him. I turned back to look at my mother, standing at the stove, to see if she would answer their calls for help. But Ma moved deliberately from task to task, her face showing no emotion. I realized then that she would not rescue her children from being chased down, cornered, and whipped one by one. I remember thinking, doesn't Ma love them?

I wasn't much older before I knew she would have given her life for ours. I can only guess that she determined it was safer to allow Pops to chase her four kids around the cellar with a belt than for her to confront her husband and have him come at all of them with a punch or a broken wine bottle. If nothing else, she knew that when Pops was confronted, he got angrier. His drinking made him dangerous. But there was something deeper and darker that drove his behavior. It had always been that way.

CHAPTER 5

Love Makes a Family

The afternoon after our family fight, the front door banged open and backpacks thudded on the floor above. Footsteps roamed from room to room. Then Mariah's voice. Her words came through clearest when she passed overhead, close to the basement door.

"Is he coming home?"

Todd's reply came from further away, in the kitchen. I leaned toward a corner of the cellar and strained to hear him.

"Poppy needs to take a break" is all I could make out.

I assumed Todd knew I was here in the shadows, listening to them live their lives without me. Earlier I'd come home from work and slipped back into the cellar before everyone else came home. When I passed through the hallway, I noticed Todd had picked up the pieces of broken glass from the night before and straightened the framed family photos on the wall. The picture of my family was back in its spot. It still looked out of place alongside the photos of Todd's family. I could imagine a day far in the future when people sorting through used frames in a thrift store might come across this curious family portrait of a mother and her five children. They would point out the youngest and wonder aloud about the sole white face in this family of dark brown.

When the kids were little and I framed the picture to place on the wall, they too were confused. "Who's that?" they asked. They smeared their fingers across the glass and stopped at the two-year-old wearing a red checked jacket from the sale pile at Sears. That's me, I explained. They looked at me in wide-eyed wonder. I moved their tiny fingers toward the people who look like strangers but who are surrounding me in the photo.

"That was my family. Now, *you* are my family."

Now I wondered what would become of the people who occupied the photo at the center of our wall upstairs. Were they still a family? And if so, were they a better one without me?

Later that night, the basement door squeaked open. It had grown quiet upstairs. I assumed the kids were in bed, but the footfalls on the stairs sounded less sure than Todd's more solid gait. After a few seconds they stopped halfway down. A thin voice echoed across the emptiness of the basement.

"Poppy?" Mariah called.

"Yeah," I said.

I got up from the love seat and walked toward the bottom of the stairs. Slowly, a step at a time, Mariah drifted down until she stopped on the last step and waited. She eyed me warily. I reached out my arms. After a long minute, she leaned forward and let me fold my arms around her. The warmth from her head felt familiar and brought me back to a time when she fit comfortably between the hollow of my neck and the bottom of my chest.

Todd and I had meant to take our time before starting a family. After we met, there were more coffee dates, then dinners, vacations, and finally visits to meet his family before we even talked about moving in together. During that time I started to tell him bits and pieces about my own family. He laughed when I described my Bible-quoting, hard-cussing grandma who lived on one side of me as I grew up and my big, brawny, brawling aunt Bonnie who lived on the other. His eyes widened when I explained the down-home drama they caused in our daily lives. But I intentionally tried to lighten the tone with some humor. I had hundreds of these dark funny stories about my family, and I thought I had plenty of time to tell him the more troubling ones before things got serious.

Then, a year and a half after we met, on that perfect fall day, time compressed. Todd and I sat on a windowsill of my new apartment over-looking Brooklyn's Prospect Park. Toward the towering city skyline, a gray plume billowed into the cloudless blue sky and now hovered over lower Manhattan. Inside, the TV played loops of jets piercing the towers of the World Trade Center. Life seemed suddenly uncertain and time too short.

Over the next few weeks, we rarely saw each other. I was hunkered down for twelve to sixteen hours at a time inside the cavernous studios of MSNBC, where I'd recently started to work as a news producer. After each shift I'd stumble out into the fresh air and see a world quickly changing around me. One night, back in Brooklyn, it was me who suggested getting serious.

"This is crazy," I said. "We're splitting time between our two places. I'm commuting to New Jersey, and we never see one another."

The Boy Scout in Todd was prepared for any situation. Within months, he sold his Brooklyn co-op and we went in together on a three-bed, two-bath Colonial in South Orange, New Jersey, a leafy commuter suburb that was just 20 miles from Manhattan. At the time, only a small part of me recognized that buying a house might mean buying into Todd's idea of having a family one day. Todd was the first person I'd ever dated. But I knew I'd found love and, for the first time, the kind of security and stability I never had growing up.

Once we were settled into our new home, I threw myself into my job. I'd been promoted and now worked alongside Lester Holt, then just a rising cable news host. Todd, meanwhile, focused on creating a home for us. First there were renovations. The house had sat empty for a few years. Todd joked it had the good bones of the 1940s but the decorating scars of the 1970s. There was money and time left over for trips to Hawaii and Mexico and frequent visits to Florida to see Todd's family. While it was clear that we were building a life together, the next step seemed to make things "official." In December of 2002, we exchanged vows in a commitment ceremony. My colleagues at MSNBC threw us a surprise reception. When Todd and I arrived at Lester's home one night, dozens of my coworkers were waiting there to wish us a happy future together. This was a life I could never have conceived of, growing up as a poor "black" kid. I had an exciting well-paying job, a big house with a yard and a picket fence in the back, and someone who loved me as I was, even if I was still unsure of who I was myself.

It should have come as no surprise that before long Todd and I began talking about the very thing he'd been looking for in a partner back when we met—someone to raise a family with. We were now in our late thirties, and so it made sense to us to start planning for it. I was the first to suggest we start thinking about adoption. It was a complicated process that could sometimes take years, especially for a gay or lesbian couple at the time. Fortunately, we found out that New Jersey was one of the few states in the country where both partners of gay and lesbian couples could be listed as parents on a birth certificate. The next step was to find a private adoption agency that would work with gay parents, and the "gayby boom" had ensured there were enough of those in business. By late 2003, everything was in place: paperwork, background checks, and home visits from officious social workers to approve us. Everyone cautioned us the wait for an infant might be at least two to four years. That was fine with us. We were still a relatively new couple. We could use the time for more home improvements, vacations, and getting to know one another better. And there would still be time for me to tell Todd some of those stories about my childhood—the ones that both defined who I was today and bound me to a past I wanted to forget.

Six months later, on a mild day in August 2004, the time for me to prepare Todd suddenly ran out. I was at the gym one afternoon when I received a life-changing call. On the other end was an adoption agency that had made a match. A birth mother had chosen us. There would be no need to meet her to convince her of what great parents we would be. We wouldn't have to share in her feelings of anticipation and excitement during her months of pregnancy and then look past her feelings of loss and shame the day she delivered. That process was already done. The mother had given birth the day before. Her newborn girl was waiting for us in northeast Ohio.

I hung up the phone and walked outside to sit on the curb. Then I dialed Todd and asked him if he was sitting down.

It had been a normal delivery and the baby was healthy, I remember shouting into the phone. The mother had waived all parental rights, and the birth father was apparently missing, possibly in jail. Todd listened and laughed nervously.

"She's African American," I said. Then I stopped to listen.

"All right," he said, laughing. "What else do we need to know?"

The only unknown was our answer. If it was yes, we had to pack and get on a plane to Ohio the next morning. Knowing that some prospective parents wait years for this type of call made our answer easy. Our future family, the baby we had dreamed about years before, was ready right now.

What happened next was a whirlwind: the celebratory dinner for two that night at a local Italian restaurant, a frenzied dash the next morning to the airport, where we remembered to buy a teddy bear, and then the circuitous drive through the outskirts of Akron to the adoption agency.

As Todd pulled the rental car off the busy suburban street and into a small gravel driveway, I looked at the squat brown building that sat several hundred feet back from the parking lot. From its appearance, it might at one time have been someone's home, a place where a family lived. Now it was a way station, an adoption agency where some families ended so that others could begin.

Todd turned the car off. It clicked and hissed in the summer heat as we sat there lost in our thoughts for a moment. Long ago I'd learned to mute my emotions and damp any feelings that might be too intoxicating or too full of sorrow. It was a survival skill, the only way to not feel disappointed when good fortune turned bad or to feel broken if it all turned to shit.

A part of me was excited about this brand-new life we were about to hold and how it would change ours forever. Another part must have felt amazed at how much my own life had changed in the years since I'd left home. And inside there was also room for a bit of fear about what it would take for two gay men to raise a daughter. But all my life I'd learned you didn't have the luxury of sitting around regretting the past or worrying about the present. You just had to keep moving.

I got out of the car and headed toward the front door. Todd did a quick jog and caught up to me. We stood on the threshold and paused. Todd looked over at me.

"Ready?" he asked.

I pushed open the door.

Just inside the doorway stood a tall auburn-haired woman. I wondered if she'd been watching from the window. This was Krissy, the adoption agency director. She gave us both a quick pumping handshake and then a big smile.

"Okay, which one's Todd, and which is Steve?" she said with an overly loud laugh.

She pointed to an adjoining conference room and followed us inside.

"I know we've got a lot of paperwork and things to discuss, but I know you're dying to first see your new baby, right?"

Todd nervously ran his hand from his forehead back through his hair. I gently clapped him on the shoulder.

"I hope you're ready, because she's a beauty!" said Krissy. At her announcement, another staffer walked into the conference room, cradling a tiny figure wrapped in a cream-colored blanket. Todd opened his arms and she placed the bundle inside.

Krissy was right. This baby was Gerber-baby beautiful. She had rich brown skin and almond-shaped eyes that were wide open. She stared at Todd and me as if she was trying to figure us out. After a few minutes, Todd gently handed her to me. I looked up to see him wiping away tears with the back of his hand.

The baby felt feather-light in my arms. I couldn't imagine the day this tiny life might ever be too much for me to bear. I swayed back and forth for a few minutes, searching for the right footing to make her feel as safe and as comforted as possible.

"I can tell you guys are going to be naturals!" Krissy said.

I looked over at Todd. He gave me a quick nod of assurance.

For the next two and a half weeks we were stuck living in a nearby Holiday Inn. The last-minute cross-state adoption meant we had to wait for a legal waiver to bring the baby back to New Jersey. In some ways it was a blessing. We had nothing ready at home.

On our first night in the hotel, I sat on a burnt orange ottoman, slowly moving my body back and forth like a rocking chair while I cradled Mariah. Todd watched me from one of the lumpy twin beds across the room, where he lay resting. I inspected our daughter's full head of curly hair, her tiny fingers, toes, ears, and scalp. Suddenly a thought popped into my head.

"A baby's skin color changes, you know," I said.

After what seemed like a long time, Todd mumbled back, "What?"

"Her skin," I said. "She's probably going to be even darker than she is right now."

The only response was Todd's light snoring.

I'd read about the importance of skin-to-skin contact to help boost bonding with a newborn in the first hours after birth. We didn't know if that had happened with her mother. I unbuttoned the top of my shirt and lay Mariah's tiny warm body on my chest, so her head tucked snugly under my chin. She fit perfectly. I massaged small circles across her back until finally the pace of her breathing matched mine.

Growing up, I knew what it felt like to be out of synch with everyone around me. I was the white sheep in an all-black family. Now I had a child who would look different from me, and I prayed it would never make a difference to her.

Just a year later, I followed Todd through the lens of our video camera as he kissed the top of Mariah's head. He hustled around the table to cut pieces of birthday cake for the screaming group of guests. Mariah had already scooped her hand into the purple icing on her plate. There was pure delight in her one-year-old eyes. As I panned the camcorder around the children's play zone, I saw the white, brown, and Black toddlers, and their families who had come to celebrate with us. An especially slight boy toppled backward off a bench, landing on his back. His dad ran to scoop him up. He immediately held out his arms for his mother.

The birthday party was our official coming out as suburban gay dads. Some of the moms already knew Todd as a stay-at-home parent. He'd stopped working so he could take Mariah to playdates, tot music classes and "mommy-and-me" playgroups. I was working long hours, so I made rare appearances around our tree-lined neighborhood, pushing the stroller up and down the hills before bedtime or during weekend trips to the playground. I remembered, with a small bit of shame, how I had felt out in public with my own mother as a child. I was embarrassed to look different from her, and I often looked away to avoid the gaze of others. Now when I took those trips with Mariah alone, I intentionally sought out the faces of strangers and mentally invited them to look at us. My dark brown daughter felt almost like a badge of honor to me, a way to affirm a side of me that others couldn't see, the Black side.

It was the public outings with both Todd and the baby that made me unsure about myself. When strangers looked at us, did they think they saw two white men and one Black baby? In my head I wanted to tell them, "But I'm Black too!" And was it obvious now that we were gay?

I told myself I shouldn't care what they thought when they first looked at us. But I knew the embarrassment was a function of how and where I had grown up. As a white-looking kid growing up in a Black family that lived in a nearly all-white town, I'd wanted nothing more than to fit in. Now I realized I could no longer hide in plain sight.

It helped that our first year together as a family was in a progressive bubble where my neighbors were Black, white, and brown, not to mention politically blue. When I looked closer, I noticed that the neighbors smiled widely at us while strangers on the street didn't give us a second look. A good number of folks in our community most likely worked alongside LGBTQ people all day in New York City. When they commuted home, they lived next door to other gays and lesbians who renovated historic homes in their quiet neighborhoods. As long as Todd and I paid our taxes and kept our lawn trimmed, they didn't seem to care that we were gay parents or that our daughter looked different from us.

As for Todd, that first year of parenting appeared to come easy. It was like just another scouting badge he had to earn. Mariah slept peacefully, walked early, and played easily. Some weeks before her first birthday party, I was confident enough about our parenting skills and our future that I popped the question this time.

"You ever want another?"

Todd was elbows deep that night in a dirty diaper. He shifted his eyes toward me and offered something between a smile and a sneer.

"Sure. Someday," he said, then laughed.

"Someday" turned out to be the magic word again. Ten days after Mariah's first birthday party, on August 1, 2005, my cell phone buzzed. After I hung up, I asked Todd to sit down. We'd hit the adoption lottery again. Though we hadn't asked, Krissy had found another newborn for us. It turned out to be Mariah's biological sister. That night Todd and I talked for hours. The decision didn't come as quickly. Todd would have to leave work permanently and stay at home with a newborn and a toddler in diapers. But in the end, we agreed. There were so many kids waiting for families. It just seemed right that Mariah and her sister should grow up together.

Within twenty-four hours we were back in Ohio. This time as we stepped out of the rental car outside the adoption agency, Mariah toddled along at our side. She tugged nervously at her sundress as we walked in the door.

"Oh my gosh, you're walking!!" Krissy gushed at Mariah.

After giving her a quick hug, Krissy shooed us all into a small conference room where she excitedly urged us to close our eyes. She stepped outside, but a moment later the door swung open and we heard a whoop of "Surprise!" I opened my eyes and studied the infant Krissy held in her arms. Something didn't look right about the baby. I realized it was her skin color. This baby looked as white as the hospital blanket it was wrapped in. Todd and I exchanged a look. Before either of us could speak, Krissy winked.

"Just kidding!" she said.

She handed the baby to a staffer and swapped it for another infant that had been waiting in the arms of a woman outside the door. This little girl was a bit duskier than the first—the color of light brown toast.

"Here's your baby!" Krissy squealed. She sounded vaguely like a carnival barker awarding a stuffed animal. Her joke seemed in poor taste. I gave Todd another side glance, but by now I could see he was busy smiling down at the baby. As Krissy handed the infant over to him, she rattled off the birth details. "Normal delivery," she said, "no signs of drugs or alcohol, good vitals, breathing, and reflexes." I drew a deep breath. There was one bit of information she didn't mention. It was conspicuously left out during her first call to us. Now its absence seemed even more striking.

"The birth father?" I prompted.

"Oh yes, the same as your other daughter's," she said, smiling. Then she laughed too loudly.

A skeptical "Humph" escaped from the back of my throat before I could catch myself. In my head it translated as "We'll see."

Later that night, we settled back into another temporary home at a hotel with the baby we would name Rachel. Mariah slept soundly on one of the twin beds while Todd fed the baby.

Before we took turns trying to catch a few hours of sleep, I had to tell Todd something I'd noticed.

"You know why Krissy brought out the wrong baby first?" I asked.

I peeked at Mariah to make sure she was still sleeping. Even if she'd been awake, she wouldn't understand what I was saying. Still I dropped my voice even more.

"She wanted to lessen the shock for us when she brought Rachel out," I said. "No matter what their mother claims, there's no way these kids have the same birth father."

Todd stroked the baby's fingers and thought for a minute. He was wired to believe the best about everybody.

"How can you be sure?" he asked.

Right then and there, I couldn't prove it. But looking at Rachel's face, I was sure. And one day, she too would be just as certain about it, no matter what anyone else said.

CHAPTER 6

Light, Bright,
and Almost White

I had a big question on my six-year-old mind, but I was afraid to ask it. One afternoon, as my big sister Neecie and I left the single-screen movie theater in town, it popped into my head. I hadn't been aware that it was on my mind until that moment. The question had been forming somewhere in the back of my developing brain, waiting until I understood what it meant. Now I realized that asking it might make Neecie mad at me. So while we waited for Ma to pick us up, I dragged my grubby, ripped Buster Browns along the complex patterns on the tiled entryway and tried to work up my nerve. I eventually forced out the words.

"Am I 'dopted?"

Neecie set her hands on her wide hips and leaned over to give me one of her looks. Nine years older, she always proclaimed herself "large and in charge" of me. I peered at the sole of my shoe. It hung loose like a tongue. I flopped it back and forth along the ground. My sister's big round eyes glared at me. Where, I kept thinking, was Ma? I hoped she would drive up in our broken-down brown station wagon. Then I could dive into the third-row seat that faced away from everybody and pretend I hadn't asked that question. As I looked up at Neecie towering over me, I realized she wasn't about to let me forget.

"What?!" Neecie said in her froggy voice.

"Never mind," I said, and darted away toward the movie posters beneath the marquee.

Neecie followed, yanked the back of my T-shirt, and whirled me around so fast I stumbled. She liked to do that to get my attention.

"*What* did you say?"

I didn't respond. She popped her eyes even wider and crossed her arms to show me she meant business.

"I'm *talking* to you."

"It was kids at the playground," I sputtered. "They said I was 'dopted cuz I'm not Black like you."

Neecie's eyes narrowed.

"Are Ma and Pops Black? Are Jim-Jim and the rest of us Black?"

After I nodded each time, she delivered her opinion.

"Then, baby brother, you're Black. And don't you *ever* forget it."

I knew Neecie wouldn't lie to me, because she cared about me. But it didn't make sense. If I was Black, then why didn't I look like Ma and Pops or anybody else? They ranged in shade from black coffee to hot chocolate. I was skim milk. Grandma called me "high yella." Others joked I was "light, bright, and almost white." I thought about coming out of Ma's belly. How could you get something white from something black? But I didn't want to ask that right now. I needed Neecie to answer another burning question.

"You won't tell Ma, what I said?"

Neecie shot me another of her no-nonsense expressions. She was studying me. Time was running out. Any second the sound of a missing muffler would announce our old station wagon had arrived.

"Humph" is what she finally muttered. That really meant, we'll see.

It felt hot under the July sun and even more uncomfortable under Neecie's glare. I was glad when Ma finally pulled up in the car with Jim-Jim, Rickie, and Mike. Neecie and I got in. We were barely out of the parking lot when Neecie croaked, "Ma, guess what Stevie just asked me?"

I felt so ashamed I slunk down onto the dirty floor in the third row. Then I turned and bent over the bench seat, burying my small head in the deepest corner of the worn and ripped red vinyl. My face smooshed into a place where the old french fries, gum wrappers, and pennies lived.

It smelled like sweat and cigarette smoke. But I didn't care. I just closed my eyes and covered my ears while Neecie repeated my question.

After a while I could hear Ma yelling at me to get off the floor. When I crawled back up and peeked over the back seat, I saw my mother staring back at me in the rearview mirror. She frowned at me, and my six-year-old self realized I had made her sad. To this day I can't recall exactly what she said on that long ride home, but I do remember she tried to answer the question herself. That answer never really explained why I looked white or convinced me that I belonged to this strange Black family. The truth about who I was seemed to have been shoved into a dark place, and no amount of digging could uncover it. But that didn't mean I would stop trying.

The kids on the school playground weren't the only ones who questioned where my light, bright complexion came from. So did my first friend in life, my cousin Cathleen.

Only six months in age and a few yards of crabgrass separated me and Aunt Bonnie's daughter, so from the time we were toddlers, we were inseparable. The grownups said where you saw one of us, you saw the other, and they took to calling us salt and pepper. They thought it was funny, and so did Cathleen and I until it occurred to both of us one day that our nickname didn't just mean we naturally went together. We'd already started comparing ourselves—our height, our speed, what made me a boy and her a girl. Now we began to place our hands and arms side by side to see the differences everyone else saw.

"Maybe you just need a suntan," Cathleen offered as she poked at my freckled skin.

"Yeah, maybe," I said, but neither of us was really convinced.

Although I was looking for an explanation, there was another part of me that was afraid someone would tell me that I might not really belong. My raucous and raw-talking family confused and scared me, but they were all I had in the world, and as a little boy I still needed assurance that I had a place among them. I'd learned the hard way not to ask them questions, so after the incident with Ma and Neecie, I kept my doubts to myself. The exception was Cathleen. Together we'd come to understand that we lived in an extended family where bad things happened and where everyone kept those things secret. It was comforting to know Cathleen and I at least had each other to share our own secrets and sorrows. Our shared experiences of growing up in those circumstances also meant we understood each other all too well. While it was true that only Cathleen knew exactly what to say to make me laugh until my belly ached, it was also a fact that her words could just as easily bring me to bitter tears.

That happened one day while we played our favorite game of "pretend" outside. We liked to role-play rich people—the families who ate out at McDonald's or shopped at J. C. Penney's. I can't remember why we argued, but Cathleen demanded she have the last word.

"Shut up," she said, putting her hands on her hips like the grown folks did.

Although we were the same age, Cathleen stood about an inch taller than me. I was determined not to be bossed around.

"Make me," I said.

Cathleen shoved me hard until I fell on the ground. When she saw me trying to stand up, she shoved me back down and spit on me.

"How you like that, huh? Now go on and cry, with your dumb self. You think I care? Run home to your mother, with your stupid, funky *white* ass."

Her words hurt more than any physical blows could. Because in that moment, Cathleen had uttered a secret curse. She didn't say I just needed more sun or claim I was still Black like Neecie. She didn't take delight in being a part of salt and pepper. Instead she called me something that no one else had, a word she knew would hurt and confuse me. She called me white. And that meant all the terrible things I thought about myself, things nobody would ever admit, were probably true.

I ran home with hot tears and snot running down my face. I was too ashamed to repeat Cathleen's words to Ma, so I just told her we'd fought. Ma told me that things would be okay. And a few days later, things would be better, for a time. Cathleen and I would be back to giggling and "acting the fool." But after that I figured that Cathleen was like everyone else, holding back the shameful truth about who and what I was. Afterward, I learned to always hold something back, to not let her or anyone else in my family too close. Just like many of the adults in our family, Cathleen wasn't someone I could completely trust or turn to, because in a heartbeat she might turn her fists and her words on me.

Family or no family, I was beginning to realize I always had to look out for myself. It was the only way to protect my skin, let alone my heart.

CHAPTER 7

Queens of the Hill

Pops may have been a dangerous figure who loomed large in my head during my early years, but there were others in our family who seemed equally menacing. And they couldn't blame their behavior on cheap red wine.

My grandmother was one of those people. She controlled much of our lives on the country hill where we lived. She and her companion John lived in a rundown farmhouse that stood atop the peak of a country road on the outskirts of town. Grandma's youngest daughter, Aunt Bonnie, occupied a house on a smaller crest. My tiny home sat in a shallow bowl, stuck in between the two. Our closest neighbors were white farm families who had lived on acres of cornfields and had large dairy farms for generations. At times, hours would go by before the sound of a pickup truck or tractor coming down the road would break the stillness.

I suppose my mother should have taken comfort in the fact that we weren't alone. At least her kids were growing up with family around. But she didn't stay on that isolated country hill out of love. She did it for survival. Soon after marrying, she realized Pops couldn't stand up straight long enough to work and support a family. Her only choice was to move back to the place where she'd grown up. My grandmother sold her an unplowed piece of farmland next door for a buck to build a cheap, prefab house. I often doubted Ma would have accepted the deal if she'd understood she'd be repaying that debt until the day she died.

The land wasn't the only thing she owed to Grandma. In the early 1970s my mother was working as a hospital aide emptying trash cans and bedpans. Her meager check could barely feed five hungry kids, let alone support a drunk with an insatiable thirst, so for years she grudgingly turned to Grandma for support. On many days she sent us kids across the country yard to tap on the door of that falling-down farmhouse. We went so often our shoes beat a permanent path through the wild grass between the two houses.

"Grandma?" I'd call through the old wooden door when I was the designated beggar. "Do you got something to eat?"

I'd find Grandma in her usual place, all three hundred pounds of her perched on a bed in the middle of a cramped and filthy front room. It had taken me time, but I'd grown used to the stink of wood smoke from the potbellied stove used to cook and heat the house. I also grew accustomed to the stench of Grandma. Because the farmhouse had no running water, she bathed rarely and did her business in a plastic bucket. When John got around to it, he emptied her piss and shit in the back part of the small farm he ran.

But growing up, I had to put the bad smells and bad feelings aside. All that mattered was that Grandma was the difference between us eating and not eating. Her generosity, though, came at a steep price. When I'd come begging, she would sigh, suck her teeth, and make me listen as she belittled Ma for marrying Pops or mismanaging money. After she was finished, she would tell me a Christian woman couldn't just sit there and allow us poor kids to go "hawngry."

"Lawd Jesus, save me. Your mama must done shit her money away. Go to the deep freeze and git yoself a pack of pork chops and a loaf of frozen bread. They is a can of peaches up on the shelf."

I then had permission to step down into the half-earthen root cellar full of cobwebs. There Grandma kept jars of her syrupy sweet, home-canned peaches and pears, alongside rows of pickles, beets, and tomatoes. Her cellar became the grocery store we depended on year round.

My grandmother's impoverished childhood in rural Virginia had prepared her to preserve not only food but also cash. Her meager checks from sweeping the floors of one of the small factories that barely sustained the economy in our town were quickly hoarded. Whatever spare change she uncovered cleaning houses, she tucked in mason jars that she hid away from us. She tied up any crumpled dollar bills in a handkerchief that she pinned inside her massive, yellowed brassiere. She had hundreds of dollars stashed around the house, but asking her for money was much harder than begging for food. For those requests, Ma would light a cigarette and then brace herself to trudge across the yard herself.

On some of those occasions, I came with Ma as she stood looking like a panhandler in the presence of her own mother. Together we crept as close as we dared between the smoking wood stove and Grandma's hot temper. Then we waited for her sermon.

"You always putting on your little airs," Grandma began. "Spending money you don't got."

To Grandma, it wasn't just that my mother was living above her means. She thought Ma was trying to be something she was not. It rankled her that her daughter now wanted the things she didn't have growing up—a nice, clean house, store-bought clothes, and more. In Grandma's book, Ma's greater sin was acting like she deserved that kind of life, and she delighted in telling her daughter—whom she called by her middle name, Virginia—just that.

"There go Vir-jen-ya," Grandma singsonged in her deep southern accent. "She wants to be white so bad."

To Ma, her aspirations weren't to be white. She was just trying to be better than she was raised. But Grandma couldn't see that. She'd been raised in a time and world that didn't believe Black women could reach higher, so she couldn't believe in my mother's dreams. Her anger and resentment were really rooted in hopelessness about herself.

As for my mother, she knew it was useless trying to change Grandma's heart and mind. To get what she needed, she had to hold her tongue while holding out her hand. She didn't have to explain what she was really thinking to me. I saw how she looked at Grandma. Here before us was a woman willing to clean for white women until her hands smelled of Clorox, yet who willingly lived in squalor to save a few pennies.

I watched Ma take a deep drag of her cigarette and swallow what she really wanted to say.

"Mama, I need this money for the light bill. They're going to turn it off," Ma said, wringing her small hands.

"I tole you, I ain't got no fifty dollars," Grandma said, folding her big fleshy arms and sucking her gold-capped teeth.

"Please don't make me beg."

"What you want me to do? You think you can git blood from a stone?" Grandma said. She grinned. I held my breath as she rocked back in a flimsy wooden chair that groaned under her weight.

"Mama, I can't have my kids up in a cold, dark house during the winter."

Grandma whooped with laughter.

"Hell! Let them freeze they asses, what I care? No one tole you to take up with that ole drunkard."

It slowly made sense to me. Ma was trapped with Pops and Grandma. She couldn't get rid of either of them. Ma thought a moment, dragged on her cigarette a last time, and then stubbed it out on the bottom of the pot-bellied stove. She turned to go.

"Forget it, Mama. Keep your goddamn money."

I jumped back as my grandmother suddenly raised her bulk off her chair. In two giant booming steps, she advanced until she stood toe-to-toe with Ma. She put one hand on her enormous hip and used the other to shake her Christian finger in my mother's face.

"Now, jes you wait a goddamn minute. Who you cussing at, gal?"

Ma tried to back away, but Grandma grabbed her by the wrists and "jecked" her backward into a nearby chair. Ma sat there helpless. She started to cry. Even though I'd seen it before, I never got used to it. My grandmother wanted Ma to know she was in charge of our little hill. If Grandma's money didn't keep Ma in her place, then her threats certainly would.

Just as I prayed to make it off that hill one day, I sometimes prayed just as hard for my mother to find out a way out too. For years I watched her try to take a few steps away and inevitably fall back into the ample arms of my grandmother, because for the price of her dignity, she could always find a loaf of frozen bread, a warm spot by the potbellied stove, or a few crumpled dollar bills.

In our family, the threat of physical violence was always present, and my siblings and I were ready for it to be directed toward us at any moment. The reasons for punishment varied. Tearing up the house while playing was a no-no. So was doing poorly in school or getting in trouble with a teacher. But perhaps the greatest offense was crossing the line from disrespect into defiance. Most times all we had to fear was a swat on the butt and a curse-filled threat, but we knew a swat might escalate to an open-handed slap or a closed-fist beating.

Mike was the one who most often faced physical abuse, especially from our grandmother, who seemed to think his smirks and patronizing grins were a way of him displaying his disdain for her—which they often were. I can't remember what Mike did to antagonize her one day a few months later, but it was enough for Grandma to declare it was worthy of physical punishment. Worse, she expected him to help carry it out.

"Chile, you go bust me a switch off that tree and bring it here," she said.

Mike stood at the bottom of her front porch. His brown marble-like eyes filled with tears, and his bottom lip quivered.

"Noooo, I'm sorry, please. I'll be good, Grandma, I promise."

Grandma's knees had arthritis, but she jumped out of her chair and descended the steps at a trot.

"*What I say?* Don't make me come any further. I will smack the black right off you."

I watched Mike's chubby short body hop back a couple of steps. He ran to a gnarled apple tree, where he snapped off a thin branch. He and I knew that if he dragged his feet coming back or retrieved a branch that was too short, the penalty would be harder.

My grandmother pulled back her arm and the branch sliced through the air

Thwack, thwack, thwack. Thwack.

I flinched along with Mike as Grandma switched his butt and legs and he yelped in pain. I wanted to step in and save him from my grandmother, as I'd watched Jim do with Pops. Instead I stood quietly, waiting for instructions. I knew that if the blood seeped from his skin too much or the welts got too big, Grandma would tell me to go fetch her witch hazel to take away some of the sting. And if she did, I would dare not take my time.

Knowing he was her favorite target, Mike generally tried to keep out of Grandma's way. But one Saturday he couldn't avoid her or her wrath. Winter was over, and Grandma was ready to leave her hot, funky cave of a front room, so she waddled across the yard to our house.

Aunt Bonnie followed her in through our back door. Bonnie lived on the other side of our house with Uncle Hunt and Cathleen. She too had taken advantage of Grandma's sweetheart deal—a plot of land for a dollar. But unlike my mother, she wasn't afraid of Grandma. A massively overweight woman herself, she often gained the upper hand in physical fights with her mother, not to mention the rest of our family.

On this day, the two of them were in a rare easygoing mood. They plopped themselves at our kitchen table and sat for hours for a family visit. I noticed my mother, who feared them both, trying to stay out of their way. In between offering an occasional comment to their gossipy conversation, she busied herself cleaning the kitchen cabinets and waited for them to leave.

Mike and I had agreed to hide out in our bedroom to stay out of the way. It was one of the few escapes my brother Mike had from our daily lives. He especially seemed to live with a boiling anger toward the grown folks in our family. It was only years later that I'd learn it was because he felt they did little to protect him from the unwanted attention of Pops.

For a while he quietly read to me from his ripped-up Aquaman comics. Then I watched him make grubby army men from an old container of modeling clay. The grownups kept interrupting us, calling Mike out of the room. He was the oldest kid in earshot that day, so he was expected to run errands.

Our grandmother had told him to "run cross the yard" several times to get things she wanted from her house. This time she wanted her pocketbook. The first few times, she stalled her with a "hold on, I'm coming" that sounded more sarcastic than sincere. Then he shifted to an impatient "in a minute." Mike could have run across the yard and back in the time it took him to keep stalling. Later I'd learn he kept putting Grandma off because she never said please and thank you. Finally, after it seemed like he couldn't put her off any longer, he left the bedroom, ambled his chunky butt into the kitchen, and opened his mouth in a gap-toothed grin.

"I have an idea. Why don't you go get it yourself?"

Grandma's face twisted with rage. She was going to skip the threat and jump right to the beating.

"Come *here*, boy!" she hollered at the top of her lungs.

Mike realized if he got too close, our grandmother might jerk, or as Grandma called it "jeck," him by the arms and pull him toward her. Then he'd really be in for it. He darted back to the bedroom.

"Oh, hell no," Grandma declared. She rocked herself back and forth a few times until she could heave herself to her feet.

Our mother bravely stepped into her path.

"Mama, leave him alone," Ma pleaded, putting her hands up as if she were surrendering.

Grandma was enraged that her daughter might question her.

"You better move, gal, before I tangle with you!" she growled. At that point Aunt Bonnie stood up from the table and moved to squeeze her wide body between them. I went to my usual hiding spot behind a chair in the living room. I was afraid Grandma might hurt Ma and then Mike. Aunt Bonnie was the wild card. She might hurt us all. I shut my eyes, afraid to see these women raise their fists to each other, but their words hit just as hard.

"Please, leave my kids alone," I heard Ma beg.

"I will whip his ass and then beat yours," Grandma said. Then I heard her booming steps.

Ma shrieked, "*Get out!*"

It sounded like Grandma had a fist clenched around Ma's actual heart. I turned to the wall. After that I heard scuffling close by, and then Aunt Bonnie's voice over everyone's demanding that they stop this damned nonsense.

"And who are *you* talking to?" Grandma demanded.

"I'm talking to you, Mama, and you better sit yourself down right now before I beat *your* ass," Bonnie replied.

"Oh, so now you gonna whup me?"

Ma began to sob. "Stop it, pleeeeze."

"Bitch, get out my way."

I opened my eyes. The three of them stood like wild-eyed, wild-haired Medusas, with tangled limbs. They thrust against each other, moving from our tiny living room to the much smaller kitchen and finally out the door. I ran to the window in time to see Aunt Bonnie jump into her car. She slammed it into reverse so fast, gravel from our driveway shot out like bullets from beneath the wheels. Then I saw Grandma waddling and stomping across the yard to her house. She turned around every few steps to cuss at her daughters. Ma was slumped on the bottom steps of our stairs, crying. Her hands shook so badly, it took her a while to light one of the cigarettes she said calmed her nerves.

I hugged her and told her things would be all right.

But she and I knew that might not be true.

As much as we kids feared our grandmother, we came to fear Aunt Bonnie even more. Her temper was unmatched by anyone's when she was riled. When her fleshy fists were balled up, they looked like big brown softballs. Behind her back we secretly called her Moosie because of the way she charged bodies when provoked.

One of my first memories of seeing her explosive anger was a few years earlier on a spring afternoon. We had all gathered on Grandma's rickety front porch. My grandmother was making old-fashioned lye soap, just as she once had as a young girl. Jim-Jim had brought me to watch. Aunt Bonnie and Uncle Hunt were there too, but they were too busy arguing to pay attention. We always kept a close eye on them, because we knew how quickly their bickering could boil over. That day when I spotted my aunt gnawing her bottom lip—a familiar sign that she was ready to explode—I scampered off Jim's lap and to a safe corner behind Grandma's old rocking chair.

"Shut your mouth," Aunt Bonnie said to her husband, spit flying out of her mouth. "Or see if I don't take my fist up against your damned head."

Uncle Hunt was short, dark, thin, and as fragile as a matchstick. He stuttered a response. He knew he was no match for his wife. His eyes darted back and forth, and he eased up off the rusty folding chair where he was sitting and began to move toward the porch steps. He looked like a beaten dog trying to escape a whupping. I peeked at Grandma, who continued stirring the big kettle and was careful to keep the burning lye mix from getting on her skin. She too took a few steps back.

"Bonnie, leave that man alone," Grandma pleaded.

But Bonnie heard Uncle Hunt stutter-mumble something under his breath. In a flash she was up out of her seat. She balled her fists. The porch rocked under her feet as she stomped across, picked up the kettle of lye, and flung it toward Hunt's face.

Everyone screamed and scattered. Jim-Jim scooped me up under his arm like a football and bounded down the steps ahead of the caustic lye spreading on the floor. He dropped me on the dirt patch in front of Grandma's house. I peered at my bare feet, wondering if my toes might melt away. When I looked up, I saw Bonnie waddle toward the middle of our country road after Hunt. But she was too fat, and my uncle had figured out how to stay one step ahead.

From then on, I tried to avoid being anywhere within arm's reach of Aunt Bonnie. If she was enraged, I didn't want to be among those directly or indirectly caught in her crosshairs. But Cathleen usually had nowhere to run. Often, she spent her days inside her house, cooking, cleaning, and doing the smallest of chores for her mother, while Aunt Bonnie sprawled on a lopsided couch and watched daytime TV.

I made excuses when Cathleen invited me over to play. "Ma needs me at home," I explained. But there were days when my mother was working late, Pops was off on a binge, and the big kids were still at school. I had no choice then but to allow my aunt to babysit me. Ma didn't like it, but she had no other options. "Just stay out of Bonnie's way and play with your cousin Cathleen, quietly," she warned.

On those days I tried to make myself invisible, especially during my aunt's daytime "stories." Before we could play, Cathleen or I would have to bring a heaping plate of food from the kitchen to the lopsided couch where she lay in front of the TV. Then we retreated to Cathleen's room, where I loved to help her comb the long blonde hair on her broken Barbies. But once the credits rolled, we cringed because that meant it was time for Aunt Bonnie to do Cathleen's thick hair which was harder to tame than a Barbie doll.

"Cathleen! Where are you?" Bonnie bellowed. "Where is that hard-headed black bitch? Get your ass out here so I can braid that nappy hair."

Cathleen dragged her feet as she came out of the bathroom holding a comb, a container of greasy hair oil, and a handful of plastic ponytail balls. Tears welled in her eyes. Cathleen knew that at some point her mother would grow exasperated at her for squirming away from the rough yanks on her head, and when she did, she'd send me to the kitchen to find something to make Cathleen mind her.

"Get up and go get me that big spoon in the drawer," she'd yell.

I didn't dare drag my feet. In the kitchen, I pulled out the spoon and glanced at the wall clock. Only a few hours more, I told myself. I had to make it until Ma came to bring me home. It might not be any safer, but at least it was predictable. I handed Aunt Bonnie the wooden spoon and sat down. When I dared to look over, I saw her bring it down again and again on Cathleen until big welts appeared on her arms and a knot swelled on her scalp. When the spoon splintered, Aunt Bonnie reached for the wooden hairbrush and continued with the beating. I looked away.

And when Cathleen began to cry, sob, and beg me for help, I acted as if I couldn't hear her. I moved within a few inches of the TV and let the sound of *Days of Our Lives* drown her out. Cathleen and I both had a house of hell. At least on this day, mine was better than hers, and for that I was grateful.

CHAPTER 8

Whitebread

On the day I was to officially become part of Todd's family in 2002, I wanted little to do with them. So I hid. I lay in bed long after the rest of his family woke. Each time his mother gently pushed open the door to the guest bedroom, allowing a slice of the tangerine-colored Jacksonville sunshine to stream through, I lay stock still. I was afraid she might interpret any movement as an invitation to sing out a "good morning."

"Leave him be, Mom," Todd called from the next room. "He's tired."

"I will," she half sang as she eased the door shut. I could hear her pad away softly.

"But he needs to eat sometime, right?" I could picture her outside the door, palms up, giving a half shrug.

"Mom, please," I heard Todd reply.

"What! He'll be hungry, I imagine. Such a long trip."

Todd's father bellowed out next in his native Brooklyn accent.

"Marilyn, he's a grown boy."

"He's not a child, Richard," she said in her quiet but pointed scold.

"I didn't call him a child!"

"Boy. You said 'boy,' honey."

"Boy. As in male, Marilyn. A full-grown homosexual—oops. I meant 'sapiens,' Homo sapiens."

"Richard!"

"Homo *sapiens*, Marilyn, from the Latin word *homo*, meaning—"

"Oh my god. Mom, Dad, please!" Todd pleaded again.

Their back-and-forth banter, full of light nagging, small bickering, and cautious chiding of one another, was like nothing I'd ever heard in my life, and it confused me. This family of New York City Jews transplanted to Florida—with a bizarre ten-year layover in Baton Rouge, Louisiana—were my new family. At least, that's what they told me. "Call us Mom and Dad, okay?" his mother told me the night before, stroking my arm while his father massaged my shoulders for an uncomfortably long time. Todd and I had visited his parents, two sisters, and brother several times before. I'd even attended family weddings and boarded an all-family cruise celebrating his parents' fiftieth anniversary. But this trip was different. Now his family was gathering to celebrate us. We would be the ones getting "married."

The idea of having a commitment celebration had been all mine. Long before our progressive state of New Jersey passed one of the first domestic partnership laws in the country, I told Todd I wanted to have a ceremony. My eagerness to formalize our relationship surprised him. We'd been together barely two years and had yet to figure out exactly when we planned to have kids. Looking back, I couldn't explain the sense of urgency myself. All I knew was that I'd fallen in love with this nice Jewish boy with a Brooklyn heart and a Louisiana twang, and the idea of the two of us being a family had taken root in my brain.

After I'd pretended to wake up on that Saturday morning, Todd's mother hovered over me. Polite offers to fix me a snack, press my shirt, and even buy me shoe polish were all rebuffed. But still she persisted.

"I'm fine, *Mom*," I said. The word felt forced coming out and I wondered if it sounded the same to her. Mom had always been a "white" word to me, the name kids on TV used for trim, tidy women who smiled a lot and hugged their kids. It was different from Ma or Mama, the names my family gave to the women who were just as likely to grab us and shake us as they were to squeeze us affectionately into their large bosoms.

The women in Todd's family also ruled firmly over their loving children and loyal husbands, but they did it quietly and efficiently with arched eyebrows and small, disappointed frowns. I was glad there would be no woman reigning over me like this in our house after Todd and I were married. Still, sometimes even Todd would joke that his mother treated him like her favorite daughter.

The night of the ceremony, Todd's entire extended family filled the courtyard of the Victorian home where we held it. From my family, only Denise and her small brood occupied the few remaining seats. This was the first time Todd's family had met my relatives. I worried, in part, what they might think of them and, now, of me.

"Sweetheart, does your sister wish to sit up front, next to Dad and me?" Todd's mother asked. I noticed she had a unique tone that always managed to sound more like a strong recommendation than a question.

"She's fine, *Mom*," I said, remembering to smile this time.

Across the courtyard, Todd's two older sisters bustled around him, straightening his tie and brushing his lapels. I knew better than to expect Neecie to fuss over me. Instead she sat with one arm folded over her chest, supporting another that reached up to cup her cheek. I knew what that look meant: "Humph. Now ain't this something."

And it was quite a picture. Here was her light, bright, almost white, but sure as hell Black brother about to gay-marry into a Jewish family. But Neecie had long ago assured me she would embrace anybody who loved her baby brother.

Todd's brother, Lee, stepped into my line of sight. I'd asked him to handle any last-minute problems.

"So, *these* single flowers? Do you want me to put them inside a vase? We can also place them out here. Maybe we can give one to every person?"

Before I could catch myself, I said the first thing that came to mind.

"Now, how the hell should I know?"

Todd either overheard me or saw the look on his brother's face. He arched his eyebrow at me and mouthed the magic word he'd begun to use on me on situations like this.

"Tone" was all he had to say.

A few minutes later, we huddled together in a small gazebo in the courtyard lit by twinkling Christmas lights. The early December winds rattled the light strings and sent chills through his great-grandmother, who sat behind us wrapped in an expensive throw. Looking out at Denise, I knew that she was wondering what was happening. So was I. When Todd had agreed to have a ceremony, he insisted that his family's rabbi preside. The rabbi peered over his glasses at me, while Todd adjusted the yarmulke that kept slipping off my head.

As the winds kicked up, I leaned in to try to hear the Hebrew words the rabbi whispered, but then his voice boomed out in English, reciting what I would later learn were the traditional seven blessings. He pulled us in close and gently draped the two opposite ends of his shawl over our shoulders. *May you always find a refuge tucked within your love—a place to hide out, and a place to reflect.*

Todd and I had brought our own vows, which were later tucked away and forgotten in a book or album that one day will be rediscovered. All I can remember is the surprising feeling of choking back tears. And there will always be one other memory: the winds gusting so strongly that they rattled the chuppah, the ceremonial canopy Todd's family had painstakingly put up over our heads. The canopy snapped taut, then came untethered on one side. Todd's eldest sister hustled forward to hold it in place.

It was only years later that I found out what was so important that she had to fret over something that seemed to me so insignificant at the time. In the Jewish tradition, the chuppah symbolizes something very important to the two people who stand solemnly beneath it: the home they will one day build together.

A cool spring breeze settled around us the next time we gathered with Todd's family, nearly three years later. This time we spread out on an expansive deck in his sister and brother-in-law's backyard. The deck stepped down into a small loose collection of trees. Through them, you could see the exclusive golf course that anchored their gated community outside Jacksonville. Though I secretly envied their custom-built home and comfortable life, I told Todd I was put off by their lifestyle.

Todd shrugged it off.

"Eh, it's not for me, either, but they worked hard for it," he said.

I couldn't argue with him. His entire family's earnest, hardworking ethic had propelled all of them into good schools, established careers, and increasingly comfortable lives. It added to my growing feeling that I would never really fit in, no matter how often they told me I was one of them.

It wasn't just the trappings of their lives. Their entire way of living was foreign to me. Not one of them drank too much, argued too loudly, or lived too recklessly. Instead they followed every rule and law to the letter and the spirit. They took pride in upholding social standards and norms. Perhaps the first time I realized this was early on in our relationship when I was in my car with Todd and made an illegal U-turn.

He turned to me. "Are you trying to get a ticket?"

"What, there were no cops around," I answered.

"But it's against the law!"

"Did you *see* any police?"

A few blocks later, he widened his eyes at me as I changed lanes without a turn signal.

"Okay, okay, I'm sorry."

I made a show of pausing respectfully at the next stop sign and looking both ways in an exaggerated manner. Todd nodded.

But then I rolled down my window and, without thinking twice, casually tossed the core of the apple I was eating out of the window. Todd blanched.

"What now?" I asked.

He just shook his head in exasperation.

Todd would say that the best compliment his family ever received came from a cousin who was considered a bit out there because he grew up in Southern California. Of Todd's family he said, "Yeah, they're pretty square. But they're good people."

I didn't disagree. It just meant it wasn't enough to learn from his sister how to buy the best challah, I had to come to terms with what it meant to be part of a family that was pure whitebread.

I jumped at the touch of a heavy hand on my shoulder. As I turned, I came face to face with the family's rabbi.

"Mazel tov!" he exclaimed. "So, now you have little ones!" I shifted Rachel in my arms so he could take a closer look. "Oy, already a beauty." He jogged over to seek out Todd, who held Mariah by the hand. The rabbi had come to this family gathering to offer a new blessing. Todd had pressed for this ceremony in which our kids would receive their formal Hebrew names.

"They're going to be Black and Jewish?" I asked when he first told me of this plan. "Don't you think it's going to be hard enough that our kids are adopted and we're gay?"

Todd grew flustered.

"We talked about this," he said. "This is something you specifically promised me after we agreed to have kids, remember? It's important to me. I'm Jewish, and I want the kids to have that connection to me and that same tradition."

I recall starting to open my mouth to argue back. His family was Jewish lite. They ate bacon. They only went to services on a few holy days. His own brother had even converted to Christianity. "Why can't we let them grow up and decide their own faith?" I wanted to ask.

But I stopped myself. Although I believed in God, I was a lapsed Catholic. I wasn't sure what I believed anymore. It was another part of my identity that I struggled with. I decided it was unfair to allow my own ambivalence about organized religion to affect our children's faith.

"Can I stay Christian?" I asked Todd.

"Fine. But they're not going to church and eating magical crackers," he said.

I laughed. We had a deal.

The Jewish blessings were bestowed that day, and Todd's sisters and mother showered kisses and gifts on the two girls. Though I would continue to sometimes question where I fit into this upper-middle-class

Jewish family, it was clear they loved and accepted the kids into their tribe.

A few hours later I cradled Mariah on my lap, and we swung alone on a small hammock in a corner of the backyard. "Higher, Poppy!" she begged as I rocked the hammock back and forth. I wrapped her tighter in my arms as I tried to move it faster. A few feet away, I could hear Todd and his family inside, joking and cooking together. I looked up when I heard Todd opening the sliding glass door.

"What are you doing out there alone?" he called. "Come on in. My family is going to think you're avoiding them."

Mariah giggled, and I called out across the backyard. "We're fine just by ourselves, right now."

And for a few short years, we would be.

CHAPTER 9

The Big Uneasy

In the weeks after that terrible night in 2015 that reminded me so much of my childhood, my family acted like they'd invited a stranger into our home. The kids awkwardly moved aside as we brushed past each other in the kitchen. Todd let me leave the musty love seat in the basement behind and invited me upstairs, but I was only permitted to roam as far as the living room couch. It was unclear if I'd ever make it all the way back home. After circling each other for a few days, Todd and I came to a stop. We hovered at the edge of the hallway after the kids were asleep. I noticed for the first time how his shoulders had begun to stoop.

"What you did," Todd said, "I know you've said you just overreacted. But that was not normal."

He looked over his shoulder at the doors to the kids' rooms and lowered his voice.

"Mariah is struggling. But your response to her . . . She triggers something inside you, I'm not sure what. But it's scary, and it's dangerous."

"Wait a minute—"

Todd held up his hand, cutting me off.

"We're going to talk to somebody."

Then he turned, walked down the hall and into our bedroom. As I stood there, he closed the door behind him with a small click.

I had to stop myself from bursting through that door to try and defend myself, as I'd done too many times before. I could hear the explanation I always gave him: Mariah needed tough love. She needed to mind us. If she didn't listen, she could be made to listen. It was an issue of respect. But I knew this time was different. Todd was done listening to the homespun wisdom that came from the country hill where I grew up, the harsh judgments from the strong Black women who raised me.

In his mind, the issue wasn't just Mariah. The problem, now, included me.

As I wandered back out to my makeshift bed on the couch, I realized there was one more thing I wished I could have told Todd in that moment. It was that I was sorry and that we could get past this. All it would take was for us to just forget what happened. It was a bad family memory that could be buried and forgotten, as I'd done with so many others my entire life.

Yet I already knew that Todd wasn't going to let it go.

A few days later Todd announced he had invited a therapist to talk to us while the girls were at school. As we waited, I walked around the house sweeping tiny bits of household clutter into drawers or kicking it into closets. In all our years together, I'd never lost my sense of anxiety about visitors. It didn't matter that we had one of the bigger and nicer homes on the block. A childhood voice inside me said that an outsider, possibly a white person, was coming to peek into our messy lives, and that we might not measure up.

Mariah and I were alike in that way—naturally wary of new people and hyperconscious about how others might see us. It was also true that we would sometimes let that anxiety boil over into anger. I'd begun to wonder how much of my own upbringing and fractured sense of self had either shaped or colored my view of my daughter. Even though I was ready to admit there was some connection, I didn't think I needed a $150-an-hour therapist to tell me that I had a fucked-up childhood.

The therapist showed up while I was wiping down the kitchen counters. Her name was Meghan. She was white, midthirties. Her jeans, sweatshirt, and ponytail reminded me of a graduate student. As she and Todd settled into chairs in the dining room, I kept bustling around the house trying to tidy up. Todd finally let out a small impatient huff, just loud enough for me to hear. I wandered over and sat in the chair beside him.

"So," Meghan said.

She smiled slightly, turned her eyes toward me, and tilted her head. It was clear Todd had already told her what I had done. I knew I should have felt ashamed or sad or regretful, but all I could summon was resentment. Not at Mariah or Todd, but at this woman with a solicitous smile.

"Where should we begin?" she pressed.

I folded my arms and looked over at Todd.

"How about you tell me when you first began having issues as a family."

I listened to Todd recount our first years as a family—the back-to-back adoptions and the challenges of caring for two high-energy toddlers. In my head I replayed home videos of this time in our lives. Our first house. Our kids playing chase in the backyard. Their squeals of laughter. "Watch this Poppy," Mariah said into the camera. I heard myself, on the videos, giggling at her attempt at a handstand. When I watched those videos recently, it was hard to recognize that carefree voice as my own.

It was easier back then, I knew, because most of the pressures of parenting fell on Todd during those first couple of years. He'd decided to stay at home full-time to care for the kids. That freed me up to throw myself into work. Soon after Mariah's birth, I'd been promoted to work at NBC's *Weekend Today Show*. It was an exciting and well-paying gig, one that nabbed me a Manhattan office next door to Lester Holt, but it came with grueling weekend and overnight shifts and a long commute. Once Rachel was born, the work demands meant I was spending even less time at home. Two kids meant twice the effort for Todd. By the time Rachel was six months old, he admitted the pace was wearing him out.

In the winter of 2005, I thought I'd found an escape. NBC had announced a new position at their news bureau in New Orleans, helping to cover the aftermath of Hurricane Katrina. I remember emailing Todd from work.

"What do you think about moving to New Orleans?" I typed. "Better hours and cheaper cost of living. Besides, you grew up in Baton Rouge. It would be like going home."

In spite of those selling points, I knew it was a strange idea. Parts of the city were still flooded, without power, or underneath mountains of muck and debris. But Todd and I had read that the city was poised for a strong comeback. Major companies and billions of federal dollars were flowing into the city. Behind them were young entrepreneurial professionals who were moving in to take part in a historic rebuilding effort. Todd's background was in community redevelopment and urban planning, and he saw a chance to get back to work. For me it meant a modest promotion and a nine-to-five job that would pay New York wages in New Orleans. Todd and I would turn forty later that year. We told ourselves that a midlife transition would be easier before the kids were school age. So in early 2006 we packed up and moved to the Big Easy, looking for an easier way of life.

Once in New Orleans, we found a house painted the color of goldenrods in the Uptown part of the city on high ground, untouched by the floodwaters. Our new home was open, airy, and filled with light. It sat in stark contrast to some of the houses around it with porches and rooflines that sagged with age and foundations that settled unevenly on the swampy land.

The kids now had their own rooms, a huge backyard, and a large wraparound porch deep enough for them to ride their tricycles on. Even amid all the ruin and ongoing recovery, New Orleans still had a funky cultural charm, an easy way of life, and months of warm Gulf breezes. For us, it felt like an oasis. For the first time in two years I was glad to come home every night for dinner, bath time, and bedtime, and I finally felt like I was settling into parenthood again.

Looking back, though, it is clear we underestimated the effect of the sudden change on the kids, especially Mariah. She was two now, and her almond eyes looked at her new house and the world around her with some apprehension. Within a few months of our move, as we lay asleep one night, Mariah screamed. We raced into her bedroom.

I scooped her out of bed and pulled her to my chest, my eyes darting around the room.

"I'm scared. I want my mom," she whined, then squeezed her arms tighter around my neck.

I took a deep breath and looked up at Todd. We'd known this day might come. Before the adoption, counselors had warned us that even small children will mourn the loss of birth mothers they've never met. I realized, now, that my daughter was feeling the same sort of yearning I'd felt my entire life for the father I'd never known.

"I know, baby, but your mom can't be here," I said, stroking her hair. "She wanted you to come live with Daddy and Poppy."

"Remember the book we read?" Todd asked. "About the little girl who was adopted?"

"What's 'dopted?"

"You know. It means they were chosen by their parents, like you and your sister. We adopted you because we wanted to give you love and a home."

She went back to sleep, but her bad dreams would continue for a while. Sometimes she would call for "Daddy" or "Poppy," but sometimes for her mother. While we were always able to soothe her back to sleep, she never seemed completely settled.

In some ways I too felt apprehension after our move. The city's mingling of French, Latin, and African influences had always made it a cultural and racial melting pot. Like Las Vegas, it had acquired the reputation of a tourist destination where people of all backgrounds could come to shed their inhibitions and let their hair down. Its unofficial motto was "Laissez les bons temps rouler" or "Let the good times roll."

But the truth was, New Orleans was a divided city—a place where the grassy medians that separated neighborhoods were still referred to as neutral grounds, hundreds of years after the French and Spanish first fought over them.

Whether you lived Uptown or Downtown defined your income. East Bank versus West Bank—what side of the Mississippi your neighborhood fell on—determined your politics. And in some small pockets of the city, there was even the sense of a possible divide between light-skinned Creoles and dark-skinned African Americans. They each harbored a lingering suspicion that their skin color affected their social status.

Katrina's winds and storm surge had ripped off the neon overcoating of the city's touristy image and laid bare some ugly racial, social, and economic divides that had long existed within the city. It didn't take long before Todd and I noticed them and wondered how to fit in.

Back in our little liberal bubble on the East Coast, we had grown accustomed to people looking at our family with delighted curiosity. But here, in this city that sat like a basin below sea level, it seemed as if it were just us in a fishbowl. I sensed the world shifting their eyes toward us every time they saw two "white" men pulling a red wagon with two girls inside, one Black, the other obviously mixed race. Even in this multicultural city, we stood out.

The fact that we couldn't hide in plain sight became clear during our first sweltering summer in the city. We booked a room for the weekend at a French Quarter hotel. It offered maximum air conditioning, a cool indoor pool, and a chance for an overnight staycation in a place where someone would cook and clean for us. As we walked through the lobby, I felt anxious. I asked Todd to go to the registration desk by himself while I stood back with the kids. As we walked to the room, I put my fears at ease after a woman on the housekeeping staff stopped us in the hall. She scanned our kids up and down, then smiled. "They're sisters, right? I can tell."

With that, I relaxed. The hotel was mostly empty, so the staff gave the kids free run of the site and free desserts, and the weekend flew by in a flash. By Sunday morning we were relaxed, packed up and ready to return to our house across the city, but Mariah had decided she liked staying in this "big house" with a pool.

"No, I don't want to go," she announced, exercising her three-year-old independence.

"I know, sweetie," Todd said, gently. "But we can't stay. It's checkout time, and you've got preschool tomorrow."

Todd reached for her hand and tugged her out the revolving door. He struggled to pull our suitcase behind him, while keeping another bag from falling off his shoulder. They walked ahead while I pushed Rachel in the stroller. Soon they turned the corner, but I could hear Mariah's protests echo down the street.

"Noooooooo, I don't want to . . ."

"Keep walking," I called ahead to Todd. "She's just tired."

Her sobs died down. As I rounded the corner a minute later, I spotted why. A block ahead, they were stopped in the middle of the sidewalk. A middle-aged Black woman stood in their path. My chest tightened. I race-walked the stroller ahead in time, and Todd turned to reassure me.

"It's fine," he said.

But I wasn't convinced.

"What's going on?" I said. "Can we help you?"

The woman looked at me and Todd.

"I saw this little girl crying, and this man . . . well, she seemed upset," she explained.

It took only a moment to picture what she'd seen: a white man leading a little Black girl down the street as she cried, "No, I don't want to go."

"She's ours, understand?" I snapped. "Here, you want to see?"

I pulled out my wallet and thrust a family picture toward the woman.

"I'm so sorry," she said, backing away.

"Really, it's no problem," Todd said.

He offered an understanding smile. I glared at them both. All I could feel was anger. I wasn't sure if it was toward Todd, this woman, or Mariah. It would be years before I recognized it wasn't anger, but embarrassment and shame. We walked in silence for the next few blocks. Once in the car, Mariah was the first to speak.

"Why did that lady talk to us?"

I listened as Todd patiently explained the woman was worried that he wasn't her father.

"But why?" Mariah asked.

Todd sighed.

"Because we look different from you, and our family looks different from other families."

I looked in the rearview mirror and saw her looking back at Todd and me. She turned away and stared out the window at the passing houses where other families lived.

Later, after we'd had time to think about it, we would tell the kids they didn't have to explain themselves to anyone, unless they really needed help. If someone ever asked again who they were and how they belonged to us, we told them to simply say we're a family. Still, Todd and I knew that might not be enough for some. From that day forward, we agreed to carry something in our wallets that no one could argue with. Stuffed behind their baby pictures and the photos of us as a family was hard proof, copies of their birth certificates.

On them, Todd is listed as their father. I'm listed as their mother.

From then on, I became even more hyperaware of how others looked at our family. Though I couldn't affect the perceptions of strangers, I did try to manage how we presented ourselves out in public. It was a high bar, and I was always on the lookout for when we might fall short. One of those times happened at a birthday party for the son of our next-door neighbor. The little boy was Mariah's age. As his celebration wound down and the leftover cake started to melt under the sinking sun, his mother kneeled to hug and kiss him. I caught Mariah watching them closely and saw her face drop. I could tell she was missing the mother she didn't have.

"Okay, baby, we need to go," I blurted out. "Time to go home."

As I picked her up in my arms, I felt a sharp piercing sensation in the soft part of my shoulder.

"Jesus Christ!" I yelped. "You bit me."

The eyes of the parents and their kids shifted toward me. I wandered behind a tree. Todd ran over and offered to take her out of my arms, but I pulled away and hustled Mariah toward the backyard gate. Todd followed me out, offering quick apologies to the host. I waited until we were on the sidewalk. Then, low enough so not even Todd could catch my words, I hissed at Mariah and shook her once. The familiar words of my grandmother, my aunt and my mother tumbled out of my mouth before I even realized it. "You bite me again and I swear, I will slap the black right off you. Do you understand?"

I searched her wide eyes that were now brimming with tears.

"What are you doing?"

Todd sounded exasperated. He pulled my collar aside and poked at the two barely visible red spots on my shoulder. Then he studied our daughter's arms—where my fingertips had left small impressions.

"That was a little much," he said.

He shook his head disapprovingly at me, pulled Mariah out of my arms, and walked her the few steps to our front door. I saw Mariah looking back at me, her lips set in a pout. As I climbed the steps behind them, I felt a small, hot ember of anger inside my chest. By now Todd knew enough about how I'd been raised. We'd agreed never to spank our kids like the children in my family had been. I hadn't raised a hand to my daughter, but I'd seen how he looked at me. I didn't pick up a belt like Pops, or snap a thin branch off a tree like Grandma would have and smack her legs until they bled. I'd never do that. Never. But these were my kids. And they would listen to me. They would respect me. That's just what Black parents did, I told myself.

"Anything you need to add," Todd said, bringing me back to the room. I looked at him and then the therapist. I noticed he'd stopped short of talking about what had happened just days before. I wondered if, like me, a part of him wanted to forget.

I looked down again and shook my head. Meghan had been jotting notes for the better part of an hour. It was getting late. Soon the kids would come in the front door from school, eyeing the white woman who had showed up to tell us how to be a family. Listening to Meghan, I realized she had no easy answers. She told us one other thing Krissy had neglected to mention to us during her sunny, optimistic introductions all those years ago. Some adopted children will reject their families and their love. They will mourn the life they didn't have. A primal wound, experts call it: a lifelong emotional ache caused when a child and mother are separated at birth. For some, there's no mending it or closing it over, only the hope of minimizing the grief. To do that requires parents with a lot of patience and very little judging—things I never had as a kid. Now I was being asked to find those things in myself.

Mariah had her wounds and, it was becoming clear, I had my own. I stared at the table thinking of the family I'd left, the family I once dreamed of, and the one I really had. After a while Meghan gave me one of those sympathetic smiles I'd come to resent, but she also offered some advice.

"I've been sitting here thinking and wondering how we might go about starting to heal the hole in Mariah's heart," she said. "She might need more people in her life who she can relate to. Maybe someone who is African American."

Todd grabbed my hand and squeezed it hard. He jumped in and reassured Meghan that we'd surrounded the kids with Black folks all their lives. There was the ballet teacher, the singing coach, the homework tutors, the occasional babysitter, and even an after-school mentor. All of them were Black. Then Todd looked at me.

I got up to clear the table. Was this woman coming to tell me that I was not Black enough for my daughter? I shook my head at the irony of the situation.

"And, well, there's Steve's family?" Todd added.

The words hung there.

I thought about what it might mean to Mariah to have a family who looked like her in her life. Then I began to think about what it would mean for me to have those same people back in my life.

The differences between us had grown over the years.

Now they were more than skin deep.

CHAPTER 10

Oreo

"Oreos" are what my family called Black folks who betrayed their skin color. They were the ones who might look black on the outside but whose actions showed they were white on the inside. Growing up, I might have been accused of being the opposite.

It didn't matter what I looked like. When James Brown came on *Soul Train* and wailed through the TV to say it loud, I hollered back, "I'm Black and I'm proud." My brothers snickered at me, but I didn't care. Every morning I still followed them into the bathroom and buttered my arms and legs with gobs of Johnson's baby lotion when they did. It was supposed to keep black skin from looking ashy.

Mike would laugh.

"Your legs are not ashy," he once told me. "They're just dirty."

Still, I was undeterred. For a few terrible years I snuck away with Rick's hair pick. It had a handle carved to resemble a Black Power fist. I tried to lift the brown curls on my head into a "white man's Afro." The few years I wore the limp helmet of hair to school, the kids snickered and rolled their eyes at me. But I knew it wasn't to impress them. If I was stuck in my family, the least I could do was try and not stick out.

I wasn't the only one who had a complicated relationship with skin color. Everyone in my family did. Grandma had the darkest skin of us all, a deep leathery brown. But that didn't stop her from making fun of anyone darker than a paper bag. "Pitch-black, blue-black, and coal-black" is what she called dark-skinned people. She called them "dumb," "ig'nrant," or "nasty." The fact she only had a third-grade education, lived in a rundown farmhouse without running water, and crapped in a plastic pail never changed her opinion that her shit didn't stink. But Grandma saved most of her bigotry for white folk. And that troubled me. Not only did she have a grandson who was white on the outside. Her companion of almost forty years, John, was white all the way through.

The story of how they met was as complicated as their relationship. Grandma was born in Culpeper, Virginia, a sleepy southern town best known for sitting at the crossroads of several Civil War battles. Blacks and whites lived side by side in an uneasy truce there. In the late 1940s her family was among the great post–World War II migration of Black families who moved north looking for greater economic opportunity. Unlike other Blacks who settled in urban centers like Chicago, Philadelphia, and Detroit, Grandma and her husband dropped stakes right in the middle of a rural town in western New York that needed both farm labor and factory workers for small manufacturers.

Just thirty miles away in either direction, there were larger and more established Black populations. The Black community's roots in those cities dated back to slavery. After New York abolished it, in 1827, Black folks from other parts of the country traveled on the Underground Railroad to Rochester, where Frederick Douglass lived, and to surrounding communities where other abolitionists resided. More than a hundred years later, maybe my grandmother would have found more economic opportunity and a greater sense of belonging had she unpacked a little further east or west. But the decision to stop in this farming community locked my family in place for a generation.

When my grandmother and her family settled, her husband readily found work in the factories. But my grandmother's fiery temperament strained their relationship over the next few years. Fed up with her, I was told, he eventually packed his bags and headed back to Virginia, leaving her alone in this strange new place, supporting five kids.

Out in the countryside, everyone knew each other and eventually learned each other's business. That's why, at some point, my grandmother became acquainted with a white man who lived up the road. John was the oldest son in a Polish farming family. He'd spent years working on the railroads and down in the gypsum mines before his back gave out. Then he settled down to work some family farmland. Just like Ma and Pops, the story of Grandma and John doesn't include details on how this odd pairing came to be, but it was easy to guess why Grandma had fallen for him. John was compact and quiet. He'd spent years with his back bent and head down, pounding or scratching out a living. Now he'd met someone different: a big, bold woman with striking wide features and a loud, booming laugh. Grandma undoubtedly saw the opposite in him of what she'd just lived through in her failed marriage. She saw a man who, no matter how hard the task or unforgiving the environment around him, would not give up. Even their difference in race didn't seem to scare him off.

Whatever their initial attraction, it wasn't long before Grandma and her kids moved into John's farmhouse. It was the late 1940s, and their decision was brave. The risk to their lives was greater than the one to their reputations, and for a time, to the outside world, Grandma let people think she was just a tenant. But people had their suspicions, including the Ku Klux Klan. The Klan was well known in the community. Decades earlier, hundreds had rallied in our small town against new Italian immigrants. It was a public display of force designed to terrorize those who the KKK believed were threatening to take their jobs. My grandmother and John posed a different kind of threat. My mother would later recall Klansmen coming to the farmhouse more than one time in the dead of night. They'd sit in their idling trucks and cars along the road, daring this forbidden couple to show their faces.

My grandmother and John were brave in the face of those threats, but they also weren't stupid. Part of the reason they survived those early years was that they rarely left that isolated country road. They couldn't be a threat if people didn't see them. If they did have to go out in public, my grandmother would crouch down on the back floor of the car and cover herself with blankets. It took many years, but her stubbornness finally outlived those outsiders and their racist resistance. And as for any opposition from her own kids, well, she handled that immediately. If anyone had a problem, they could take it up with her. No one dared.

By the late 1960s, attitudes had changed enough for Grandma to leave the farmhouse and go to work in town. She cleaned houses there. Her crumpled dollar bills came from half a dozen white women who hired her to tidy their homes. Though she didn't trust them, she knew how to play to her audience.

"Okay, sweetheart, not a problem," Grandma cooed whenever they asked her to scour the floors on her knees or take home some of their clothes that needed mending. She'd grip the few bills they handed her afterward and tuck them into her brassiere with one hand while caressing their arm with the other. If the women threw in some outdated canned goods or a few old dresses, she'd go into what Neecie called her Stepin Fetchit routine.

"Oh, you really done *blessed* this ole colored woman," she'd say.

But once Grandma closed the door on their homes and hauled her broad backside into John's pickup truck, her demeanor changed. She grumbled about "dirty crackers" and their "old wrinkled white asses." Grandma complained that the "eye-talian" ladies couldn't be trusted, the "Jews" were tight with their money, and the "Polacks" lived dirty and funky. Never mind that she'd slept next to a Polish man for forty years, or that she had a grandson who could pass for white. According to her, white folks were "not to be trusted." She said they "only look out for themselves and might smile in your face one minute, then stab you in the back the next."

When she said these things in front of me, she never gave me a second look. Despite her strange beliefs, I knew she loved me. But still it left me to wonder whether one day I might grow up and be seen as one of these evil white people. It was more likely that Grandma had decided something about us long ago. Black, white, or in-between, it didn't matter. All the people in our family were in a crazy category all our own.

Aunt Bonnie laughed when anyone called her crazy. We were careful, though, to use that term only in humor when she told stories of her wild adventures.

Bonnie, like the rest of us, rarely had two cents to rub together, but if those few pennies bought enough gas to start her car, she had places to go and people to scam. One Saturday when I was about eight years old, she planned to set out for the fancy new mall in nearby Buffalo. It was a forty-five-minute drive, so this was a big excursion. We typically only went to the mall if we saved up money during the summer for school shopping or if Ma got a sudden windfall from her tax return. That day, Bonnie pulled her car into the driveway and asked Ma if she wanted to go. I was excited. I had dreams of a frothy Orange Julius or a sticky sweet Cinnabon. Ma searched in her purse. All she found was a pack of cigarettes and a few pieces of stale gum.

"I'm not sure, Bonnie," she said. "Do you have any money?"

"Hell no!" Bonnie said.

She threw her big head back and howled with laughter, revealing her rows of tiny teeth and big gums. Ma and I exchanged looks. We had seen Bonnie in action. She could spin a yarn to someone's face without blinking an eye. Her stories were so extraordinary; you couldn't make them up. And she told her tales in a mournful voice, one I'm sure she picked up from soap operas. Ma told Bonnie, "Maybe next time."

When Bonnie backed out of our driveway and pointed her car in the direction of the mall, I don't think she had a specific scam in mind. She probably waited until she saw something in one of those store windows that inspired her.

Sure enough, six hours later, Bonnie's car nosed back in and the horn honked. She poked her head out of the window and cackled with glee.

"Now what did you do?" Ma asked, coming out on the porch. She lit up a cigarette, figuring she was about to hear a long tale.

Bonnie could barely get the story out between her fits of laughter. She told us she had sweet-talked one of the white store owners into giving her clothes on credit. Like my grandma, my aunt knew how to play to her audience. On this trip she had acted out the role of a poor but proud Black woman. She claimed she was trying to support her hardworking husband who was sick in the hospital and couldn't work. Bonnie told the bleeding-heart store owner she needed a few new dresses to go to a job interview. As she told the story, tears of laughter rolled down her fat cheeks. Cathleen finally popped her head out of the rear window to finish the story. She said her mother used a variation of the same story all the way home with more sympathetic white folks, to fill their gas tank and their bellies.

Cathleen may have feared and despised her mother, but like the rest of us, she marveled at her boldness. For years her punchline to the story was repeated in a way that sounded like a compliment. "I think Mama's the only person in this world who can go to the mall with not a penny in her pocketbook and come home with a full tank of gas, a bucket of Kentucky Fried Chicken, and a new dress." It was the nicest thing Cathleen could ever say about her mother.

I watched my aunt and cousin convulsing with laughter.

Even my mother laughed. "Bonnie, you are crazy."

It wasn't just Grandma and Bonnie who felt white people owed us something. It was considered a fact in our family that white people wanted to control Black folks' money. As a kid, I had reason to believe that. They had the power to give. I saw that they were the ones who paid Grandma in dollar bills and handed Ma a check every two weeks. In my view, they also had the power to take it all away, as proven when they came to collect on outstanding bills. It was this latter group I grew to be wary of and dislike at a young age. If someone white came to our door, it meant they were showing up for our money.

One time my mother spied an unfamiliar car creeping into our driveway. At the sound of tires on the gravel, she sidled up to the window. When she spotted the person behind the wheel, she ducked beneath the sill.

"Don't let that white man in this house," she whispered.

I stood there, too scared to move. Ma was already in motion, crawling across our cracked linoleum floor toward the back of the house.

"Get down!"

She shooed me with her hand, but it was too late. I spun back to the door in time to see a pair of hairy knuckles thump on our screen door. It rattled the already dented aluminum so hard, the bugs caught in the screen fell on the man's hands. He wiped them off.

"Son? Son? Will you come to the door?"

Ma crawled further away. I was cornered. I walked over and tried to block his view.

"Is your mother at home, son?" he asked.

Without thinking, I glanced over my shoulder for a second and then back at this white man.

"Nope."

"Are you sure?"

I nodded.

Suddenly, he called behind me. "Mrs. Majors! Are you there? Mrs. Majors?"

He pulled at the screen door, and I jumped back. When I saw that it was locked, I crossed my arms and tried my best to throw him the kind of resentful glare Aunt Bonnie gave bill collectors.

"Son. I heard you speaking to someone when I walked up," he continued.

I believed this white man wasn't to be trusted. He might trick me to get inside, to cut off the electricity or take back our rent-to-own washer, and he wouldn't go away. I believed it was a sin to lie, but I also wanted to help my mother. Another part of me wanted to prove that I really belonged to this crazy Black family.

"It was the dog," I said. "I was teaching her to sit."

The man stood there a long time, looking at me. Then he shook his head and stuck a bill collection notice in the crease of the screen door. As I flung the wooden door shut on him, I called over my shoulder to Ma:

"Stupid white people."

One of our small town's most famous white people stood guard in the middle of downtown. His bronze statue rose in front of a huge obelisk memorial dedicated to the town's war dead. All I saw was a towering white man who stood at a dividing line. If our car passed to the left of his stern face, we were headed to the fancy part of town, Main Street, but when we veered to the right, we were going toward the city's south side—the place set aside generations earlier for working-class immigrant whites and then poor Blacks.

I suppose other people took pride in looking up at the statue of Major General Emory Upton, the hometown boy revered by the Union Army for his Civil War military tactics. Many years later, I'd wonder how they'd perceive a lesser-known piece of his history. At West Point, Upton had once had to defend himself for proudly attending an integrated college and fraternizing with Black students.

Batavia had never been legally segregated like the south. County and city schools were open to Blacks even long before my mother and her siblings attended in the 1940s, and state law had long required that public facilities be open to all. But whites and Blacks both knew that in this community it was probably best, unless otherwise necessary, to stick to your own kind.

Given the geographic and social separations, it was hard to see what some of us had in common. It was John's family who first helped me realize that some white folks didn't see Black folks as a threat, and that we shouldn't see them as one either. Long before I was born, the people he called his kin wanted little to do with John because he had taken a Black family into his home and his life. But the only person more stubborn than my grandma was John. He waited them out, and after some time they finally came to accept.

It also helped that most of John's people, as Grandma called them, were just as poor as we were. John was a struggling farmer who, when especially desperate, could always depend on his few hogs for meat, his fields for vegetables, and uncleared trees for firewood to heat the house. Members of his family knew that, and when their jobs or lives failed, their rattling cars would heave up our country hill and then collapse in John's front yard. They always said they'd just come to visit, but they didn't leave till they had a few dollars from John and some canned goods from Grandma.

John's younger brother, Roland, was the family member who needed the most help. Often he'd arrive in one of the junked cars from his front yard that he'd nursed back to life. After he swung his long bowlegs out, he'd stand beside the car for a minute looking for the sight of John's ancient tractor. As he scanned the fields, he'd spit brown juice through his missing teeth.

During one of the first visits I ever remember, I studied him from Grandma's porch. He was half shaven and wearing a sleeveless white shirt that was stained yellow with sweat.

"Git yer ass outta the car," he yelled behind him.

A stringy woman with a cigarette dangling from her mouth sat in the passenger seat. In response, she leaned into the back seat and cursed likewise. Then the back doors creaked open. My eyes lit up at the gaggle of towheaded kids crowded inside. As they tumbled out, it was hard to tell the boys and girls apart. They all had the same long, lank yellow hair and grubby faces.

When I went to greet them, they looked me up and down. Then when we ran off to play, what looked like the oldest kid of the bunch, maybe eleven, spit something brown on the ground like his dad.

"You'se a niggrrr?" he asked, wiping his lips.

I'd never been called anything like that before. I shrugged.

"I guess," I said.

He laughed and clapped me on the back.

"Well, damn. I guess that's okay."

For the next hour we played tag. Then the girls took turns pulling up their shirts at me while the boys tried to light John's sheds on fire with their stolen matches. When we got tired of that, we snuck up near the porch to listen to Grandma tell her dirty jokes to Roland's woman. They shrieked with laughter and we muffled our giggles. While hiding out, I saw Roland walking up from the fields. He patted his pocket with satisfaction and then yelled to his "goddamn kids" that it was time to go. I felt sad at losing my new friends, but Grandma told me they'd be back soon enough.

Later, as we sat on the porch, Grandma laughed and shook her head remembering the years that John's family wouldn't set foot in her house. She told me they called her a good-for-nothing nigger. In turn she'd called them all poor white trash.

"But in the end, peoples is peoples," Grandma said.

I thought that sounded right. When I looked at Roland's family, they didn't seem all that different from us.

John's family members weren't the only whites who eventually made Grandma feel at home in the community. Out in the country, our closest neighbors were white farm families, some of whom had owned land there for generations. After years of eyeing "that colored woman" with suspicion, they finally came around to just calling her John's woman. The rest of us were accepted because we were her kin. By the time I was born, those neighbors never failed to toot their horns as they drove by. They'd stop on occasion to borrow some tools or get permission to hunt on his land. John and Grandma never said no. In return, the neighbors down the road plowed our driveways during the winter and gave us extra sweet corn or beans from their fields.

Those relationships later made a difference in how my siblings and I were viewed. We came to recognize the farmers' wives as the same ladies who drove our school buses, and when their kids got on those buses smelling of manure and wood smoke, we didn't shy away from making room in our seats to let them sit down.

Though my siblings and I claimed things might have been easier had we lived next to the other few Black families in town, there was a benefit to how we grew up. Out in the country there were no railroad tracks to separate us by race, and no good and bad parts of town. Our families all shared the same land and often faced the same challenges. They all just wanted to make a living in this struggling rural community, and all wanted to make a better life for their kids.

Although he didn't know it, Pops was the person most responsible for showing me the difference between race and class. For a few years, from when I was just a toddler, Pops was able to maintain an on-and-off job at a local plant that manufactured drywall from gypsum mined in the area. When he was sober enough to work, he'd sometimes come home with white work buddies in tow. They were always thirsty after their shifts.

When they started coming, my brothers and sister and I would scurry away, suspicious of these strange white people in the house. They weren't shy about sitting at our kitchen table, either. Although Pops took delight in pointing out the evils of what he called the white devil, I noticed that none of these white men had any more devil in them than Pops. They drank just the same and cussed just as much as Pops. And if his buddies were the ones who bought the beer or liquor, Pops didn't seem to notice any difference between them, either.

A few raised their eyebrows when they first spotted this dirty-faced white boy who called their work buddy Pops, but they were mostly interested in having me get them another beer from the refrigerator. It was eye-opening for me to have these white men stop by our house for drinks. Then one day one of the men invited our entire family over to his house for a barbecue.

The morning of the backyard party, Ma fussed at us to wash our faces, put on clean clothes, and be on our best behavior. She seemed anxious that we kids didn't make a bad impression, perhaps to counter whatever crazy thing might happen with Pops.

Pops's friend from work lived further out in the country than we did, at the end of a long dirt road that suddenly appeared in the middle of a stand of trees. I poked my head up over the front seat, because I wasn't sure what to expect. There at the end of the path stood an old wooden house, a bit bigger than ours but in far worse shape. It was clear these folks didn't have much, probably less than we did.

As we piled out of the car, a solid white woman with sunburnt skin came out onto the cluttered porch to greet us. She steered Ma toward one of the wobbly kitchen chairs that she'd set up there. Pops clapped shoulders with his work friend and they wandered off, already half drunk, to try and start a fire pit.

What I remember after all these years is Jim, Rick, Neecie, Mike, and me racing off to explore the creek behind their house with the couple's kids. I couldn't tell you all that we did that day, but I know by the end we were all covered in mud. You couldn't tell that we'd been wearing nice clean clothes, while the white kids had been wearing clothes my mother would never let us wear in front of other people. As night fell, I recall a yard dimly lit by oil lanterns and fireflies and the sound of Ma laughing with the white lady, louder than I'd ever heard her laugh before.

It was also the first time I remember realizing that some white people could be poorer than Black people, and that being a poor family didn't mean you had to be a broken one.

CHAPTER 11

A Shadow of Myself

Though I never heard my own mother disparage people—Black or white—based on their race, I knew what she thought of people from a different class. Even though she never came out and admitted it, she didn't want us to go to the public schools in Batavia, where we had a better chance of seeing one or two other Black faces. And she didn't want us to attend school in the county, as she had, with the sons and daughters of farmers. She thought we had a better chance of getting ahead if we went to the private Catholic schools in our small town.

The schools had sprung up in the early 1900s to serve the first "others" in town, the children of Italian and Polish immigrants. Later they attracted the kids of middle-class parents who wanted smaller classes and more disciplined environments. Ma saw an opportunity for her own children. For years before I was born, the nuns in town had become well acquainted with my older siblings, and so I have to imagine they must have been a little unsettled when Ma tugged her last and youngest—a kid so pale he looked white—through the front doors of Sacred Heart Elementary. If they were surprised to see a Majors who looked decidedly white, the soft-spoken Franciscan sisters didn't let on. Apparently, to them, I was just another soul to be saved, another young mind needing a good Catholic education. But Ma still had to endure the looks of the white parents at my school during every Christmas pageant, PTA meeting, or parent tea. I realized how hard it must have been for her in 1973 during the first open house in my new school. Walking in that night, we held on tight to each other's hands. My elementary school teacher Sister Francelette greeted us at the door.

"Mrs. Majors, thank you for coming," she said.

"Hello, Sister. I'm very glad to be here."

I noticed my mother had that voice she used when talking to white people.

"Is your husband joining us tonight?"

"No. I'm sorry. He's tied up at work," Ma said.

I opened my mouth, but shut it when Ma squeezed my hand tight. Pops didn't have a job. Besides, anyone who glanced at the newspaper that week knew the police had jailed James R. Majors Sr. for domestic violence. I wondered if nuns read newspapers.

"That's too bad," Sister said.

I noticed she patted Ma's back.

"Stephen, can you take your mother to your seat?"

Somewhere in the middle of those tidy, straight rows of miniature metal desks and wobbly wooden chairs was one that belonged to me. That night, my shadow sat there. Days before, the class had lain down giggling on sheets of oversized white construction paper. Sister had shined a bright light on us that cast a shadow on the paper. Drawing with her careful long fingers, she then traced the outlines of each face and upper body. We used that white paper model to cut out a duplicate image on black construction paper. Mine was a contour of my head and shoulders, topped by my extra curly hair and punctuated by an upturned nose. We each taped our silhouette to the top of our chair as if we were sitting in our seats. When we got to my desk, my mother and I stood behind mine.

"This is me!" I said brightly to Ma.

She looked around the first-grade room. There she saw a roomful of white, smiling moms and dads standing alongside their smiling kids. There were two other kids who didn't have dads with them. Their parents were divorced, but I still knew I was different from them. Ma didn't say much that night. Neither did I. I watched her trying to avoid the stares of anyone looking our way. After a while I did the same. I stared down at my desk and ran my finger along the long groove at the top that held my pencil.

I was glad when the open house was over. Maybe no one would remember, I thought. But the next day I opened the newspaper. There was no report on Pops, just a big picture of Ma staring back at me. A photographer from the newspaper had snuck into our classroom for a quick snapshot. I suppose he needed another community photo to go along with those of the Kiwanis potluck dinner and the guy who bowled 400 at the lanes. In Ma's picture, she is standing in the middle of the classroom of other parents with her winter coat on, looking straight ahead. Only my silhouette stood next to her. I had taken a small step away, and the photographer apparently thought I belonged to someone else, someone who was white. At that moment I understood that I could be a shadow too. I didn't have to always be Black like my family. And I didn't have to be like the white people they hated. Sometimes, out in the world, if I was lucky, I could move and shift and paint a different portrait of myself. Sometimes I could be white, sometimes I could choose to be Black, and other times I could just be something in between, a shadow of my full self.

While I began to learn how to move between worlds on the outside, I still struggled to find my identity within my own family. No matter what Ma or Neecie or anyone said, I began to feel there was a part of me that didn't belong to this crazy clan. I knew it in my bones, and I saw it every time I looked at my face in my mother's bedroom mirror.

One day as I was standing there, I opened her closet door. I'm not sure what drew me inside. Maybe it was the sweet smell of her body powder. Maybe it was intuition that something was being concealed from me and I needed to find it. I kneeled on the gritty floor and began to root around. I pushed aside the few dresses, skirts, and colorful head scarves that hung from the clothes rack and pulled out piles of shoes. I had a vague sense of where to look. In the far corner, a cool, heavy, and metallic object met my searching hands. It was a fireproof lockbox. Ma used it to store her important papers. Although I was alone in the house, I slowly dragged it toward me, afraid someone might hear it scrape against the closet floor.

Out in the open, I noticed that the box had a locking clasp. I had watched enough TV so I thought it was possible that one of the bobby pins on her wardrobe might open it. It was such a shock when the latch clicked. Inside, everything lay in a big heap—yellowing life insurance policies, old report cards, and black-and-white pictures of Ma before she was married. I noticed she looked happy then. I put it all aside and went on searching. Then I spotted something bewildering. Tucked in a crumpled envelope I found a newspaper clipping about a man who had hit his wife with a metal stool in a Greyhound bus terminal in 1949, and there was an official letter. The return address: a mental hospital. I spotted the name of my grandfather, William. I'd never met him, because he'd mysteriously left for Virginia years ago. Now I knew why. Crazy as a bedbug. This was undoubtedly a secret, what we called "family dirt." If I listened closely, I heard most of it. The grown folks whispered it when they sat around our kitchen table at night. But this was something they'd never discussed out in the open. To me that was proof there was some dirt that got buried so deep it was never shared in the light of day. I wondered if one of those secrets concerned me. The only way to know was to keep looking.

Finally it slipped into my hands. It was as if it had been expecting me to find it one day. The manila envelope had my name typed on it. Underneath were the words "Birth Certificate." My heart thumped. I closed my eyes and pulled out the sheet of paper. I opened one eye, then the other. I read the names to myself. Then I tried them aloud.

Mother's Name: Claudine Majors—that was Ma, Claudine Virginia.

Father's Name: James R. Majors Sr.—and that was Pops.

When I thought of my mother, there was something inside me that recognized the truth. When she hugged me to her chest or held my hand, my body sensed it had once been a part of her. But as for Pops, that was a different story.

I tucked the certificate back into the envelope and crammed it toward the bottom of the pile in the lockbox. I would crawl back into that closet many times over the next few years to reexamine it and hope it might tell me more. And sometimes when I did, I stared at my hand, scarcely a shade darker than the white piece of paper I held, and tried to convince myself.

"Pops is my father," I would whisper.

In those moments I would remember what Neecie had told me outside the movie theater that day, and how Ma had looked at me so sadly on the way home.

It would take time, but eventually I decided I didn't care what my family told me or what was written on this paper. Though I couldn't prove it or even dare to speak it aloud, I knew the truth. Someone else had to be my father—someone who didn't look like Pops but instead looked more like me.

I also knew what that would mean for me, because I'd heard the ugly name they called kids who had dads not married to their moms. Those kids were bastards.

Soon I would push even that fear aside. I'd figure out being called a bastard would be far better than being known as Pops's son.

CHAPTER 12

The House on the Hill

One of my favorite stories as a kid was the tale of how my family almost died in a fire. That near tragedy was retold as a comedy in our family.

"Tell me again how your hair burned off," I would beg my mother.

Ma scratched the short, light brown thatch that felt like straw and flew out at all angles when she was upset. When she sighed, Jim-Jim jumped in to talk for her.

"This knucklehead decided he wanted to play with Ma's cigarette lighter," Jim-Jim said, tilting his head at Rickie.

"That's a lie! It was your idea," Rick said, smiling.

"Naw, naw. You took it out of her pocketbook, and when the curtains caught fire, you were afraid to wake up Ma."

Neecie raised her eyebrows. The fact that my brothers had accidentally burned down our family's first home, a trailer on John's property, was undisputed. But it still sparked arguments over who was ultimately to blame.

"I tried to tell the both of you, you'd get your asses in trouble!" Neecie said with certainty. She always thought the boys caused most of the problems in our house.

"Shut up, ugly. Before I pop you upside the head," Jim-Jim said, half-jokingly.

Denise bristled. "Who you are calling ugly?"

Jim-Jim was the oldest, the loudest, and the strongest, but even as a kid Denise refused to buckle to him. I suppose she saw the way Ma backed down from Pops and decided she would never give in to a bully. She flipped Jim the bird.

Jim-Jim reached over and cuffed her ear. Then it was on—hair pulling, scratching, biting, and even punching. By the time I was eight, I learned that if you couldn't win an argument in our house, then you could get your way through force. As kids we were unruly, not to be trusted with matches or with our own tempers. Ma, who often worked late into the night, came home to find holes in the wall, broken lamps, busted lips, and bruises even when Pops wasn't around to do the damage himself. Her kids had burned down one home, and it took all her energy to keep us from destroying this one.

"*Stop it! Stop it! Stop it!* What the hell is *wrong* with you kids?" she shrieked.

We didn't think there was anything wrong with us. We considered it just normal sibling warfare. We'd grown up seeing the smallest disagreements among adults explode into free-for-alls. It was no wonder we believed that to get what we needed in life, someone else might have to lose what they already had.

When there were store-bought groceries in the house, there were spoils to be fought over, and so the battles intensified. We never knew, from one day to the next, when we might be standing on Grandma's doorstep begging for a loaf of her frozen Wonder Bread, so when we had food, we fought to get our fair share.

That's what happened the night Ma splurged and spent the last few dollars of her paycheck on takeout pizza. As we sat there, Jim-Jim, Rickie, and Mike eyed the last couple of slices and squabbled over who got last dibs. Denise sat back on the couch, satisfied. She'd been smart. She convinced Ma to order her a small container of BBQ chicken wings instead. She savored every bite, sucking the remaining bits of meat from the bone. We stared as she wiped the small spots of savory-sweet BBQ sauce from her lips. Jim-Jim cocked an eyebrow, plotting.

"Denise! Give me of one of those," Jim-Jim said.

Denise pulled the box tighter to her and calculated the risks. She didn't want to give Jim-Jim anything, but unless she negotiated some terms, he might take what he wanted by force.

"What you gonna give me?"

Jim-Jim grinned slyly. "Let's do this. Trade me, Rick, Mike, and Steve one wing each for the rest of the pizza," he said.

Denise was mulling the offer over when Jim-Jim suddenly reached over and snatched the box out of her hands. He held it above her head in a game of keep-away. In our house you did not fool around with someone's food. Soon we were wrestling over a chicken wing. Ma came flying in. By the time she put a stop to it, the coffee table full of food was overturned. I started to cry. Now no one would have more to eat.

"Who started it?" Ma demanded. No one would answer, but I was so upset I needed someone to blame, anyone. So I pointed at Neecie.

She burst into tears. It was less about the lost food than the fact she'd lost the fight. It was yet another reminder to her that the males in our house always held the power and would use it to get whatever they wanted. It would take decades for me to learn how Pops exercised that same cruel power over Denise.

As the youngest, I used the only power I had. While the big kids fought and scrapped, I saw that I could get my way by doing the opposite. I set myself up to be the good kid. I followed all the rules and snitched on the big kids when they didn't. In a house where it was every man for himself and the strongest survived, I worked to ensure that Ma would reward me for being well behaved. The big kids called me spoiled, tender, a brown nose, and the "golden heifer" of the family. I didn't mind. The only problem was when my goody-two-shoes ways made me a target of my siblings' spite.

The one person who really resented my status as the good son was Rick. Like me, he fought for attention, but in all the wrong ways. I'm not sure why, because he had more going for him than the rest of us. He was tall, slim, smooth-skinned, with a perfect Afro and a high-wattage grin. Arguably he was the best looking of our bunch and the most charming.

He strutted around school in his one pair of hip-hugging jeans, plat-form shoes, and tight shirts, attracting the attention of even the white kids. He didn't want the kids on our bus or in school to think he was just one of those "nigger" kids from the hill, so he worked hard to fit in, but it was with the wrong crowd. By high school he was known as the cool Black kid who could drink and smoke weed with the white farm boys and then go racing down the country roads in their dads' borrowed pickups. When he did, he left the rest of us in his dust.

I realized he would leave us all behind for good one day. Then sud-denly, one winter night, he climbed out of our bedroom window and stood there, resting, a few inches below the sill. Jim-Jim, Mike, and I looked out at him.

"Rickie, if you get caught, Ma's gonna bust your ass wide open," Jim-Jim called through the open window.

Jim-Jim knelt on all fours like he did when he wrestled at school. He blocked my view. I crawled beneath his crouched stance and peeked at Rickie standing outside all by himself in the snow.

"Yeah, and who's going to open their big mouth, Ma's little white baby?" Rickie nodded in my direction.

I felt Jim-Jim's body coil and tighten like it did before the coach's whis-tle blew during his matches. Jim-Jim was quiet for a minute. If I could guess what he was thinking, it would have been this: We might call each other all kinds of names, cuss each other out, steal clothes, money, and food from each other, and sometimes throw a punch or two. But faced with a common enemy—Pops, Bonnie, Grandma, even Ma—we kids were all in it together. Rickie had just declared I wasn't one of them. Mike sat cross-legged on top of a bunk bed across the room. He let out a long "oooh."

Jim-Jim was silent as he came to a decision in his head.

"Know what, Rickie? Fuck you."

He closed the window with a bang, perhaps loud enough for Ma to hear. By then Rickie was already racing off toward a car down the coun-try road. He turned, grinned, and flipped the bird. I wondered if it was for Jim-Jim, for me, or for all of us. As much as I felt betrayed, I also felt relieved. Now I knew for sure where I stood with Rickie. He didn't think I belonged.

Later I realized the funny thing was, neither did he. He didn't want any part of our family. Because, given the chance, he always found the fastest way out, even if it was the bedroom window. He also wanted to get as far away as he could from our small town and the life he thought a young Black man would have if he stayed there. But no matter how fast or far Rickie ran, he would never be able to fully escape his past. Neither would I. In fact, in years to come, I'd not only have to stop running from my family, I'd also have to make my way back to them.

CHAPTER 13

While We're Still Talking

The idea that the family I'd left behind, years before, might somehow save the family I had today seemed strange to me. While the therapist hinted that perhaps it might benefit Mariah, Todd perceived that it might also unlock something for me.

"When's the last time you spoke to your sister?" he asked in that spring of 2006.

"It's not like she's called me," I shot back.

Todd shifted his eyes and murmured to himself.

Though I didn't want to admit it, I had to think back eight years to one of the last times we had spoken. Calls weren't just to catch up. Instead they delivered news of family deaths, divorces, and dysfunction. Yet I didn't blame Denise for being the bearer of bad news. For a time that's all she had to share.

That changed one day in 2007 when I picked up the phone and unexpectedly heard her gravelly voice.

"Stevie, it's me, Denise."

I braced for whatever bad news she had.

"I'm not getting any younger," she croaked. "And I know we don't see each other enough."

I listened as Denise explained her plan to visit us in New Orleans and bring along her kids and grandkids. Altogether, she and my brothers had twelve children and grandchildren among them, who ranged in age from elementary school to twentysomethings. That day she talked about the need to keep the younger generation connected.

"These kids are growing up and have no idea of who their cousins are."

At the time, Todd and I were just beginning to understand the challenge of raising two toddlers on our own, with no family around. Todd had long complained that I kept my family at arm's length. He thought it wasn't healthy for our kids. He pressed me to say yes.

"And you guys need some family around you," Denise had added, as if reading Todd's mind.

I finally agreed.

Over the next few months, the plan came together. Denise would bring her two grown daughters and three grandchildren. She would also bring Rick's oldest child, little Rickie, who now had his own school-aged daughter. In many ways my two nieces and nephew had benefited from the breakup of our family. They'd avoided most of the trauma we carried from growing up on our chaotic country hill. They'd been raised away from an older generation who battled their personal demons, in between battling each other.

There was a part of me eager to see how they'd grown up. I also wanted to see what kind of family we might be. My kids were excited to see their Aunt Denise and spend time with their older cousins. For days they flipped through a photo album, trying to memorize their faces.

At the airport, Denise bustled ahead of her brood.

"Come here, my brother," Denise said. "It is so good to see you."

She grabbed my arm and planted a kiss on my cheek. She smelled of perfume and a bit of the rum I knew she sometimes drank for courage. I hugged her back. It was the most affection we'd ever shown one another.

Behind Denise straggled her two adult daughters, both the color of weak tea. I hadn't seen Joni and Pam in years. Denise had raised them on her own, after her husband had died of a sudden heart attack when the kids were small. I looked at my nieces now. Both were taller than me. I awkwardly hugged them and then turned to Pam's kids. There were two boys and a girl, all in elementary school. The boys were cherry brown and the girl pale with blond hair. They'd grown up knowing they had different dads.

"Uncle Steve!"

Little Rickie and his daughter came next. It had been years since we last saw one another. He was a grown man now, so I hesitated for a moment trying to decide whether to hug him or shake his hand. He stepped into me before I knew it and grabbed me in a bear hug. He had his father's charm and good looks. But over the next few days, he was eager to show me he was his own man. He and his cousins were easygoing, warm, and unburdened by the same secrets and history as my siblings. I too wanted them to see that I was different from the rest of my family. I had a nice home, a good job, and a solid relationship. I realized it was less about impressing them. Instead, I wanted them to like me.

Mariah too seemed especially fascinated with making a good impression on them. More than once I caught her holding up her little brown hand next to my sister and my niece's sons. She'd always known that my family came in all colors, but now she seemed delighted that one of those colors looked like her. She swung on her boy cousins' shoulders and climbed into their laps, putting her face close to theirs whenever possible.

While my kids were trying to get to know their cousins, I found myself trying to connect with my nieces and nephew. In moving around the country, I had missed out on the chance to see them grow up. Now they were adults. I watched how they parented their kids with a mix of humor and no-nonsense authority. Unlike the older generation, they didn't need to use belts or to berate.

"Okay, you guys, go sit down before I knock you down," my niece said jokingly to her sons as they started to wrestle. I doubted she'd ever raised a hand to her kids, but they quickly untangled themselves and plopped on the couch.

As the week rolled by, I began to accept the idea that things were changing in the younger generation of my family. They were different people from me and my siblings, raised away from the isolated place where we grew up and outside of the influence of the people who raised us. I decided I had to let go of the shame that had made me separate myself from parts of my family so many years ago. Then, on the second to last night of their stay, I saw a different side of them that reminded me of the past, one that frightened me.

"The big kids are going out tonight," Denise announced. "They want to see the French Quarter. You and Todd good to help me entertain the kids?"

Todd and I looked at one another. It shouldn't have come as a surprise that my nieces and nephew might want to have fun away from the older folks and even their own children. We agreed they deserved a night out on their own, but we warned them about the dark side to New Orleans. Drunk tourists wandering around the French Quarter, with Mardi Gras beads and red cups of booze, could easily end up being rolled for their wallets or raped in dark alleys.

"Just give us a key and we'll let us ourselves in," my niece Pam promised. "That way we won't wake you."

Denise, Todd, and I kept the gaggle of kids entertained until bedtime and then turned in. In the middle of the night I heard the front door creak, and I relaxed. When morning came, I found the kids up early and asking questions.

"Do you know where our mom is?" Pam's older son asked.

"Isn't she here?" I asked.

They shook their heads no, over their bowls of cereal.

My chest tightened. I couldn't tell if it was fear or just anger. By late morning, it was decidedly fear. Her cell phone had gone unanswered. I suggested going back to the bar where her sister and cousin last saw her. Denise shrugged her shoulders.

"She's a grown woman," Denise explained. In my mind, though, she was unaccounted for in a strange city, with a notorious reputation for swallowing up the occasional wayward tourist. By noon even Denise started to worry. Then a car pulled up to the cracked sidewalk and deposited my niece on the curb. She leaned inside and thanked the male driver, then staggered slightly up to the front steps.

"What did I miss?" she said.

My family laughed, but I stewed. I had thought the next generation were different from the rest of my family, or at least I wanted them to be. They considered their adventure just a wild night in New Orleans. It was a great family story to be told one day, nothing more. But I thought this drunken night out was careless and reckless. They'd heard enough of our family's past and should have realized that alcoholism and addiction was in our blood. Part of me felt embarrassed about how they acted, while another part felt ashamed for thinking I was better than them. If nothing else, I wanted them gone so I wouldn't have to feel anything at all.

A day later, as they prepared to leave, I put on my best face. We hugged and high-fived and promised that we'd make it an annual tradition, but that never happened. More than a decade would pass before I ever saw them again. Though we would invite them back many times, they never came or returned our calls. After a while we gave up. Instead I followed their lives at a distance, on social media. Denise had been right: they were adults now. They were free to make their own decisions and lead their own lives. They had to find their own way in life, and it might be without us. Yet I couldn't shake the feeling they were choosing to keep their distance, not only from me, but sometimes from their own parents. For as different as they were from my generation, maybe we had passed something of ourselves on to them. Maybe, I thought, they had inherited our family shame. No matter the reason, I took their emotional distance as a final sign that I should move on from the rest of my family.

In the five years after my family visited, we settled into our new home in New Orleans. I came to believe it would be the place we set down roots. The kids had become acclimated to the hot, humid summers. They looked forward to Mardi Gras and the seemingly endless parade of other citywide celebrations, and Todd and I appreciated the slower pace of life. Even the city's racial divide had abated some. In 2008 the city bucked the rest of Louisiana by voting for the nation's first Black president. Just a few years later, it came together to elect its first white mayor in more than thirty years. But over the next couple of years, there were signs those things might not be enough to make us completely feel at home. The annual hurricane season kept us in a perpetual state of vigilance. Then there was the out-of-control crime, the city's shaky infrastructure, and its uneven economic recovery. Add to that the still struggling public school system.

In effect, it meant if we wanted to live in a neighborhood protected from future storms, with the best performing schools for the kids and the lowest crime rate, our kids would grow up in the parts of New Orleans that were traditionally white and affluent. We'd come in part because the city was a cultural gumbo, yet we felt lost in the sauce. And there was one more concern that was solely Todd's.

"I think we need to be somewhere where we have more family around us," he said one day as we put the kids to bed.

What he meant was more of his family. I couldn't understand why. He spoke to his parents several times a week. He and his siblings texted each other, something they called their daily gratitude. On birthdays, just sending a card was considered impersonal. The entire clan took turns calling to sing an off-key chorus of "Happy Birthday." Wasn't that enough? I couldn't remember the last time my brothers and sister had wished each other a happy birthday. It had been so long, we didn't recall each other's actual birth dates.

"I don't think you understand," he answered. "This isn't for me. It's for the kids."

He explained that without a mother our adopted kids might need more than just two parents as a replacement. They might need to see that they were part of something bigger—an extended family. After a few months, I gave in. We would move back east. It seemed that for more than half of our time together, Todd and I been on the move, seeking the perfect setting for the family we wanted to be. Now we hoped we'd find a home in a quiet, leafy Maryland suburb just outside Washington, D.C.

Our new home, Takoma Park, was founded as the first real commuter suburb of Washington during the late 1800s. For the next 150 years, mostly white families moved in, attracted by its affordable housing and good schools. While some whites fled in the wake of desegregation, some remained. And the progressive politics of those who stayed would later make it a welcoming place for a growing number of Hispanic, Caribbean, African, and Asian immigrants.

We arrived in a neighborhood of 1940s brick boxes built for middle-class whites but that now included families from Korea, India, and Ethiopia. Todd had gone to great pains to find a place where our own melting pot of a family wouldn't stick out so much, and I was hopeful it might make a difference.

In 2011, when we settled in, we tried pointing out all the good things about our new home and neighborhood to the kids. Both Mariah and Rachel would have their own big-girl rooms, painted their favorite colors. There was a big yard for playing, a quiet street for them to ride bikes, and a nearby playground with kids of all ages and shades. But by that fall, Mariah looked around and told us what was still missing.

"I just want my mom."

The sad request came one day after school when a new friend she'd met in the playground over the summer said she wasn't allowed to visit our house because we were gay.

"Do you want us to call her parents?" we asked. Mariah shook her head hard enough for her braids to swing wildly. My heart was breaking for her. I knew there would always be other friends, but I couldn't replace the one thing she really wanted, her mother.

As the new school year progressed, Mariah slowly did make other friends. Their parents couldn't care less about whether Todd or I were gay. Soon we hosted playdates and sleepovers and joined the list of trusted carpool parents. But that did little to quell Mariah's feeling that she was different from the other kids and that we were responsible. Over the next two years, her list of grievances grew. A mom would always say yes to a third, fourth, and fifth piece of candy, she informed us. A mom would let her stay up past bedtime. A mom would buy her fake nails, high heels, crop tops, or an iPhone. And a mom would love her so much, she would only praise and never punish.

At first Todd and I tried to fill her emotional void with hugs and reassuring talks. While she accepted our comfort, she continued to demand something we could never give her. She wanted her mother. Instead she had gay parents who didn't seem to understand her.

Todd hoped that trips to visit his mother and sisters might provide the kind of maternal nurturing that Mariah craved. Then we invited a parade of Black women hair stylists, ballet teachers, voice coaches, homework tutors, and mentors into her life. Maybe it made some positive difference, but at the end of any trip and at the end of every day, Mariah came home to a family that looked different from her and one that looked different from everyone else.

By the time she was nine, that hurt became anguish and sometimes anger. She would scream until she was hoarse, sob until she was spent, and slam a bedroom door repeatedly until a full-length mirror shattered. Her gay dads "hated her," "didn't love her," "weren't her real parents," and "should never have adopted her."

For as many times as I endured her angry outbursts, understanding and empathizing with the deep pain underlying it, there were other times when I couldn't contain my own anger and feelings of rejection.

It was those times that I fell back on what I'd learned from my family about the way to contain children who wouldn't listen to you. I was raised to believe you grab them by the arms, shake them once or twice, and then scream, "Who do you think you're playing with? Do you want me to slap the black off you? You better stop that screaming before I give you something to scream about."

Looking back, it's clear that this was the beginning of what Todd now called "my problem." In his estimation, those increasingly charged episodes were what finally led up to that awful fight in our home. Now, after I and my birth family had seemingly agreed to go our separate ways, he was telling me I needed to invite them back into our lives. I was confused and angry. "They haven't called in years. Why should I be the one to make an effort?" I complained. Todd conceded my family was broken and fractured. But he said if we were to help Mariah deal with the pain and regret over the birth family she had lost, perhaps I had to reconcile my feelings of shame and anger over the family I had given up on. Yet even Todd agreed that it wasn't that simple. While I was possibly reliving some of the trauma of my childhood, Mariah was experiencing a kind of trauma that was uniquely her own. It was the kind of deep emotional distress often experienced by adopted children. The therapist and adoption counselor told us that years of study had shown that children separated at birth from their mothers feel a "primal wound" that leads to feelings of anxiety, abandonment, and loss. Was Mariah rejecting us to mask her own rejection? And if so, what emotions did it trigger in me if this child who represented the family that I had always wanted was now pushing me away?

An incident that happened several months later made me confront those questions. It was supposed to be family time, something the therapist had recommended to help us begin to heal the fractures that had emerged between us. That afternoon, Todd and I took the girls to an ice cream parlor in a neighboring community. Mariah had increasingly been reluctant to be seen in public with us. I looked at Mariah in the rearview mirror. Those almond eyes refused to look back at me.

Todd parked the car. I got out first and waited by Mariah's door. Before I could speak, she jumped out of the back seat, slammed the door behind her, and shouted, "I told you I didn't want to come. It's not fair that you're making me."

"Here we go," I muttered to myself.

Rachel slowly came around the other side of the car and offered me a sympathetic look. With her skin the color of a deep summer tan, she could walk next to her sister and be perceived as being one race or walk next to Todd and be seen as another. Unlike Mariah, but like me, she might always be able to move between worlds.

I took a deep breath and watched Mariah stalk up the small inclined sidewalk ahead of the rest of us. I slowly jogged to catch up.

"Wait up!"

"*No!*" she yelled back at me. A man and woman walking the opposite way eyed us both. I stood there for a minute, trying not to let my public embarrassment turn into anger.

Within a few minutes the four of us sat together inside the ice cream shop. For the moment, Mariah had put the last few minutes behind us. She was at ease knowing that we were the only customers inside. Todd told her that ice cream was the best kind of therapy. She smiled. I wondered whether we might even be able to laugh about this someday. As I sat there staring into space, Mariah suddenly took my arm and squeezed it. I looked up.

"Why are the police here?" she asked. She pointed to the front of the store.

Three officers in bulletproof vests were standing there. Two seemed to be talking to the counter person, while the third surveyed the room. Occasionally his eyes seemed to catch mine.

"He wants your ice cream," I joked, turning back to the kids, but they both kept glancing over my shoulder.

Then I saw Mariah's eyes shift. Two of the officers were headed for the door, and the third walked straight toward our table.

"Could you join us outside," the officer said to Todd. "The rest of you don't leave. Stay right here."

Todd slowly stood up. The officer followed him out the door.

None of us said a word. Out the front window, we could see Todd shaking his head and then fumbling for his wallet. Part of me realized the kids were scared and that I should stay there with them, but another part knew exactly what was happening. I jumped out of my chair and swung open the door.

"What's going on? What's the matter?" I demanded.

Todd saw the look on my face and placed his palm out toward me, signaling that I should stand back.

"Who are you?" the officer in charge asked.

"I'm his partner, his *gay* partner. And these are our kids. Now can you tell me what this is about?"

"Can I see your ID?"

I tensed and opened my mouth, ready to ask for his badge number. Todd slowly shook his head.

"Someone saw us on the street and thought something didn't look right," Todd said. "They called the police."

I turned to look at Mariah and Rachel watching us from the window, then I turned around and slowly reached for my wallet to dig for the folded copies of the birth certificates that I had stuffed inside years before.

As the officers looked at them and began to match them against our IDs and the family photos Todd had in his wallet, I flashed back to the time the woman had stopped to question us in New Orleans, and to the church ladies who once called the mall cops on us in a parking lot.

How much of their actions had been because of their perception that all families should look alike? And how much of it had been because they looked closely at us and decided we didn't look anything like a family?

Though I couldn't admit it, that interaction and others like it started to shake my faith in my ability to hold us together as a family.

A few weeks later I stepped out onto the front steps of the house and searched through my contacts. After dialing the number, I waited for her voice to reach through the line. We didn't even need to say hello.

"Stevie!" my sister asked in her familiar croak. "What's the matter?"

I could hear the anxiety in Denise's voice as soon as she picked up. It had been years since we'd talked, let alone been in the same room together. I remembered that the kids were toddlers the last time she saw them. One thing I always appreciated about Denise was that there was never any need for small talk between us.

"What is it? Tell me?" she pressed.

I thought I had called her to share what had happened in the ice cream shop. In my head I had rehearsed what my outrage would sound like.

"Neecie, some white people called the police on me and the kids," I planned to say.

Instead, before I knew it, I was recounting everything else that had led up to it, all the problems of the last few years between me and Todd and the kids. Her gruff "Humph's" and "Hunh's" punctuated the conversation along with the occasional emphatic curse. Finally I stopped, unsure what I had called to ask her for.

"Well," she said. "Ain't this some shit." She thought a moment. "If all this has been going on, why didn't you call me before?"

I didn't answer. We both knew I didn't need to. Finally she filled the silence. "I should have known. Things were just too damn quiet all these years. Even for you."

Denise knew me better than anyone in my family. She understood I'd built a new life since leaving home decades before—one far different from the one we had grown up in. If I was reaching back across the years to call anyone for help, even her, it meant I had run out of options.

"Oh, Stevie," she sighed. "What do you want me to do?"

"I don't know," I admitted.

If nothing else, Denise and I shared a perspective that Todd or any therapist didn't have. We remembered what it was like waking up thinking we didn't belong, that maybe we had been dropped out of the sky into a life, a family, an identity that didn't fit. Denise had refused to be bullied like my mother or be a batterer like my grandmother or aunt. I, meantime, couldn't change myself to look or act like any of the men. She reminded me of how we had gotten through it. As she spoke, I could almost see her, hands on hips, eyes wide, and head tilted forward as if she were giving me what she called a home truth.

"Listen," she said. "This child might not have chosen to be a part of your family. She might not *want* to be the only chocolate brown girl in a family with one white and one light, bright gay dad. But tell me this: Where the hell is she going to go? Back to her mother? Is she going to go get her own apartment at age thirteen? You know what I'm saying?"

I realized Denise had me between tears and laughter, as only she could. I waited for the payoff. "She's got two parents who love her. Two parents who keep her brown ass fed, clothed, and safe. And two parents who are trying to give her a hell of a better start in life than she might have had otherwise. That's a hell of a lot more than some kids ever get in life. It's damn sure a lot more than we got. Now if she don't want to hear that truth from you? I'm damn sure prepared to come down there and tell her what's what."

CHAPTER 14

Neecie

Denise had always been a kind of second mother to me, and she had a tough, take-no-shit attitude that made for a pragmatic style of parenting. Oftentimes she dragged me out of bed, scoured the nearly empty fridge for my breakfast, and then yanked a comb through my rat's nest hair before school. Summers were different. There were no other boys my age for miles around. With Ma at work all day and my brothers off running wild somewhere, Neecie was solely responsible for me. And because we were too poor for things like daycare or summer camp, Neecie was caretaker, coach, and camp counselor all rolled into one.

Generally, she wasn't thrilled about it.

"Neecie, I'm bored," I cried every day during the summer I turned eight.

She rolled her eyes, but I knew if I bugged her long enough, she might hand out some of her hoarded snacks, a few lyrics of a pop song, or something to spark my imagination.

One Saturday that summer of 1974, I found her sitting on the living room floor listening to Casey Kasem's *American Top 40* and thumping her thick brown thighs up and down in alternation. She told me she was trying to tone them. That fall, Neecie was going to try out for cheerleading at her high school. It didn't matter to her that she'd be the only Black, curvy girl trying out for the squad. She had those soda-straw-thin white girls in her sights, and now I was distracting her from her workout.

"Neecie, I don't have nuttin' to do," I whined. I put my hands beneath her knees to feel them slap my palms as they descended.

"Jee-zus Christ. Go out and play, why don't ya?" she huffed.

"I don't know what to play!"

"Well, what the hell do you want me to do about it?"

Neecie stared at me a long time. I must have looked especially pathetic that day, because she suddenly stood up and dragged me outside. While I watched, she took an old bedsheet and used a piece of frayed rope to tie a poor man's hammock underneath the tree in our front yard. Then she grabbed the beat-up clock radio off the kitchen table and used an extension cord so that it reached outside. Finally, she found two old half-rotten lemons in the fridge and a half cup of hardened brown sugar in the cabinet. Within minutes I imagined I was on a sunny beach, sipping lemonade to the sounds of Paul McCartney and Wings.

Her resolve to make something out of nothing was the result of her frustration with our circumstances. She believed we deserved something better than the life we were living. While most of my family kept people away, afraid they would find out just how poor we were, Denise invited the whole world in; she wasn't afraid or suspicious of outsiders. By the time she was a high school senior, she had gaggles of white girls sleeping on our grubby living room floor during slumber parties. She joined the Drama Club, the Yearbook Club, the student newspaper, and the National Honor Society. She had cracked open the door to a better world and was determined to barge right through it. It helped that she had an oversized personality. That, along with her salty language and nonstop banter, helped her attract everyone from the pious nuns and priests at the Catholic high school to the popular girls who looked like they stepped right out of Pepsi commercials. She didn't care that her own nappy hair barely grew a couple of inches. She bought wigs, so she could fling her locks at every house party and school dance she was invited to.

It was at one of these parties that Neecie learned there were limits to who she could be. She came home one night crying to our mother.

"These girls pulled my wig off my head," she sobbed. "They laughed at me, Ma."

My sister had discovered another existence beyond the four walls of our cramped and crazy home. But as a Black girl, she'd learned she might not be fully embraced by everyone. Neecie's brashness didn't always make her friends. She had definite thoughts about the way people lived their lives, and that was true inside our own family as well. For example, she wasn't shy about telling Ma she needed to kick Pops to the curb for good. She also lectured our grandmother, our aunt, and other women in our family about their name-calling, back-stabbing, and finger-wagging ways. And she didn't hold her tongue in telling some of the men they had no backbones or balls. It didn't matter that she was probably right. My family called her mouthy and "mannish."

Outweighed by my brothers, there were many times she should have backed down from a sibling battle, but Neecie's motto was "I ain't going down without a fight." Many times, Ma would come home from work to find the house in tatters and Denise bruised and sobbing.

"Denise, why?" Ma would ask wringing her hands. "Why are you going to try to stand up there and fight a boy?"

"Because I will not let *anyone* tell me what to do or who I have to be, least of all these stupid motherfuckers."

There were a lot of things my big sister gave me as a kid. But there was one thing that she offered freely and that I never had to ask for—a conviction that we deserved something better and an idea that we might belong somewhere else. Her ambitions and dreams for herself showed me I could also find a different and less troubled way of life. Looking back, I realize that without that, we both might have grown up trapped by our circumstances and settling for rotten lemons instead of some bittersweet lemonade.

While Denise and my brothers continued to be at odds with one another, I came to see how united they could become when confronted by a common enemy.

The year I turned nine, our worst foe—Pops—was moving in and out of our lives every few months. Increasingly, he was landing in jail on a charge of domestic assault or resisting arrest. Other times, he was sleeping off a binge with his father, brothers, and sisters. If he wasn't in one of those places, he was likely somewhere in Rochester in a flop-house, drinking and drugging with his buddies and a few women. But those times he was home, he was at his most uncontrollable, often beat-ing my mother. She had never been strong enough, emotionally or phys-ically, to push him out of our lives. But things had changed now. She wouldn't have to battle him alone.

We'd had many fights with Pops inside our home over the years. The walls bore scuffs and patched holes as evidence. And my siblings had their scars; some of them would remain hidden for years. But they also had grown stronger. Tired of being victims of his abuse, they started to openly challenge his power. Rick was now taller than Pops, and Jim-Jim easily outweighed him. Denise and Mike might never match Pops in terms of strength, but out of all of us, they despised him the most. He had treated them the most cruelly. It was an awful secret they carried, which we wouldn't learn until years later. Now they spoke openly of doing whatever it took to see Pops either dead or gone. All they needed was the right moment.

That moment came one night early in 1975. Pops had begun drink-ing early. That itself wasn't unusual. Normally when he drank himself into a stupor, he'd slump in his favorite ratty armchair and talk back to episodes of *Gunsmoke*. But that night, he was just shy of a tank full. He stumbled to the wall phone, announcing on the way that he was inviting the "fellas" to come and drink with him. By the time he hung up, each of us looked for our bunker. Mike, Rick, and Jim-Jim headed to our cramped bedroom to hole up. I sat with Neecie in her room.

Less than an hour later, a smear of headlights flashed through our living room window. The stones in the gravel driveway crunched and popped under the wheels of Uncle Clarence's late-sixties sedan. From Neecie's room, just off the living room, I could hear our back door open, then the rustle of paper sacks and finally the clank of liquor bottles. As I stared through the wallpaper and listened, I could picture what was happening just a few feet away.

I knew my uncle's voice by the sound of his noisy cussing, and there were two other men out there with Pops and his brother. I turned up the volume on the ancient black-and-white TV with the bent rabbit ears in Neecie's room, but it wouldn't drown out the voices that kept cursing and laughing, louder and louder.

"How the hell you drink this?" Clarence asked. "It don't give you the shits?"

I could almost see him holding up the jug of Pops's favorite—Mogen David blackberry wine.

"Give me my goddamn, mother-fucking bottle," Pops slurred.

My mother was quiet. She was only out there at Pops's command. I knew she was trying to keep away from these men. But I could predict what was going to happen. I'd seen my leering Uncle Clarence do it before. He'd slip behind her and grab her around the waist. Those times, Pops would just smirk. It wasn't long before I heard it happen.

"Get your hands off me," Ma snapped.

"Aww, come *on*, Virginia. You know I'm just playing," Clarence said.

Suddenly I heard Pops on the move. His voice echoed down the short hall to the boys' bedroom.

"Wake up and get your asses out here," he shouted, pounding on their door.

I scrambled beneath Neecie's bed and pulled the ripped dust ruffle in place behind me. I heard someone open her door. The mattress sagging over my head suddenly lifted as she was pulled off the bed and out into the living room. Pops was going to put on a show, I thought, and he wanted us as an audience.

From beneath the bed, I heard Pops tell the boys to go get his guitar. For a few short minutes I thought I was safe, until a pair of rough hands reached under the bed.

"Get out here, boy."

The hard nap of the rug scuffed my back as my uncle's sweaty hands dragged me by the feet out into the living room.

The next few hours we took our usual places on the broken couch listening to him. Ma warily circled the living room trying to keep the tables and floors clear of empty booze bottles and overflowing ashtrays.

She stopped only once to rush over and angrily yank Mike away from one of Pops's friends who had strangely pulled my thirteen-year-old brother up onto his knee. Way past midnight, when the bottles were empty, two of the men called a taxi and left. Pops and Clarence were the only two drunks remaining. Silently I prayed they would pass out at the same time. But they didn't.

None of us can remember what lit the fuse. Clarence might have insulted Pops. Pops might have hit Ma. Or Jim-Jim, with his newly hard and massive chest, might have looked over at Pops and seen his skinny ribs sticking out of his white "wife beater" and decided he would end this night quickly. All I know is that all of us quickly realized this was our final chance to take him down.

Within minutes the wooden legs on the coffee table snapped. Pictures crashed off the wall. Lamps tipped over, creating shadows of wrestling bodies on the fly-specked ceiling. All of it was happening so fast, I didn't have time to hide. Now that I was old enough, my job was to run from my hiding place behind the chair or couch to Grandma's and ask for help. That was important if Pops pulled the phone off the wall and there was no chance to call the police.

But tonight, I couldn't find a way around the bodies that were blocking my path. Through them, I saw Jim-Jim and Pops rolling around on the kitchen floor with bared teeth. The floor was slick with their sweat and spilled wine. Pops had Jim-Jim in a headlock, but Jim-Jim was trying to punch his way out, while Ma and Rick tried to get between them. Mike, still too short for direct combat, aimed choppy kicks at the pile of legs. Then Neecie picked up one of Pops's empty wine bottles.

"Hold him still!" she screamed.

From over her head, she brought it down in a wide arc, missing the top of Pops's thinning scalp but clubbing him partly over his ear. Blood pulsed out.

Pops roared. He scrambled to get up off the floor, lashing out with his fists and feet. It was a desperate attempt to hurt anyone he could reach. As he kicked wildly, his foot connected with the underside of the aluminum and Formica kitchen table—the one where I read the funny papers on Sunday morning. It slowly tipped up and then toppled over with a hard slam. And when it did, I wasn't hiding behind a chair or under a bed. I wasn't running across the yard to Grandma's house, where I could safely watch the shadows of my family fight through the window, like a Punch and Judy show. I was crawling under that table when it fell. When it did, the heavy edge came right across my slim neck. I don't know whether I blacked out or if I've blocked it out of my memory in the years since then, but I don't remember much more about that night.

The story that I heard, and that's been told proudly to others over the years, is that Denise and Mike yanked the table off me and everyone crowded around to make sure I was breathing. Rick cradled me in his arms. Then Jim-Jim went after Pops with such madness in his eyes, Ma was sure he would kill him. Mike was the one who ran for help. Within minutes, Aunt Bonnie came charging through the front door like a moose and went into battle. My grandmother hobbled across the yard with John behind her, carrying a rusty old shotgun that hadn't been fired in decades. But it was enough of a threat. The only thing that saved Pops that night was that the police arrived moments later.

Many years later, as Pops lay dying of chronic alcoholism in a Rochester hospital, Jim-Jim, Rick, Denise, and Mike traveled to see him one last time. Denise said they all just needed to lay eyes on him again, to make sure he was finally going to die. At the time I didn't understand. It seemed to me they already had a lifetime of bad memories of him to live with. I was content with my own final memory of Pops. It is of him sitting in the back of a county sheriff's car in our driveway that night, battered, bloody, and broken.

Today the case of domestic violence and potential manslaughter is a treasured story in our family. It is a badge of honor that we share. The big throw-down, we called it, or the night Stevie almost died and we almost killed Pops. I'm not sure how close any of those things really came to happening, but embellished story or not, I believe that because of my family I lived to fight another day. From then on, I took perverse pride in a crazy-ass clan willing to do anything to save ourselves and one other.

CHAPTER 15

Wild Child

When the years of accumulated guilt I felt for turning my back on my siblings got too great, I tried to remind myself that I was not the only one who didn't feel at home within our family. Rickie had long ago decided he wanted no part of us. Like Denise, he shared a disdain for our chaotic and dysfunctional lives, but I always wondered if there was also something about us as people that he disliked, especially me.

Back then, I was too young to understand why. To me, Rickie was just the wildest child of our wild bunch—the one who broke all the rules and got into the most trouble. He argued with Ma about going to school. If he went, he'd skip classes. Then he avoided coming home to the consequences. On the nights he did come home, he'd sneak back out after everyone was asleep to be with his friends. He had started to hang with white farm boys who always had engine grease under their nails, cow shit on their sneakers, and cheap beer on their breath.

After Pops was gone, Rick's wild ways became the new source of our family feuds. While I'm sure he was angry at Pops and the painful circumstances in our lives, he began to take his frustrations out on me. At first I thought it was because I was young and an easy target, or because I was the spoiled baby of the family, but in time I realized it was something he saw in me that he resented. He told me as much during a family argument I'll never forget.

"Admit it, you love him more," Rick had said, pointing his finger in Ma's face. "You make the rest of us take a back seat to him. He's your favorite because he looks white."

Ma rarely raised a hand to us, but this time she exploded and slapped Rick dead across the face. He didn't flinch. He did, though, suddenly raise his fist, ready to strike back. Mercifully, he stopped short. I watched Rick run out of the house. I wondered if he was gone for good. But a few weeks later, he came home. I remember him shuffling his feet and looking at the floor as he apologized. Occasionally he'd steal a pouting glance up at Ma. Rick had learned to use his "bad boy good looks" charm to get his way other times. But this time, Ma stared at him. I imagined she was trying to tell whether he was sorry—not so much for threatening to hit his own mother, but for striking a blow with words that he knew would hurt her. After a few minutes, Ma murmured that she accepted his apology, but after that night and for the rest of her life Ma never looked at him the same ever again. Neither could I.

By his senior year of high school, Rick was spending more and more time away from our house. He'd met a girl. A few months before his graduation, he brought her home to meet us. Things were slowly changing in our small town. It was 1975. Still, we all stood around our shabby living room gaping at this middle-class girl. She had freckles, a long, pale face, and straight hair that she kept flipping nervously. Ma tried to act as if it were the most normal thing in the world that a white girl named Mary was standing in front of us, tightly gripping Rickie's hand. It was only after Mary left that my mother questioned Rickie.

"Are you crazy? Do her parents know? What are you thinking?"

"We're in love, Ma," he said. "And we're getting married, after graduation."

Ma slumped into a kitchen chair. Her hands shook as she tried to light her cigarette. The rest of us huddled around, waiting to see how this would play out.

"Married? Then what? Are you going to bring a baby into this world?

What kind of life will this child have with a Black father and a white mother?"

Things had changed in our small town since Grandma and John had first begun living together in secret. And things were different since Ma had brought home her little light, bright, almost white secret a decade before. But to Ma, people's attitudes in our town had not changed.

I looked at her, but she didn't look back at me. Ma wondered what kind of life a mixed-race child would have in this world. I didn't say it, but I thought she should be worrying about what kind of life it would have in a family like ours. As it was, we didn't have to wait long to find out. Rick and Mary snuck off to the Justice of the Peace and got married right after graduation. Just as Ma feared, Mary soon announced she was pregnant. Their son, "little Rickie," was born a few months later. When they brought him home from the hospital, Rick petted him like a baby deer. He showered him with kisses and called him sweetheart and dolly. Little Rickie was a beautiful baby, and he also didn't look a thing like Rick. He was as pale as his mother, with light eyes and freckles.

I watched as Ma held her first grandson in her arms and whispered to him. I could tell she had set aside her anxiety about what it would mean to bring another biracial child into the world and this family. She had also, for the time being, reconciled with Rick. Together they rejoiced in this life that represented a new start for him, while my brother, for his part, rejoiced in his creation—a beautiful, white-looking baby boy. Rick held his son almost like a talisman.

"Look at what I made!" is what I almost imagined him saying to the world.

I got my chance to hold this new baby, and I looked at him a long, long time. I marveled at this tiny, pale, squirming life that had come, in part, from my caramel-skinned brother. Here, finally, was someone in my family who looked just like me—high yella.

As I handed the baby back to Rick, I guessed our family reconciliation with Rick would be temporary. He now had a family of his own, one that gave him things he had missed growing up—safety, stability, unconditional love. I suspected, though, that he thought his new child and wife gave him something more, something he thought I had—an invitation to a different life, in the white world. One day we would both have to come to terms with the truth that even if we gained entree to that world, it wouldn't fundamentally change who we were, or where we had come from.

The next year would be a pivotal one in the history of my family. It was 1976, and around us we watched as the country celebrated its bicentennial. During that time, elaborate fireworks displays exploded across the country, and tall ships paraded into New York and Boston Harbors. In our small town there seemed to be bicentennial sales on everything. Red, white, and blue bunting decorated the insides of virtually every window display.

The celebration was timely. There was a sense of optimism about the future. Vietnam, Watergate, and the oil-crisis-induced recession were in the rearview mirror, and in our family we'd finally said goodbye to Pops and slowly begun a climb up the economic ladder.

That summer I turned ten years old, and my four older siblings, born a year apart, now turned eighteen to twenty-one. They were all old enough to work, drink, drive, and live on their own, and they were enjoying the kind of freedoms they'd never had before in their lives. While I envied the fact they had all moved out of the house and could go their own way in life, my mother wasn't as impressed. She worried her kids had all just gone buck wild, but she couldn't stop them. Jim and Rick scraped together enough money from their part-time jobs to buy used muscle cars. After they'd had a few beers, they'd drag-race their old Dodge Chargers side by side down our country roads, throwing up clouds of dust and throwing my mother into a panic. Mike preferred the high speeds of an old motorcycle, which he'd received as payment for working with a nearby farmer. Even Neecie, who refused to drive herself, seemed to court danger. Each night that summer her rowdy friends would cajole her into their cars for late-night trips to their beer-soaked parties.

My siblings' drinking had started long before that summer. In high school, Rick had tried to keep his vices a secret, but Ma heard the empty beer cans rattling around in the car trunk and smelled cigarettes on his breath. That alone was enough to spark arguments. But then there was the telltale odor of reefer. Ma asked Rick to think about all the bad things that addiction had done to our family, but Rick wouldn't listen. He just wanted to have a good time, and he was not alone. To my siblings, the dangers that Ma warned them about were nothing compared to those we'd experienced growing up. They also sensed that our country and even our rural community were changing. Sex, drugs, and disco had finally come to our country town. And as poor Black kids from the countryside, my siblings felt they finally had a chance to taste the freedoms everyone else seemed to be enjoying.

I watched their transformations. Rick began bodybuilding. Overnight his lean frame swelled until his chest strained against the gold chains he wore. Jim traded his faded jeans for flared slacks, and Mike ditched his denim jacket for a leather coat. Neecie tottered on platform shoes in multiple colors. Each night I saw my brothers and sister leave our house in a cloud of cigarette smoke and variations of musk cologne, headed for Big Daddy's, the small disco that had opened on the edge of town. Rick had earned a job there as a weekend bouncer.

When they returned, I lay awake hoping to hear them laugh and talk too loudly about their exploits. Sometimes in the morning I'd find a sprawl of their feather-haired friends sleeping off their hangovers in the living room. It shocked me to see so many white people here in our tiny house. But times had changed. Once we had been snubbed by the old Italian, Polish and Irish families in our town. Now their kids thought nothing of hanging out with Black friends.

Though my mother didn't realize it at the time, some of those friends were there for more than just sleepovers. My siblings also enjoyed some of the sexual freedom of that era. Denise had found herself a white farm boy, who wasn't afraid of disapproving looks and snide comments from others. Mike had begun to entice and date a series of young-looking and naïve girls. They were apparently taken in by his pose as a tough motorcycle rider. Even Rick, who had a wife and son at home, didn't let married life stand in his way. At work at the disco, he attracted a legion of groupies who hung out near the door waiting for his shift to end each night.

Over the next year I saw signs that all this newfound freedom might come with a price. Jim's partying nearly caused him to flunk out of school. Mike flipped his motorcycle in a horrific accident. And Denise announced she was pregnant and leaving college. But it was Rick who seemed to be living life on the very edge. He loved his life as a disco bouncer and the admiration he gained as a bodybuilder. He and his new wife began to fight more as he came home later each night or sometimes not at all. Ma saw all this. She had put her kids in the small Catholic schools in town, hoping to give them a better education. After their graduations, she had begged and borrowed money so they could apply at least to the community college in town. Now she worried they had squandered those opportunities. Her concerns came to a head during a Christmas gathering around that time. That night, Ma watched disapprovingly as my brothers and sister carried in a few cases of beer and bottles of liquor along with some gifts. I saw the look on her face but noticed she held her tongue. I guessed she'd figured that at least her kids were together, safe and in once place.

But Grandma wasn't about to keep quiet. She eyed Ma.

"Why you let them kids drink that ole nasty beer?" Grandma asked.

"Mama, they're grown now. None of them live under my roof, and they make their own decisions."

Grandma may have realized her power over our lives was diminishing. Maybe that's why she lashed out.

"Y'all fuckin' kids ain't no better than that ole damn drunkard father of y'all's," she declared.

Then she stood up, flipped us the bird, and waddled out the door.

As the night wore on, empty beer bottles began to pile up on the kitchen table faster than Ma could clear them away. I was excited to see my siblings smoke, drink, and cuss like the grownups we were once told we had to obey but not be like. When the beer ran out, they turned to the liquor bottles. It was just a matter of time before their jokes and teasing got rougher.

"Well, at least I'm not dating jailbait," Rick said, nodding his head at Mike. When he laughed, it sounded like a hyena.

"Okay," Mike slurred. "How about we talk about your love life. Or should we say love *lives?*"

Rick's eyes narrowed. He edged forward in his seat. Sitting next to him, his wife Mary shifted uncomfortably.

"All right, fellas," Denise said. She gestured a time-out. "Let's knock off this happy horseshit. Let's talk about the future. New Year's resolutions or wishes."

She pointed her beer at our mother.

"Ma, you go first."

Ma slowly walked out of the kitchen drying her hands on a dish towel. She stood in the middle of the living room and took a deep breath. She'd been quiet as the night went on. Now she spoke in a clear voice.

"My wish for the new year is that my kids stop running the streets, stop drinking, stop carrying on . . ." She paused. "And quit using drugs."

She pointedly stared at Rick.

"Why the hell you looking at me?" he demanded.

Ma didn't break her gaze. She had heard enough of the loose talk among Rick's friends and some of the gossip in town. There were rumors that Rick was using cocaine and possibly even dealing it himself while working as a bouncer. If Ma had heard it, surely Jim, Denise, and Mike had as well. Maybe they'd seen Rick using or even done it themselves.

It didn't matter. They rallied to Rick's defense, and quite possibly their own.

"Ma, really?" "How can you say that, Ma?" "Do you know this for a fact?"

Our mother slowly shook her head back and forth. She could have been signaling no, but I thought it looked more like a sign of resignation.

My siblings were growing up in a time where doing drugs wasn't the same as being what people called a drug user. That seemed more hardcore. Doing drugs was just smoking some weed and maybe doing a little recreational coke. But my brothers and sister couldn't say that to Ma. That might risk outing their own behavior.

I noticed Rick never denied anything. If he was doing cocaine, it's clear he didn't see it as a problem, or as his mother's business. He furiously began gathering his things and shoved his wife out of the house. He yelled from the driveway, vowing never to come back.

I closed the door behind him.

The rest of my siblings were rattled, but they respected Ma too much to just walk out and leave her alone on Christmas Eve. One by one, they put down their drinks and began to help her clean up. It was clear to us all that the party was over.

CHAPTER 16

Making Do Without

In honor of Father's Day, Sister Mary Jennifer pulled out the black and white construction paper and the safety scissors. She set everyone in class to work on the backgrounds. We started at the same place—a black border and a piece of white paper cut out to resemble a shirt collar. After that, she said we could use the colored construction paper, Elmer's Glue, and markers to make the personalized neckties. Sister peeked at my paper tie.

"Think about your fathers, children. Make the sort of ties they'd like to wear."

I smiled at her. Sister knew I didn't have anything close to a real father at home, but she acted as if I did. I played along, and when it was done, I showed it proudly to her. Then I dropped the sticky shirt and tie card at the bottom of my book bag, where it found a home with the crumpled applications from Boy Scouts and an invitation to a father-and-son pancake breakfast.

Even though I wanted a dad, there never was much room for any father, good or bad. From wiping your ass to whupping your ass, Grandma, Aunt Bonnie, and Ma made it seem like we didn't need more than a mother.

It was no wonder that the men in our family—husbands, ex-husbands, boyfriends, brothers, and sons—faltered at fatherhood.

"Black men ain't worth shit," Grandma said one day, to a female relative having "man problems." They were huddled over a massive iron pot on Grandma's porch, shucking peas.

"Ain't that the truth?" the relative replied, rolling her eyes.

It was a familiar call-and-response in our family. I glanced up from Grandma's heavily lined brown hands to her wide face. She hated Pops, for good reason, and gave little thought to Uncle Hunt. She cursed her ex-husband at every opportunity. I wondered if she really believed all Black men were worthless. Did she also mean her sons, her grandsons? I didn't dare ask, but when Grandma repeated her assessment aloud, the women in our family always nodded to themselves. Meantime the men shuffled their feet and looked away.

For many years I wondered about the origin of Grandma's belief. Like all truths in our family, you could find it buried in the stories. One of Grandma's favorites was one about her own childhood. Over the years, she repeated this story so many times I can still hear her voice in my head.

"Wes Richards was his name," my grandmother would begin. "And he was good with his hands, my daddy. White folks came from miles around to get him to make things, like tables and chifforobes. He didn't have any book learning, but he had common sense. Daddy was good at figgerin' numbers, so the white folks couldn't fool him out of his money. I really loved that man. But then, my mama died. Oh, Lawd. She got that cancer. She was a beautiful woman, my mama—light-skinned, high cheekbones. People say she was part Cherokee. But when she passed, it felt like it break my daddy's heart. He had to work and couldn't care for us chillun. So he carried us to different people's houses. I remember my brothers went to my uncle's houses. My sisters Kate and Carrie went with some of Daddy's sisters. Now, me and Dorothy was twins, you know. You couldn't separate us. We was like this."

At this point, Grandma would twin her wrinkled fingers together.

"Me and my twin went everywhere together. But they said I wouldn't listen. I was headstrong as a chile, you know. Daddy's people tried to send me back to him. But by then, Daddy got remarried, and that woman didn't want no other woman's chillun up in her house. So Daddy couldn't bring me to live with them. I wasn't but eleven or twelve. He took me to our old home, where Mama died, and I stayed there, by myself."

I would pause her there, surprised every time.

"All alone, Grandma?"

"Yes indeed. I was just a little girl. And many a day I sat in that window and watched out and waited for Daddy to get me. But he never come. It was a hard life."

Grandma used to tell dozens of stories on that porch, and as a result she taught us a lot of lessons about life—both good and bad. Her heart had been broken by one man, her father, and her head nearly broken in by another, her husband. To Grandma, these weren't just painful personal experiences. They were painful lessons. And for whatever reason she wanted us to learn them too.

Perhaps we have learned one lesson too well:

When it comes to a father, you can always make do without.

Despite my grandmother's attempt to diminish the role of fathers and demean any of the men who tried to take on that role, she ironically was the one who gave me a positive male role model in life. As I look back on my memories, the man who was my father, if not by blood but certainly by example, was there all along. He was a few yards away, across the well-beaten path that led to my grandmother's house.

Every day, Grandma stood on the rotting porch steps of their old farmhouse in a huge flowered housedress and hollered as loud as she could for John. When he didn't answer right away, she would whisper to herself:

"Where is that ole damned Polack?"

It didn't matter that John was hard of hearing and yards away behind his barn, she kept yelling. She got lucky when the wind was blowing the right way. Pretty soon John would yell back.

"What the hell you screaming about, woman?"

"Come up out the barn and go fetch me my pocketbook out the truck."

Grandma would then stomp back in the house, which was fifteen feet from the parked truck.

"Ah, *bullshit!*" John would yell up toward the house.

But he would drop what he was doing and lope up the dirt farm road leading to their buckling house, stopping here and there to spit his tobacco and grumble about how crazy Grandma was. From the time I could walk, I'd tag along behind him, stepping inside his muddy boot tracks. I knew John wasn't my grandfather. He wasn't even married to Grandma. But he came to be the closest thing to a father I ever had. Those muddy tracks he left for me represented the only clear path I could follow about how to be a man.

The few photos that were ever taken of him made him look like he stepped out of the pages of the 1930s Dust Bowl. There wasn't much to him, physically. He'd always been short, and age and farm work had shrunk him to no more than five foot five. His dirty blond hair had gone gray. He cut it himself when it started to stick out of his cap. He was less worried about the few days' growth of ash-white stubble—what he called his "whiskers." Those he used to scrape clean with a straight razor and boiling water when he got around to it. John had ice-blue eyes and was lean, with ropy muscles that crossed his sunbaked forearms from years of manual labor. He probably never owned more than two or three pairs of mud-caked work pants and an equal number of filthy cotton shirts. He would wash out those items and his long johns in a basin when they got too ripe—the same basin he would occasionally use to scrub himself, just from the neck up and only from the elbows down. Aunt Bonnie said he smelled like shit, but he only smelled like a hard-blowing winter wind to me.

John didn't talk much. He muttered most of the time. But he was one of the few people who dared talk back to Grandma. Normally he let Grandma jabber on. She nagged him about things he needed to buy, cook, or clean for her. Those times John would just grunt back to keep her happy. It was only when she tried to talk about life outside their little world together in that farmhouse that he lost his patience. She might have been the queen of our hill, but John knew she couldn't speak with authority about life elsewhere.

The one time I recall she tried, Grandma said she thought she heard on the radio about President Nixon. It was a basic fact about civics that any fifth-grader would know. But Grandma had never finished the third grade.

"What are you talking about, woman?" John asked. "That's ignorant. It makes no sense."

Grandma was poor, Black, illiterate, and dependent on John for the roof over her head and protection from a world she struggled to understand. But if you challenged her authority, she would literally throw her weight around. I watched my grandmother heave her tremendous bulk up from the daybed where she was shucking corn and hobble over on her arthritic knees to where John was sitting on a stool unlacing his boots.

"You is the ignorant one," she said, pointing her finger in his face.

"*Bullshit!*" John roared.

After those types of fights, eventually John would get tired of listening to Grandma. He'd lace his muddy boots, stomp out of the house, and go tramping down to his ramshackle barn to stare at the few cows and pigs he raised or repair something on his ancient tractor. An hour later, Grandma would be yelling for him again. This time she'd call him sweetheart and doll, and I noticed he seemed to hear her right away.

I knew Grandma and John would never break up. For as many times as I saw them so mad that they were practically spitting in each other's faces, I saw the other times when Grandma grabbed John's wrinkled hand as they rode in the truck together or John rubbed Grandma's broad back after she came home from cleaning houses. Their arguments set the rhythms of their days. Unlike Ma, who had to physically fight off her abusive drunk husband, and Aunt Bonnie, who physically dominated her own household, Grandma had fights with John that were at least predictable.

I learned to overlook their crazy outbursts because they were only directed at one another. I never felt like they would hurt me. In fact, they indulged me, more so than any of the other kids. It didn't seem to matter that I looked different from any of Grandma's other grandbabies. It always felt like she gave me special attention. In a family where everyone was angry, I took attention and affection wherever I could find it.

"Give Grandmama some sugar," she would say, turning her chocolate brown cheek to me.

I held my breath so as not to smell her funky sweat and pecked her quick.

"*Oh*, Grandmama's baby done give her good sugar," she said. "You hawngry?"

I gave a little nod.

"John!!" she shrieked.

"Quit your screaming, woman." John poked his head out of the kitchen, which doubled as the place where he washed up. "What do you want?"

"Make this boy a sandwich."

I thought of the mouse droppings that I saw on their kitchen table all the time.

"Grandma, I don't want a sandwich," I said, climbing into her enormous lap and giving her a hug. "Can you and John take me out to eat? I want a hamburger and french fries."

"Why can't he eat a sandwich?" John muttered.

Grandma put her meaty brown hand on my back and nudged me up onto her enormous chest.

"John, can't you see the boy is hawngry."

"Aww, bullshit." John pulled his head back through the swinging kitchen door. I knew I'd won.

Minutes later, there I would be, sitting on the front seat of John's Ford pickup. I didn't need a safety belt, and Grandma and John didn't believe in them. I was safe enough between John in his dusty dungarees and Grandma who was wide enough to take up her seat and most of mine. They seemed proud to have me ride to town with them. I didn't know then that their riding together in a car had been forbidden by custom for at least the first decade of their life together.

During those years, when John and Grandma would have to drive off their little country road, Grandma would lie on the floor of John's truck, head covered with a coat so that neighbors and the local Klan wouldn't see her. She would wait until they were in friendlier territory before daring to show her face.

It took years for Grandma and John to wait out the prejudice, hate, and bigotry that was directed toward them. They'd done it with a mix of aww-shucks and shuck-and-jive. John was the aww-shucks one. He didn't have to try hard to fit that role. When he and Grandma weren't arguing, John was an amiable old fart. The folks up at the seed mill, down at the livestock auctions, and around the John Deere tractor store knew John was someone they could trust. If he was bartering something, John would tell them whatever might be wrong with what he was offering. If there was a small grievance, an extra cigar or a swig from a flask would appear to fix it. In his quiet way, he could put people at ease.

Grandma, on the other hand, had mastered the art of shucking and jiving—making people, especially white people, believe that this big Black woman liked them, even though she generally didn't. She called white ladies names like "sweetheart," "sugar," "honey," and "darling" in every encounter, while showing her gold-capped teeth and folding her hands primly in front. With the men—those farmers and workingmen who were part of John's world—she used humor, telling them dirty jokes and haw-hawing along with them.

In the early years together, it was a survival instinct. If they were to live together in a small farming community of mostly white people and raise Grandma's five Black children together, they had to find a way to interact with their neighbors in a way that wouldn't get them killed. But by the time I came along, I suppose it was just habit. They'd fallen into these public roles and simply couldn't conceive of behaving any other way. Over time, it was that consistency of how they showed up that gave them permission to go anywhere with anyone—even with a little pale-faced boy who walked down the street between them, swinging both their hands.

John never bothered to explain his relationship to Grandma, so he saw no reason to explain who he was to me. Then again, I really wasn't anything to him, officially. If someone who knew them asked, he'd mumble in between chews of his tobacco, "It's Claudine's grandbaby," nothing more. Anyone else just got the silent treatment. Still, occasionally I tried to force an answer out of him.

My favorite place to do this was at the local hamburger stand where Grandma would make John take me whenever I sucked in my dirty cheeks to look extra "hawngry." At the counter, John and I would always encounter some nice white lady who thought we made quite a picture.

"Oh, how cute. What's your name, little fella?"

"Stevie," I said.

"Oh, and this must be your grandpa."

I hesitated and looked up at John. Was he going to say anything this time? He just gave the white lady a wink that made her giggle.

"Go on, tell the lady what you want," he mumbled out of the side of his mouth.

Later, sitting back in John's truck, I wiped the french fry grease off my lips with a sleeve and told Grandma about the mix-up.

"They thought John was my grandpa!"

Grandma laughed. The corner of John's mouth curled up at me. The woman's mistake wasn't far from the truth, in my mind. This man, in every word and gesture of affection, was my father figure. He had made peace with the fact that most of the world saw him as just John—that bachelor farmer who owned a few dozen acres up on that hill, or that Polack who had taken in that colored woman and her children a long time ago. I knew different.

My lasting memory is of me squeezed between them on the front seat of John's old pickup, heading home after another adventurous trip into town. No matter the time of day, someone would be behind us honking at John, who poked along the highway way under the speed limit. John and Grandma were in no hurry, so John would pull the truck all the way over to the shoulder to make way for a world that was passing them by.

Though the world around them changed during their nearly fifty years together, they never did. That steady presence helped them survive, and it also wore away resistance, paving the way for the rest of my family in that town. And while they may have influenced outsiders, they also profoundly affected how we came to see others. Their new relationship in the late 1940s introduced our Black family to the white world, in a way that would shape it for generations. I'm sure that's not what they set out to do. All they ever wanted to do was create a space between two worlds where they could be together.

On a country hill and in a world where so many things were black and white, John taught me that love was not. And in his own quiet way, he taught me that I didn't need a dad to have a father figure.

CHAPTER 17

Don't Trust That Bitch

We called our extended family by names like Fartcha-Meat, Horse Face, Cancer Belly, Light Fingers, Crazy Ass, Hussy Ass, and Hot Ass.

They were the kind of taunts a foul-mouthed kid might throw out to make fun of someone on the playground, but the grown folks in my family used them like names and pronouns. They weren't brave enough to use these dirty names out in the open, though. The crude nicknames were reserved for the moment a distrusted relative was out of earshot, whether in person or on the phone.

A typical phone call might end like this: "Okay, mmm hmm, all right, sweetie, we'll talk to you again soon, doll. Bye-bye!"

Then the wait for the dial tone.

"I hate that ole black bitch."

Listening from the next room, I would mouth the naughty name to myself, trying it out. After hearing enough of these conversations, I came to understand the rules of the name-calling game. It didn't matter if someone was white or Black, it was okay to use their race in the nickname. The best names always included some part of their anatomy, like calling someone an "ole buck-tooth black bitch." And if you thought up a name that made everyone else laugh, you scored extra points. One of my favorites was made up by Aunt Bonnie to describe a "friend" whose large pendulous boobs overtopped every bra and tended to swing freely whenever she walked. She was known to us by a name that is still the most outrageous ever given by anyone in our family. Forever after, behind her back, she was called "that ole swangle-tittied black hussy bitch."

Aunt Bonnie's and Ma's first cousin Shireen was the queen of handing out these titles. If she bestowed an especially outrageous nickname on someone, it stuck for years. When they visited one another, Bonnie and Shireen were thick as thieves. What Cousin Shireen didn't realize was that my aunt couldn't wait for her to leave. Sitting in Aunt Bonnie's living room, I waited for the busted storm door to hit Cousin Shireen in the butt and then slam shut behind her. A few seconds later, Aunt Bonnie let loose.

"Ole black pop-eyed Shireen, with her stupid ass and light fingers," Bonnie muttered just loud enough for us to hear.

I put my hand over my mouth and giggled. By listening closely, I had figured out why she earned that name. Shireen's eyes *did* pop out of her head when she laughed. She was also *light-fingered* and occasionally shoplifted cheap items out of dime stores. And I supposed that if she didn't know Bonnie laughed with her one minute but talked trash about her the next, she was also *stupid-assed*.

While blood relatives weren't spared from this name-calling, anyone who was related through marriage was especially vulnerable. My uncles' wives were often the primary targets. Grandma's three sons had packed up and moved to the city long before I was born. As Black men in the 1960s, they rightly concluded they would find more opportunity in the thriving Black neighborhoods of Rochester than in the white rural community of Batavia. In the city, they found solid jobs and wives. They also got away from my grandmother. But their departures just made Grandma resentful. "They think they shit don't stink," she complained. It never occurred to her that anyone would have ambition, let alone a dream worth supporting. She thought that anyone who left the hill must have thought they were too good for the rest of us, and in my grandmother's mind, any outsider you brought back with you must think the same. My grandmother's distrust of her daughters-in-law was reaffirmed when all my uncles' wives eventually divorced them. Even I could see it was because my uncles enjoyed drinking, gambling, and chasing other women, but that was irrelevant to our family. We justified their breakups by claiming, "That black bitch just wanted his money" or "That crazy-ass bitch couldn't even cook" or "That lazy-ass black bitch never lifted a finger."

Still, the lesson for me was clear. People outside our immediate family couldn't be trusted. To be fair, out of everyone, my mother was more accepting of outsiders than her mother and sister. She rolled her eyes whenever Grandma called herself a churchgoing woman in one breath and cussed somebody out the next, and she shook her head in disapproval when Bonnie started her name-calling. Ma realized that not only were we poor and Black, but we were held back by our own prejudices.

Still, when it came to her own kids, Ma had a hard time trusting the people her kids brought home. She always wondered if they were good enough for us. In some cases, I'm sure they weren't, but it never occurred to her that sometimes the problem was her own kids.

When Rick was the first one to bring a stranger into our family, Ma did her best to overcome her initial wariness of her white daughter-in-law and fears for her mixed-race grandson. But barely two years later, the marriage was over. Rick did what he'd done as a kid. He came home late. He didn't come home at all. Finally he left his wife and son altogether on one side of their double house and walked six steps next door to live with another woman, who was also white and soon to be pregnant with his daughter.

It didn't matter that Rick was to blame for the breakup of his marriage. Our entire family circled the wagons. We helped Rick strip their tiny one-bedroom apartment of all the furniture, even the bed, before my sister-in-law got home from work one day. We went from sitting across from her at the dinner table at Thanksgiving to giving her dirty looks in the checkout line of the grocery store in town at Christmas.

There, in the parking lot of that store, Aunt Bonnie used her car to block Mary in as she was pulling out of a parking space. Bonnie cranked down her window, leaned her big face out, and cussed Mary out in front of slack-jawed strangers. When we heard how Mary cried of embarrassment, we all thought it was funny. Thanks to Bonnie, soon the woman we called "Rick's wife, Mary" became "That-flat-faced white bitch Mary."

Given my family's inherent distrust of anyone different from us, it's a wonder that my brothers and sister ever dared to date, let alone bring someone home. If the relationship didn't last, Ma was likely to stab her cigarette into an ashtray for emphasis, cough a few times, and then say, "See, I told you. Lie down with dogs, get up with fleas." Anyone who really knew us would wonder whether we were the dogs or the fleas, but my siblings did their best. As Jim, Denise, and Mike grew older, they brought home a string of people over the next few years. In our small community, they were fishing in a small pond, so it was no surprise all the people were white. By the late 1970s, interracial dating wasn't as much a taboo as when I'd come along. My siblings didn't have to hide, like Grandma and John, or pretend I was something I wasn't, like Ma. As a result, there was a slow but steady change in the complexion of our family. Although it happened in about a decade, one day I suddenly looked up and realized that I wasn't the only light face around the crowded holiday dinner table. Now I was among several spouses and grandchildren who came in shades from light cocoa to pure cream. I don't remember anyone acknowledging this difference, just as they still refused to admit that I was white or biracial.

My family was only capable of changing so much, and despite the fact there were more diverse faces at our table, they continued to hold on to an innate distrust of anyone white. They might bring out their best manners and biggest smiles to welcome the growing number of white spouses at our family gatherings, but they still felt the need to voice their prejudice. Barely had the door hit "someone on the ass" on their way out and my family was clucking, gossiping, and making up names. As a kid, it left me confused. Was my Black family pretending to like me too? Is it possible they hugged me, bought me gifts, and took me places but then secretly rolled their eyes and made fun of me?

In time when I moved off the hill and out into the world, I realized I had to choose: take a chance and trust the outsiders who were invited into our family to date and marry and have children, or trust the people who raised me. Over time, it became an easy choice for me to make.

CHAPTER 18

The Boy Scout

For years Todd and I had talked about a trip to Paris to celebrate our fiftieth birthdays, which fell just a few weeks apart. However, when the time arrived in June of 2016, I instead used a Groupon for a local hotel where I binged on Netflix and splurged on room service. He stayed home and washed our used Prius. Our dreams had grown smaller. So had our love. We were stressed and frustrated. Our relationship frayed while we fought over the one thing that had at one time brought us closer, our children. In the months since that awful night, we'd been to countless family therapy sessions, but Todd and I had yet to heal our relationship. We talked openly about whether we had what it took to stay together and whether it might be better to raise the kids apart.

There had been other lows in our time together. After we adopted Rachel, neither of us had foreseen how hard it would be for Todd to be at home alone all day, raising a rambunctious one-year-old and a newborn. But one night I came home from work to find him near an emotional collapse.

"What is wrong with her?" Todd pleaded.

Rachel had woken from a nap at four and started to cry. Now it was eight-thirty. She had an intense form of colic. We fed her, changed her, bathed her, and rocked her, but the keening wails went on past midnight, and they returned every night for months. At its worst, Rachel would arch her back as if in terrible pain and scratch at her face. She rejected bottles, pacifiers, and all our attempts at comfort. Todd and I began to stay in separate parts of the house every evening—one of us to sleep, the other to rock the baby for as long as it took to calm her, sometimes until our arms felt numb. One night when the crying wouldn't stop, Todd rolled out of bed at two o'clock and stumbled downstairs to relieve me. The room stank of sweat. He found me standing there holding our baby by her arms, seemingly ready to shake her quiet.

"*Steve!*" he shouted.

I froze.

"Give her to me, now!" he commanded. "Go to bed. You're exhausted."

Later I'd learn how parents, both new and old, are advised to walk away from colicky babies during times of stress to avoid shaken baby syndrome, and I thanked God that Todd was there for me in the moment when I needed him the most. Together we eventually learned to soothe Rachel by simulating conditions in the womb. A blacked-out room, a white noise machine, and a vibrating cradle swing finally eased her distress. Still, in time, Todd and I would find that when it came to their birth mother, there were other things that we could never be able to re-create or replace.

Todd and I had faltered in our relationship at other times over the years. While he had dated and been in several relationships before we met, I had jumped from coming out as gay into a life with two kids, a house, and a dog. A few years into our relationship, I made the mistake of trying to see what I had missed. Long after he'd gone to sleep, I came home late from work one night and eased beneath the sheets, careful not to wake him.

"Where you've been?" he mumbled.

"There was a ton of traffic in the tunnel," I said.

I pulled the covers up and turned away. I didn't want him to smell the alcohol on my breath. He shifted to look at the clock on his nightstand. Then I could feel him turn back toward me. But he didn't say anything. Neither did I, until the next day. It was a weekend, and I went out of my way to help with the kids, taking them to the playground for most of the day. I was trying to hide my guilt and a hangover. However, by that evening I was still fighting both. With the kids in bed, we sat staring at the TV.

"I want to tell you something, but I don't know how," I said, my voice surprising even myself.

"Tell me what?"

"Last night, I did something," I said. "I met some guy on the way home, and we kind of fooled around a little."

Todd turned back to stare straight at the TV.

"But we didn't have sex," I added. "I swear. I don't know what I was thinking. I had a couple of beers after work and . . ."

We sat quietly for a long time. I felt like burying my head in the seats of the couch, so I'd never have to think about it again. Maybe one day it would just be one of the stories we could laugh about. "Remember that time . . . ?"

Slowly Todd stood up. As he moved to the door, he turned back to me.

"You might think you can make this all okay by just telling me. You can't."

Unlike in my family, there would be no spinning a story of bad behavior into a funny one. This wasn't going to be forgiven as a drunken mistake. After that night, we never spoke about it again. Todd's silence told me he might forgive but would never forget.

Over the years, the rifts that opened up between us often triggered deep-rooted insecurities. For example, I thought that he judged the way I had grown up. On the rare occasions when he met members of my family, I saw how his eyes widened at the way they smoked, ate, and drank to excess. I watched him cringe at the easy way they cussed at strangers and at each other. Over the years, the stories I told him about their ongoing faults and foibles didn't make him laugh as much. Instead, he would shake his head in shock.

Though he never said a word against my family, I began to wonder what he really thought of them, and of me. I knew there was a part of him that was relieved that I didn't seem to struggle with alcohol and drugs as others did in my family. Yet when he did see a side of them in me, it gave him pause. For example, he soon learned that I was quick to anger. During an argument I could lash out with words that hit hard. I was also noticeably wary around his family, friends, and neighbors. If I considered them outsiders, I was likely to roll my eyes, cluck my tongue, and pick apart their faults before they could mine. That insecurity was most obvious when he tried to invite anyone into our home for meals.

"I work all week," I would complain. "Why the hell are you bringing people here?"

Despite his assurances that this was how normal people socialized, soon after any guests arrived, I would often retreat into the bedroom or make an excuse so I could leave altogether.

"What is the matter with you?" he demanded.

I knew what was wrong, but I couldn't easily explain what growing up in social isolation had done to me. As a kid, I'd wanted nothing more than to escape the crowded and chaotic confines of our tiny house. Yet at the same time, I'd been taught to keep away from outsiders and be skeptical of anyone who tried to get too close—especially if they were white.

Now I had to figure out what that meant for the person I loved.

As Todd's birthday approached, that third week of June, I wrestled with what to do. I wondered whether this might be our last shared celebration. The arguments over how best to raise our kids, especially Mariah, had exposed the fundamental differences in our own upbringings. And although we didn't want to openly admit it, there was a question of what that meant for our future.

A few days before his birthday, it was our daughter Rachel who helped break the emotional stalemate.

"Soooo, Dad's birthday. We're doing something, right?"

I shrugged my shoulders. Finally we agreed on a photo slideshow of him, set to the song "Somewhere over the Rainbow." I wondered how to capture the fullness of a person's life in two dimensions. I knew I had to try, if not for us, then for the kids. They needed to see the entire story of our family from the beginning and even possibly to the end.

Together Rachel and I crawled into my bedroom closet and pulled old photo albums out of the back corner. One of the first photos I came across was of Todd and his late brother. Lee was just five years older, married and with two kids who were near the same age as our children. Because they were closest in age, Todd and Lee shared a special connection. We vacationed with him and his wife, and our kids grew up as close cousins. Then Lee was diagnosed with cancer. Over the next three years, Todd researched treatments, counseled his brother, and traveled to care for his wife and kids. But all his efforts weren't enough. As he went to visit his brother for what would be the last time, he called me from an airport layover, his voice hoarse. "I didn't make it in time. He's gone." The death of his brother devastated him. The two children Lee left behind would grow up and eventually have only fleeting memories of their dad. I knew that memory weighed on Todd as we tried to hold together our own family.

From the back of the closet, I pulled more photos. There was Todd with his sisters, his mother, and then his father, who just a few years after Lee's death had succumbed to Alzheimer's disease after a long and slow decline. I remembered the talkative man from Brooklyn and his bounding optimism about everything.

"I know life is hard—you got work, bills, kids," he often said, squeezing my shoulder blades. "But you got each other, okay? You and Todd."

Finally, I pulled down the albums of our own family and remembered all the times, good and bad, that had come before today.

A few days later, on his birthday, the four of us watched the photos play out on a laptop I had dragged out to the backyard table for his impromptu party presentation. There were pictures of Todd on his first bike; perched on his father's shoulders; arm in arm with his late brother—year after year after year, with the same crooked smile. They seamlessly transitioned to that shirtless photo of him in Israel and then to ones of us together, with Mariah and Rachel in our arms, in strollers, on our shoulders and laps, and finally as almost teenagers at our sides. The slideshow ended with us frozen in time.

I sat there, remembering the man I had met sixteen years ago. The nice Jewish boy, the Boy Scout, the good son and the loyal brother. I'd once almost passed him up in a coffee shop. He was still by my side, for better or for worse. Here was the type of man I had never known in my childhood. Here was the one I realized I still loved. Nobody spoke. The kids glanced back and forth between us. Todd sat, staring at the last slide. Finally he looked at me and we both began to cry.

"Oh. My. God." Rachel rolled her eyes at us. The four of us began to laugh.

Later that night, Todd and I talked in a way we hadn't for a long time. Though I liked to tease him about his Boy Scout virtues, Todd knew he wasn't perfect. He admitted he could be controlling about the little things in our lives and yet indecisive about the big decisions. He was stubborn and sometimes only saw the world through the eyes of someone who had grown up unburdened by some of the things I had experienced.

It had taken him time, but he now understood the impact of the trauma I'd experienced as a kid, and he saw the echoes of it in my relationship with him and the kids—especially Mariah. Yet he told me he saw something else in me, all those years ago and even now: a tough grit and resilience. It was the kind that had helped me survive my childhood. It was also what he had come to rely on, during the deaths of his father and brother and during all the difficult times in our relationship. It was also something he thought I was somehow passing on to our kids. Mariah, especially, he thought would need that in her life.

Still I knew he didn't have endless compassion for my faults. He wasn't Ma. If it got to the point again where he had to ask me to leave or I left on my own, I knew there would be no coming back for me, or for us. Many years ago, when we adopted the kids, the counselors had explained to us that we were committing to be their forever family. It was a commitment we had made to our kids and, now he reminded me, to each other.

No matter how difficult our lives, he was determined to hold me to that promise.

CHAPTER 19

Acting White,
Acting Black

In 2015, I stood inside a packed commuter train as it moved along sluggishly, a few inches at a time. Sweat collected between my backpack and dress shirt. As I looked around, I could see other passengers worried the train might be stalled inside the tunnel, as D.C.'s Metro trains were known to do at times. Moments earlier, I'd missed a call that had gone straight to voicemail. Then I recognized the number.

Listening to the message, my heart sank. "Please call us here at the middle school. It's regarding your daughter." My heart thudded as I waited for the train to lurch into the station. Finally I stood on the crowded platform and cupped my hand over the phone.

"Wait, tell me again," I insisted. "You had security remove her from the classroom? This doesn't sound right. She's never had a problem in school, never. I'm coming down there right now."

By the time I reached Todd, he'd received a call as well, but the story he'd heard was different. Mariah had been upset and crying in class. A teacher's aide escorted her to the guidance office to calm her. Still, I fumed at the picture in my head. As I headed for the school, I remembered recent viral videos of school discipline officers wrestling tiny Black girls out of their chairs and to the floor. I walked into the school's front office ready for battle. Mariah's face disarmed me. I looked at her, tear streaks staining her face, and pulled her into a hug.

"Poppy, I'm sorry. I was just upset. Sixth grade is just hard."

I'd always impressed upon the kids the importance of school, just as my family had. Even my grandmother, who seemed to believe there were limits to dreams, encouraged her own kids and grandkids to try and do well in school. With only just her third-grade education, Grandma still preached about doing well in school. I'd often make my kids laugh, mimicking her southern dialect. "You got to learn them books!" But even in elementary school, Mariah struggled. Testing revealed her learning differences. Behavior in the classroom had never been an issue, but now her problems at home and with schoolwork began to boil over into frustration and then spill out in tears.

A few weeks later, Todd and I returned to the school. We sat in a beige cinder block room on plastic chairs across from a row of white women. They introduced themselves as the IEP team, the staff responsible for creating Individualized Education Plans for students with special learning needs. I looked around impatiently as I waited for them to organize their files. We had doctors, counselors, therapists, mentors, and now school psychiatrists in Mariah's life. All the king's horses, all the king's men, I kept thinking.

Reams of paper were shuffled back and forth in front of us. We had come to ask for the type of intense support that schools can sometimes provide. Historically, schools handed it out grudgingly because of tight budgets and reduced staffs. Todd had coached me beforehand. "Know your audience," he said. He'd seen me in these types of situations before. All I could do was promise him I'd "act white and be polite." He laughed despite himself, but now that we were sitting here, even his face looked grim. The IEP team explained they were doing all they could, within the boundaries of the law. I folded my arms. Then I felt the woman next to me, a learning specialist from the district office, reach over and stroke my arm.

"You know, I think you came in here already feeling aggrieved."

I stopped. I imagined how I must appear to her—well educated, white, entitled, possibly even defensive because I was one of those gay parents, the ones with the chips on their shoulders. Maybe that was all true. But she didn't see all of me—the one who was raised poor, Black, and suspicious of how institutions treated Black people.

"Look," I said, snapping my head back and forth and wagging a finger directly in her face. "You. Don't. Know. Me. And I've never laid eyes on you before today. Don't you *dare* tell me how you *think* I feel. And let me tell you another thing . . ."

I stopped short. Looking around, I noticed the group of white women staring at me in openmouthed disbelief. Then I saw Todd. He wasn't looking at me, but he was sending me the clearest possible signal. His head lay in his hands, moving slowly left to right.

What these people also didn't know was that at work I was now an advocate for kids in schools—especially poor kids. My job was head of communications for a national nonprofit that worked with primarily low-income kids of color. Research had shown that poor Black and brown kids often don't have many of the same basic resources as their white counterparts. A kid comes to school hungry, in shabby clothes, or with an untreated toothache, and that kid is less likely to be able to focus on learning. The same is true if they need extra academic support. I was determined to make sure my own daughter would have the supports she needed. Todd might not have liked my approach, but by the time we left the meeting, we had what we came for.

There were other small incidents like the one in Mariah's school, which embarrassed my kids when they witnessed them. They cringed and accused me of "talking black" or "giving attitude." They pointed out I used a Black affect when I felt demeaned by someone who was white or when I wanted to subtly signal to other Black folks that I was one of them. Code-switching, or moving between two different styles of language depending on setting and audience, wasn't something I was conscious of doing. Still, when friends of the kids who were Black came over to play, I noticed how my speech and inflections changed to match theirs and their parents'.

"Poppy, stop trying to act Black," Mariah hissed at me after I greeted a friend's dad with a "wassup" and an awkward hand dap.

Despite believing that I would always have more in common with Black people, especially poor Black people, my climb up the economic ladder had threatened to change me, and in some ways that I was ashamed to admit. Later that year, an experience with one of Rachel's friends from Girl Scouts made me confront that.

The little girl and her mom had showed up on our doorstep a few weeks after the start of school. The black garbage bags they were carrying bulged in places. I could see the outline of a stuffed animal in one straining against the plastic. The little girl, Lilliana, untied it and reached in, pulling the animal free from atop the pile of clothes, books, and toiletries. Rachel and I watched her unpack from the top of our basement stairs.

This wasn't the first time Lilliana had stayed with us. Half a dozen times before, the little girl with cornrows and a bright smile had marched into our home with her Minnie Mouse backpack, carrying everything a ten-year-old needs for a sleepover—PJs, toothbrush, and hair scrunchies. Now she had everything she owned in the world jammed tight inside those garbage bags. Her mom had been evicted. Their well-worn furniture, lumpy mattresses, and boxes of scuffed pots and pans were dumped in a sad pile in front of their apartment complex. When Rachel's scout troop learned of their situation, families organized and began hosting Lilliana and her mom for a few weeks at a time. Now it was our turn, and they were camping out inside our musty-smelling basement.

"How long are they staying?" Rachel whispered to me.

I gently tugged her back from the doorway, giving Lilliana and her mom some privacy.

"Just until they find a new place to stay," I said. "Only a few weeks. I think."

The first week, we tiptoed around them. Todd greeted them with dinner at the end of the day. I kept the bathrooms stocked with extra towels and toilet paper, and the kids made sure to poke their heads into the basement to wish them goodnight. I told the kids we were living the same Girl Scout values I heard Rachel recite at meetings—about help-ing people all the time. But as I watched their piles of unwashed clothes spread across the basement floor and snack food wrappers multiply in the trash, I began to question their values. My critical eye fell on Lilliana one night at our dinner table as she heaped her plate with everything but vegetables.

"Slow down, sweetie," I said.

Mariah gave me the pointed, private look that I sometimes reserved for her and Rachel in public spaces. You're embarrassing yourself, it said.

And she was right. Yet as the days wore on, I couldn't help myself.

"Just how far behind were they on their rent?" I asked Todd.

"Does it really matter?" he asked.

I shrugged as if it didn't. But it did, to me, because as a kid I'd come to believe that poverty and homelessness were the cost of marrying poorly, or at least of making poor choices. I hadn't been much older than Lilliana when my own mother emptied our dresser drawers into paper sacks from the grocery store and loaded them into the back of our bat-tered station wagon. We were running away from Pops, yet again. My siblings and I arrived on the doorstep of a family friend's home, where they passed out cups of hot cocoa, borrowed blankets, and reassuring pats on the head. But I didn't feel comforted. I just felt ashamed.

In all the years since I left home, I was determined to not make the same mistakes as Ma. People who had stable homes and families had worked hard, saved wisely, and made good choices about spending. If they didn't, everyone paid the price, especially the kids. One night, well into our guests' stay, I practically said as much to Lilliana. She was play-ing in Rachel's room, and as bedtime approached, she asked if she could play longer and maybe spend the night in my daughter's comfortable bed. Before I could catch myself, I opened the door to the basement. On the floor below was a sleeping bag and air mattress.

"It's a school night, sweetie, you should go home to your mom."

As the door closed behind her, I finally realized what my boorish behavior had been saying: *Welcome to my nice home. Let me show you around. You can look, but don't touch. Over here is a symbol of what a good family we are. And down there is a sign of your choices in life.*

I never got the chance to apologize to Lilliana and her mom. Within a day they were gone. Their garbage bags were hauled away in another family's car. Our basement floor was left spotless and the bathroom sinks scrubbed to a gleam. Shortly after, they found a new apartment. Rachel stayed friendly with Lilliana, but their playdates and sleepovers became less frequent. Finally they just stopped.

Looking back, I felt ashamed of what I'd done. Lilliana needed someone to look past her present circumstances and see a different future. It was the kind of thing that someone had once done for me, long ago, and it had taught me I didn't have to share the same fate as my troubled family.

CHAPTER 20

One Step Forward

Three girls in plaid Catholic school jumpers pushed me up against the brick wall of St. Anthony's Middle School and held me there. I struggled but couldn't break free.

"Your ears are dirty," one pointed out. She was right.

"Why don't you brush your teeth?" another asked. Sometimes I just forgot to.

"Don't you even own an iron?" the third asked. Yes, I said to myself. But it's busted.

I was ten and had just started middle school, and my new classmates could easily see that I didn't fit in with the other carefully groomed and dressed kids. What I couldn't tell these mean girls is that my old way of life at home was falling apart. Neecie was getting ready to move out. I had counted on her to take care of me while Ma worked. Consequently, I didn't know how to comb my own hair for school. The silky mass of curls—what my family called "good hair" or "white folks' hair"—hung in near-tangles. With Neecie not around to scold me, my teeth didn't get brushed, my ears didn't get cleaned, and my school clothes were picked out of the dirty laundry. Ma's nightly menu of fried anything and potatoes had also finally caught up with me, and now I was pudgy. The kids on the bus and the playground knew me as the fat half-breed with uncombed hair, wax-filled ears, and skunk breath. The nuns began to send home polite hints in the form of pamphlets on personal hygiene. Ma was so offended, she threatened, "I'm going to go down to talk to that school." I shook my head no and told her I could handle it. It was bad enough I looked like white trash. I didn't want everyone at my new school to meet my Black mother.

Whereas the nuns in my elementary school seemed to have sympathy for me, these sisters wrinkled their noses and pulled their lips into a tight frown whenever I was around. Just a few years earlier, teachers sent home glowing comments on my report cards that were filled with A's and B's. Now the new nuns looked at me, then at my grades, and shook their heads in disbelief. They accused me of cheating on tests and having someone do my homework for me. I felt bullied by both the teachers and the kids.

One morning, I sat contemplating my horrible life in the small church that adjoined the school. The entire school was there for a mandatory Catholic Mass. The sister patrolled the pews daring anyone to fidget. Maybe it was the half-spoiled milk I'd had with my cereal that morning or the accumulated shame and fear that curdled in my belly. Either way, I could hear my gut churning loudly and felt a roiling in my bowels.

"Shush! Sit still," one of the sisters hissed. Within the folds of the sleeves of her brown habit, I could see a ruler peeking out. She carried it to enforce her rules. A much larger wooden stick—a paddle—waited in her office for bigger infractions. The gurgling and sharp ache kept building. As I squirmed around, I weighed the thought of that paddle on my butt against the pressure building inside. Finally I figured it wouldn't matter. I was going to be in trouble either way, so I stood up and ran out the back of the church. I raced toward the toilet in the school next door with the desperation of someone who has a ticking bomb in their pants about to explode.

I didn't make it. From then on, I knew my grades and practiced manners in class would never matter to the sisters or these kids who had two parents and nice houses and someone to comb their hair in the morning. They would always think I was a piece of shit. Now I had proved them right.

My saving grace came toward the middle of the next school year. My current fifth-grade teacher, Sister Anine, was sent away mysteriously. We'd become used to her bouts of anger. But one day as we sat with our heads on our wooden desks waiting for Sister to arrive, the principal walked in and announced that Sister needed recess for the rest of the year. A few days later, a substitute appeared in our classroom. With all the nuns currently assigned to other duties, the school had to settle on someone who hadn't been trained in the martial arts of wooden rulers and paddles. That lay teacher was Mrs. Marone. She was in her early fifties. She clicked into our classroom on a pair of pumps and amid a cloud of perfume. Every conversation came with a warm touch on your back and an encouraging smile. She never yelled or threatened. Very soon she pulled me aside to offer me something else. She'd taken note that I didn't seem to fit in with many of the other kids. By now I felt I was different. I didn't want to roughhouse or play kickball with the boys. Instead I liked to jump rope with the girls. That and my poor hygiene made me a big target for the bullies. But Mrs. Marone also noticed that in lieu of friends, I spent much of my time with books. My grades were good, and so was my behavior. That earned me her attention at first, and then slowly other rewards. First there were some new bookmarks. Then it was a pack of mints, and finally more private gifts like a brush and comb kit from the drugstore. From then on, I was willing to do anything just to earn her praise and attention, whether that meant reading more books or even combing my hair and brushing my teeth.

"Stephen, you're very bright, you know," she said one day toward the end of the school year. "What are you going to be after you go away to college?"

"College? I don't know, Mrs. Marone. What do *you* want me to be?"

She looked at me, smiled, and patted my hand. In all her years of teaching, she'd probably become accustomed to schoolboy crushes. She was well past the age for that, and she must have realized I had feelings for her not because of her looks but because of the looks she gave me. It didn't matter how I appeared to Mrs. Marone—Black, white, rich or poor. She noticed something different inside me, something that might carry me away from this little school, this small town, my country hill. And because of her, I now recognized it in myself.

Neecie was already on her way to a better life. She was leaving for college that fall after cobbling together grants, student loans, and work-study. As she got ready to depart, Ma wanted to be sure that Denise could hold her head up high when she walked onto her mostly white campus. The day of Denise's departure fell on Ma's payday. Our newest used car, a rusty Buick Skylark, was packed to the roof with boxes and borrowed suitcases. There was only one obstacle to my sister starting her higher education. Neecie absolutely wanted a new pair of platform shoes. It would mean a hasty trip to town before we hit the highway for the five-hour trip. Ma just couldn't say no.

Our little town was still bustling with Saturday shoppers during the late 1970s. There were often few places to park. Ma agreed to circle the block while Neecie ran in to buy a pair of shoes in one of the two department stores.

"Ma, it'll only take me a minute," Denise said, bounding out of the car at a red light.

My mother nodded, her cigarette bobbing up and down. After the third trip around the block, Denise had still not appeared. Suddenly Ma felt something familiar, and I felt sick to my stomach.

The car jerked a few times and the engine sputtered.

Ma sighed. "We're out of gas."

Many times, we had "driven to town on fumes," praying to make it to a gas station. Some of those times we ended up stranded on a country road, praying for a farmer to come along with a good soul and a few gallons of gas in his barn. We had come so far since then. Pops was gone. Jim and Denise were in college. It felt like we were on a road to respectability. Instead we were stuck on Main Street, with a long line of drivers behind us, honking. Ma's spendthrift ways, poor planning, and habit of living above our means had caught up with her. Our shame was on full public display. Ma laid her head down on the steering wheel and cried. Her battle for control over her life and our war for respectability were lost that day, all for the want of platform shoes.

Sitting in the back of the car, ducking down to hide from it all, I remembered something Neecie had once said to me.

"You can take the colored folks out of the country, but you can never take the country out of the colored folks."

That year, Ma was still trying to find her own place in our new world. For decades Pops had taken away her freedom. Grandma had controlled her life by holding a few dollars above her head. And her kids had taken most of her energy. Now she had more time to think. Most nights, she sat under the brightest lamp in the living room, sometimes with her Bible, other times a romance novel. Most of the time the books lay open on her lap while she looked around at the four walls. All her life she'd seen herself as Grandma's daughter, a high school dropout, a battered wife and then a single mother. Now she had a chance to be someone else.

She started with those walls, marked up with scuffs, patched holes, and a thin film caused by years of cigarette smoke. In fits of frenzy she would climb up and down ladders, scrubbing until her hands reeked of vinegar. Then she figured it was time to paint or paper over. In the years that followed, if someone had bored a hole into our living room walls, they would have come away with a plug of wood, striped with layers of Sherwin Williams paint and wallpaper. Each represented another attempt by Ma to cover up the past and start anew.

Grandma would hobble over and watch, sucking her teeth. She began calling it Ma's little dollhouse. She insisted Ma was wasting her time and money.

"Vir-jen-ya, why you fret so much about this little house when you ain't got a pot to piss in?" she'd often ask.

Even I had to admit that the dollhouse was built on shaky ground. Our house began to sport new curtains and carpets, but Ma still scrambled to find money to make sure the electricity stayed on. Still, my mother began to have an unshakeable confidence that the freedom she'd dreamed of so many years ago was finally within reach. That's why one April she opened an envelope from the IRS and began waving her short brown arms wildly in the air. "Ohhhhhhh!!!!" she screamed. It was rare to see her face light up with pure joy. I'd seen it when my siblings graduated from high school, and then again at the birth of her first grandchild. But this was something different. This was ecstasy.

She waved the piece of paper in front of my face. It was a check for one thousand, five hundred dollars.

"I want to hold it!" I said.

I too felt its power. The only thing better than holding this golden ticket was the moment after Ma cashed it. I fingered the stacks of tens, twenties, and fifties stuffed into the bank envelope. To her credit, Ma did make sure the electric bill was paid, that groceries were in the refrigerator and gas in the car. But we also ate in restaurants and made several trips to the shopping mall. Within three days of her cashing that check, it was all gone.

Grandma held out her open palm to Ma, with fingers spread.

"Money goes through your hands, jest like water, Jen-ya," she cackled.

Aside from tax season, Christmas was the other time of year my mother looked forward to. There wasn't any windfall, but with her children gathered together, this was her opportunity to show them how much she loved them. The more presents she purchased, the happier she was. Her shopping strategy depended on her payday. If it fell a week or less before Christmas, she was flush with cash. If not, she bought on credit. The holiday bills could wait like all the others. Like a brown Mrs. Santa Claus, Ma loaded up the trunk of her shabby car with sacks of new clothes, boxes of electronics, and enough stuff to fill a small catalog. Every year's holiday haul was bigger than the last.

The most extravagant Christmas celebration she pulled off became more than a good family story. It's now a legend. Among the mountain of presents under the tree were expensive jewelry, leather boots, top-of-the-line stereo equipment, high-end apparel, an electric guitar, two new bikes, and roller skates. Everyone also received a complete set of Samsonite luggage, and everything was charged on credit, of course. We had no money to travel, but we looked like we were going places. To top it all off, Ma decided that home-cooked turkey and ham weren't good enough for her kids that year. She mail-ordered steak and lobster for dinner.

We walked into our living room and our jaws dropped. It didn't look like a solemn celebration of Jesus's birth. It damned near looked like Jesus was getting married and Ma was throwing a reception of biblical proportions.

"I can't help myself." Ma giggled as she poured out Mimosas.

She couldn't help herself, and neither could her mother. As soon as Grandma hobbled into the house, she began clucking her tongue.

"How you spend all that money on them little trinkets? You watch, a few weeks and y'all gonna be wondering where that money went. Mark my words, hard times are coming."

We rolled our eyes and laughed. With that, Grandma started cursing us under her breath and called for John to take her across the yard to their house. As they left, I looked out the window. John's aging knees were trying to hold up under the weight of Grandma, who was leaning heavily on him as they trudged through the snow. Grandma finally struggled up the steps of her porch, which half sagged into the ground in places. The foundation of the house was collapsing beneath them. Just next door we enjoyed Ma's newly redecorated dollhouse. That night, Ma basked in the glow of the twinkling Christmas tree lights and enjoyed the warmth of the butter dripping down her chin from the lobster. But then February rolled around. When there wasn't enough money to buy heating oil, Ma huddled over our space heater with the frayed electrical cord and looked through the stack of bills that had piled up on the kitchen counter. The glint in her eyes was gone.

I was only a kid, but I knew I might have a future off our hill. All Ma had to look forward to was another trip across the yard to visit Grandma, her potbellied stove, and her deep freezer.

CHAPTER 21

Truth, Lies, and Secrets

One night in March of 2015, Todd hunched over a stack of folders strewn across our bed, while I crouched on the hardwood floor of our bedroom closet, rooting around in the past. We'd agreed it was time to hand our kids the adoption documents we'd been hauling in moving boxes for more than a decade.

They weren't exactly a family secret. They hadn't been locked away from our kids, but the watertight plastic storage bins had been conveniently pushed into the corner, shoved away where it was easy to forget. I slowly pulled the lid off a bin, knowing everything would be out in the open now—the names, photos, and some of the details that they were once too young to understand. These artifacts of their first years were certain to answer some of their questions and perhaps put some of their lingering anxieties about adoption to rest. They would also reveal facts about their birth family that might be deeply painful.

Both adoptions had been open from the start, and we had shared what we knew with the kids. Their birth mom was single, and at each birth she faced a choice. Five times she kept her children. After the birth of her sixth, seventh, and eight children, she did not. Our daughters were the sixth and seventh in line. A younger brother, the eighth child, had been adopted into another family. I pulled a few photos of the older siblings from the bin. They flashed wide smiles for the camera as they sat at a hospital cafeteria. The adoption counselor, Krissy, had taken the photos while their mom was giving birth to Mariah. They'd surely known their mother was pregnant. What did they think each time they left the hospital without a younger sibling? What did she tell them? What did they know, even now? These were questions we might never be able to answer.

There was another photo of their mom inside the container. This was a duplicate of the one Mariah and Rachel had already. Long ago we'd pasted it inside each of their scrapbooks to help them understand the story of their adoption. The picture shows their mother looking sleepy-eyed and exhausted, shortly after giving birth.

As I looked through the rest of the photos, I thought of my mother giving birth to me and the story she concocted the moment the nurse placed me in her arms. She, Pops, and her four other children were Black. I was paler than white bread. I'm sure there were questioning looks. But at that moment, in an out-of-town hospital where she'd chosen to give birth, thirty miles from our small town, she would have needed to settle on a story that she would tell from that day forward. I'll never know what she said to the nurses, but from then on, she stuck to an explanation that was simple. She told me that I just came out with lighter skin.

"Here it is," Todd said. He handed me a photo of the man named as our daughters' birth dad. It had been years since I'd seen it. We'd never shown the picture to the kids before. In it a hulking, muscular, dark-skinned man stares straight at the camera. It's clear that someone directed him to do that. It's a mug shot. The man's almond-shaped eyes were Mariah's. Years before, when I first saw the photo, I knew immediately that Mariah might one day be delighted when she noticed the resemblance. At the same time, I knew it would cause Rachel pain and confusion. She would look at it and suspect that this man was not her birth father. I wondered if, like me, she might spend the rest of her life speculating about that missing piece of her history.

As I calculated how best to introduce this small photo that said so much about their story, Todd created piles atop our bedspread—birth certificates, medical records, adoption decrees. It was the first proof of their place in this world. Off to the side there was something that didn't fit into any pile. It was something I hadn't seen in years. I picked up the stapled, glossy booklet. It was part scrapbook, part sales pitch. As prospective parents, the adoption agency had encouraged us to create a brochure to introduce ourselves to birth mothers. When we'd first shown it to the kids, years ago, they were excited by it.

"How did our mother get it?" "Did she like the pictures?" "Did she write you back?"

I remembered their disappointment when they learned it was a copy, not the original that was touched by their mother's hands. Our youngest had then read over the words I wrote describing my own family. It accompanied the childhood photo of me with my family, the same one that hung in our hallway. It was at that moment that Rachel began to connect my story to her own.

"*Sooo*, I guess I get why my mother gave us up for adoption. She had other kids, right, and, well, she was poor and stuff?"

At the time, I nodded and reached over to pull her in for a hug. She gently pulled back from me.

"She was just like your mom, right?"

"Well . . ."

"Wait, I got a question," Rachel asked. "Why did your mom keep you?"

Back then, I told her that parents who know they can give a child a good life often decide to keep their baby. Some who can't, choose adoption. But I had no answer for her next questions: "What if parents choose the wrong thing?"

Now, years later, Todd and I called our kids into our bedroom to learn the consequences of our choices.

"We think you're old enough to look at some more things related to your adoption," Todd said. "Come have a seat."

The room was quiet. Todd handed them each a small pile of official documents related to their adoptions. I watched them as they slowly turned over each paper in their hands, trying to pull some other detail about their pasts from them. There was very little new, but still they handled them like precious artifacts.

After a few minutes I looked at Todd. He nodded okay and I pulled out an envelope.

"So, we've told you we didn't have a picture of your birth dad," I said. "That's kind of true. We've really only had this."

Our kids dropped everything else and huddled over the photo.

"He looks just like Mariah," Rachel said. Her round brown eyes looked disappointed.

"He's not your dad," Mariah said.

"You mean, *birth* dad," Todd corrected.

"I'm sorry," Mariah said to her sister over her shoulder. She headed out of the room, to place the photo inside her scrapbook.

I turned to Rachel. "Does it bother you, not knowing your birth dad?"

She thought a minute, then shrugged.

"I guess my dad was just a random dude she . . . well, you know, slept with."

Todd raised his eyebrows.

"What? It's kind of true," she said with half a smile.

She paused to think some more. Then she finally blurted out what I'd feared she was thinking all along.

"You guys lied."

"We didn't," I sputtered. "We've always told you the truth."

"But you didn't tell us everything. You had all of this stuff and this picture and didn't give it to us."

"We wanted to wait until you were old enough to understand."

She considered that, but then shook her head.

"No, Poppy. You lied."

She handed me the rest of the photos and walked out. I couldn't bring myself to admit she was right. I also wanted to tell her that all parents tell their children lies. One day I hoped she'd learn that they mostly do it to protect their children's feelings. And sometimes they just do it to protect themselves. As a kid, I had learned that determining those true motivations was often a messy business.

CHAPTER 22

Ole Hot Ass

Aside from bill collectors and extended family, people rarely came to visit our house. So when a brand-new Cadillac pulled into Aunt Bonnie's driveway next door and I saw her chunky legs wobbling out on tiny heels to get into it, I was curious. I spied on her from my bedroom window as a strange man opened the car door for her. And when she rode off in the passenger seat of that car every day after Uncle Hunt left for work, I shook my head and muttered our family motto for anything dubious: Unh-unh-unh-unh-unh. It roughly translated as "Ain't that some shit."

Before that Cadillac showed up around 1977, Bonnie spent most days in a housedress, plopped on a couch, eating plates of greasy food and watching soap operas. Suddenly she was leaving home each day with her hair done up and a full face of makeup. Bonnie returned from these chauffeured visits with new dresses, jewelry, and doggie bags from nice restaurants. We realized she couldn't be spinning tales to that many shop owners. When it became clear what was happening, we weren't shocked. Titillated was more like it.

For years I'd heard the scandalous stories about relatives who were "hot-assed." That meant they were horny and looking for satisfaction anywhere they could find it. Ironically, Bonnie was often the one sucking her tiny teeth in disapproval while telling their stories.

One day not long after I started tracking Aunt Bonnie's coming and goings from my bedroom window, she marched into our kitchen out of breath. Ma got down from her stepladder where she was trying to scrub the years of grime off our kitchen cabinets. I put down my book and hovered close to the kitchen. If Aunt Bonnie came unexpectedly, my mother and I knew we were about to hear a jaw-dropping story.

"Jen-ya, guess who I saw creeping around up in Buffalo yesterday?"

Ma sighed. "Who?"

"Ole black Maxine's husband, Ollie, looking like an ole damn black peacock."

"Bonnie!"

Even my mother couldn't help laughing at this nickname.

"He was sitting up there with some damn purple zoot suit from back in the day and a damn hat with a feather poking up from it. He looked like a damn black peacock!

"I look over and see this light-skinned gal sitting next to him in the passenger seat, looking no older than a teenager. I kept waving and tooting my horn, and finally he cracked his window, looking all sheepish. He said, 'Well, hello, Bonnie, I didn't notice you over there.' I said, 'Well, Ollie, I was sure that was you. How are you doing? How is Maxine these days? Is this y'all's daughter?' When the light turned green, he stepped on the gas and beat it out of there like it was nobody's business."

I watched the two of them double over till tears rolled down their faces. When the laughs died to a titter, Bonnie offered the moral of the story:

"He ought to go sit his ole hot ass down somewhere."

Ma offered her amen: "Unh-unh-unh-unh-unhhhhh."

Though I was used to hearing these stories, nothing could prepare me for when I began to hear them about my mother. Before then, I'd always thought of her as better than the other women in our family. Unlike Grandma and Aunt Bonnie, she was neither hot-tempered nor hot-assed. I was old enough to realize she wasn't a saint. She gossiped a bit and cussed a lot when she got mad. But other than that, she had always just done her best, even when she didn't have the courage to leave Pops. But she wasn't a sinner to me, more like a full-time martyr. She put up with Grandma and encouraged her kids to do better. For that reason, I figured her soul was like her kitchen cabinets—just dusty and in need of occasional cleaning.

At least, that's what I thought until a freshly washed and waxed gold Buick crept into our driveway. It was a Sunday, so I knew it wasn't a bill collector. I watched from Grandma's house. Ma had sent me "cross the yard" before the man in the Buick got there.

"But why?" I had asked. "Why can't I stay home? I want to watch TV!"

"I'm visiting with a friend. Go over to Grandma's and don't come back until I tell you."

I left but took my sweet time, walking the path my feet had carved out of the crabgrass over the years. Ma yelled from the back porch.

"Go on, hurry up. It's just for an hour."

I couldn't understand why Ma would let a stranger come over to our house. When I got to Grandma's, I tried to distract myself from the smell of the slop bucket and the pan of dirty dishwater boiling on the potbellied stove. When I saw the Buick pull in, I pressed my face to Grandma's fly-specked window. The fancy car parked right next to our back porch, and a man hopped out on the passenger side. He scurried up our three concrete steps and raced behind the screen door that Ma was holding open for him. No one went in and out of our houses without someone spying them from some window. It was clear that Ma was trying to hide the identity of this person, but she couldn't hide what I saw. His bald head peeked out from beneath his old-fashioned hat. This man was white.

The mystery man came to our back door every Sunday, and before he arrived, Ma told me to leave. I knew better than to ask grown folks about their business, but this was Ma, and so I had to keep asking. I whined, cried, and carried on, hoping she might eventually answer.

"Why do I have to go? Ma! Who's coming over?"

"Just a friend."

It was winter now. Ma zipped the coat up tight beneath my chin, spun me around, and nudged me out the door.

Later I sprawled across the unwashed bedspread atop Grandma's daybed in the living room. As I peeked out the window and saw this man scuttle like a bug inside our back door, I realized Grandma might know something about Ma's secrets. For all her faults, I guessed she loved me enough to wait until I asked who this "friend" was.

"She steppin' out with ole cancer-belly," she said as she picked her teeth. "He run the barber shop in town. I don't know why Jen-ya got to mess with that eye-talian man. He almost twenty years older. Besides, he already got a wife."

There was more. Grandma said there was talk around town that he did small favors for a mob family that was based in Buffalo. The "Mahf-ee-yat" she pronounced it.

I left the window. As much as I had wanted to know the truth, now I wished I hadn't asked. Now I had to put it out of my mind. When you grow up half expecting and half-fearing that the electricity will be shut off, that the car will run out of gas, that a family meal might end in a fistfight, or that Pops might reappear in the middle of the night, you train yourself never to feel shocked or at least never to show it.

Anything can happen. Somebody else can be your father. You can be white. You can be Black. You might be adopted. Or your mother might invite a married man over to your house. You can't be surprised. You just have to be numb and stay that way.

While I learned to bury a lot of my feelings as a kid, there was one I could not escape. It was fear of deprivation. I couldn't pretend it wasn't happening, and Ma couldn't create a wild story to explain it away. The evidence was incontrovertible. First, our lights went out. With that, I knew our empty refrigerator would stop humming and the black-and-white TV would refuse to turn on when it was time for *Happy Days*. If all that happened, I knew for sure the electric company was out to get us again and that other bill collectors were on their heels.

Every day when I came home from school, I threw all the bills from the mailbox into the growing pile Ma kept in a raggedy wicker basket on the kitchen table. She ignored them until payday. Even then, she might shuffle through them all and just put them back in the stack for another day. But our routine changed if an envelope came with a big red stripe on the outside and the words "Final Disconnection Notice." If I found it in the mail, I ran to the phone to call Ma at work.

"Ma, they're gonna turn the electricity off," I whispered.

I heard a quiet hiss, a crackle, and a sudden breath as she smoked and thought.

"What's the date on it?" she asked.

She was counting the days before her next paycheck. Even if we had time, there was always the risk that someone might send a utility van out to the house a day or two early. Time had run out if I came home and saw a paper notice fluttering in the screen door. It looked like a death warrant. *Service terminated.* I would get back on the phone. My crying calls to Ma set off a chain reaction. She made crying calls to the billing office and a crying visit to Grandma's house to ask for money. The electric bill wasn't her only problem. Routinely, our phone was disconnected, we ran out of heating oil, the car stalled in traffic without enough gas, and creditors threatened to sue. Ma just treated it like it was her fate in life, and I worried it might be mine as well.

But then in 1978 something began to change. Even while dodging debt collectors, Ma had managed to send Jim and Denise off to college. Though it was through lots of college loans and generous grants, it was an achievement. By this time Rick also was off on his own, somewhere, now on his second wife and kids. Even Mike was living independently, working blue-collar jobs and paying his own bills. For the first time, Ma had only two mouths to feed in our house. That freed her up from the loans and loaves of frozen bread from my grandmother. With the extra money, she was now able to keep the lights on and the house heated, and she still had some left over to begin to replace some of the patched furniture and the badly painted-over wood paneling from the 1960s.

Ma had yet to make her own transformation, though. Denise must have sensed that Ma wanted it but didn't know how to go about it. During one of her visits home from college that year, she sat at the kitchen table with our mother. I peeked around the corner and listened.

"Ma, you're still young. You're a good-looking woman," Denise said, tapping her own cigarette on the ashtray. "Why don't you get out there and date? You don't have to be alone your entire life."

Ma pulled at the elastic band on her frayed cotton-poly-blend pants.

"I am too old to be out there, sitting up in some bar or running the streets," she said.

"And what are you going to do in a few years when Stevie is gone and you're up here on this hill all by yourself—still be up here dealing with Grandma and Bonnie and all this happy horseshit?"

Ma didn't answer, but she did a lot of quiet thinking over the next year about how she could change her life. One day that change arrived in a pink vinyl case. Inside were shades from ivory to beige to bronze and lots of other colors, along with a consultant script and a business card. It said that Ma was now a Mary Kay Cosmetics consultant. As I ran my hands over the tubes and cases, brushes and makeup wands, I was struck by the thought of a magical transformation. My mother was a divorced, working-class, Black single mother. She had spent her life quietly trying to dress up her shabby life and attempting to shape her kids into the best possible versions of themselves. This pink case was more than just a choice to bring out the best in other people with the right palette. Its arrival meant that Ma was ready to transform herself.

Suddenly she was leaving the house most nights and weekends, armed with makeup samples and order forms. She spent hours on the phone, not trading gossip with Bonnie, but booking appointments. Her calendar was filled with makeup parties and consultations. She didn't dare leave the house without looking professional, as her Mary Kay mentor suggested. Soon there were weekly hair appointments, nail appointments, visits to Weight Watchers.

Within a year she lost thirty pounds and hung her glitzy glamour shot on the wall next to everyone's high school graduation photos. She was now earning more money than ever, between her job at the hospital and Mary Kay. All her life she'd seen herself as the woman who made a detour after school that set her on a path to poverty. Now when she looked in the mirror, she saw that woman on a road to a different future.

It wasn't just the makeup. My mother also glowed with what I supposed was love. I had watched her mysterious boyfriend come and go from our house every Sunday for more than four years. I knew little about him other than what my grandmother had told me, but I could plainly see his tiny bald head and paunchy belly as he snuck into the house. I assumed he was still afraid of getting caught, by whom I'm not sure. I couldn't imagine his wife looking for him on our country hill. And Grandma and Aunt Bonnie certainly saw his comings and goings. Ma had hidden the truth about the white man who was my father since I was born. Still, it surprised me that now she tried to keep this man a secret from me, too.

Ma must have realized I knew more than what she'd told me. One early Sunday morning when I was twelve, she cracked open the door to my bedroom. Trying to sound nonchalant, she told me to come out and meet her friend. Walking out of my pitch-black room and into the living room, I remember the sharp winter sunlight glaring off the snow outside. There her boyfriend stood in a gray pin-striped three-piece suit and snow boots.

"This is Louie," Ma said. "Say hello."

He gave me a soft, damp handshake. It didn't seem he was capable of much more. He was barely five feet and much older than he looked from Grandma's window. I mumbled a weak hello. I couldn't believe this round and little old Italian man was Ma's boyfriend. I was taller than him. He also didn't measure up in other ways. I thought back to when I was younger and used to lie awake in bed and imagine what would happen if Ma got married again. I prayed to have a new dad to show me how to throw a football, so the kids wouldn't make fun of me. Sometimes in my daydreams he was Black. Sometimes he was white. But he never looked like Louie.

"I'm going to Grandma's," I said.

Ma would continue to try and get me to talk to Louie or at least acknowledge his presence. Sunday after Sunday he would arrive with something. Sometimes it would be pastries, other times ingredients for Italian dishes that he would cook, but I noticed he'd also tuck money into her hand before leaving. Generally it was fifty dollars but sometimes a hundred. Sometimes he'd try to hand me a ten-dollar bill, but I'd push it back toward him. I didn't know if his money bought Ma's attention, but it would not buy mine.

His visits continued until one Sunday morning after I entered junior high school. That day Ma let me sleep in, and by the time I woke up it was almost noon. As I rubbed my eyes and walked into the kitchen, I saw her sitting at the table alone. She said Louie wouldn't be coming anymore. Over the next few months, she withdrew into herself and returned to the stack of romance novels on her nightstand. I never asked Ma whether his wife had found out, whether the cancer was back in his belly, or whether they'd just had enough of each other.

I knew I should have felt sad that after all these years my mother had finally found love but then lost it. But I was still angry that she had tried to hide the relationship from me and then lied about who this man was. I told myself his presence in my mother's life had no effect on me.

Instead, I was now more determined to confront her about the other white man in her life, and what their relationship meant about who I was.

All I had to do was wait for the right moment.

CHAPTER 23

The Traveling Salesman

By middle school I decided that no one would ever mistake me again for being just a poor Black kid. I started each morning by combing my tight cropped hair, ironing a crease into my pants, and dousing myself with a bottle of Old Spice that Pops had left behind in the cabinet years before. Once I got off the school bus in the morning, few people realized where I had come from.

Looking the part was just the beginning. Now I had to fit in. I soon discovered that being known as a smart kid gave me access to a new class of friends. I was too ashamed to ever invite them to my house. So I spent time in their tidy suburban ranch houses, where I gawked at their color TVs with something called cable. I might not have been born with their lifestyle and privilege, but soon I coveted it. Keds sneakers, Sony Walkmans, and Big Macs. I pestered Ma for all of the trappings of the typical 1980s white middle-class teens in my school. Ma seemed happy that I was beginning to explore a better life off the hill. When she had the money, she gladly handed it over, and when she didn't, she grudgingly borrowed it from Grandma.

By the time I reached high school, I was moving exclusively in a circle of white friends. I made sure my clothes, speech, taste in music, and mannerisms mimicked theirs. I joined the Yearbook Club, Drama Club, Student Council, and Honor Society—anyplace where I thought I could be and not have someone question whether I belonged. For years

I had tried to fit into my own family by acting Black. Now I'd grown comfortable playing the part of a middle-class white kid.

Money became another equalizer. For the first time in my life, I realized that I didn't have to be limited by Ma's paycheck and Grandma's handouts. My junior year, I walked into the local McDonald's and talked my way into an after-school job. Now I had money to make sure that all my clothes came from the mall and that I could go out with friends to movies or the skating rink. As much 1980s teenaged freedom as our rinky-dink town had to offer, I made sure to enjoy it.

In her own way, Ma had encouraged this. Growing up, we heard her tell stories of wearing worn hand-me-downs from her older cousins and going to school with holes in her shoes. She didn't want her own kids to experience that shame, so she went into debt every year trying to buy us new clothes and sneakers from fancy department stores. She wanted us to measure up to the other kids in school. So she didn't blink when I came home one year with a flier advertising a language club trip to France and Spain over spring break. Ma owed my Catholic high school thousands of dollars in back tuition. Her car needed repairs, and the roof needed replacing. But two of her paychecks and some loans from friends sent me off to Paris and Madrid.

When I returned home, Grandma and Aunt Bonnie rolled their eyes, but even worse, my school principal was irate. He wondered why I didn't show up over the break for the work-study program that helped pay off my tuition bill. He glared at the expensive pair of leather shoes I'd bought in Paris. He fired off a letter to my mother, expressing his disappointment that we'd neglected to meet an important obligation. Ma just tucked it behind the bundle of other bills in the kitchen. She might get to it, eventually. For her, providing me that opportunity was worth the added debt and embarrassment.

That experience was just one of many that Ma apparently decided were worth an investment. With all her older children gone, she threw whatever money she had, along with postdated checks and maxed credit cards, at my future. There were more school trips, club fees, appointments for contact lenses, and new clothes. To a few in my family, especially Rick, it confirmed suspicions that I *was* the favored child. But I knew it came down to supply and demand. She had only one child left to support, and she was determined to use all her remaining blood, sweat, and bounced checks to ensure that one of her kids made it as far away from our small town as he could go.

Ma's dreams for me began to help me realize there might be a bigger world beyond the community colleges and state schools that were financially in our reach. By senior year I was applying to colleges across the country. That spring I learned my better-than-average grades were just good enough to get me into a small but prestigious engineering school at the tip of upstate New York. It didn't take long to realize that student loans and grants wouldn't be enough to cover the costs. I needed scholarships. There was only one way to ensure they would give those to me. I realized I had to present myself differently. I had perfected the art of shapeshifting and code-switching as a kid. It didn't matter what I looked like, how I saw myself or even the white world of high school that I had become comfortable operating in. For the purposes of getting away, on my college admission and loan applications I made sure to check all the boxes. Now I was a low-income Black kid from a rural community, just looking for an opportunity to make something better of himself.

In the fall of 1984, I sat on a lumpy bed and looked around at my new home. My mother sat next to me, twisting the straps on her purse and looking uncomfortable. We sat for a few minutes and watched a procession of well-to-do parents hustle their kids past the open door to my new dorm room and down the hallway. Finally she stood up.

"You all settled?"

"Yep."

I tried to sound relaxed, but the truth was, I was impatient for her to be on her way. I told myself it was just because I didn't want her hovering, but I wondered later if I was embarrassed that people would see this Black woman and stare at me. I loved my mother, deeply, but back then I thought that if she wanted to launch me into a different world and different life, there might not always be room for her.

I walked her down the stairs and to her used car. I remember trying not to look around to see if anyone was staring.

"Okay, don't worry about me. I'll call you this weekend," I promised.

Then I leaned over to give her a hug. As Ma pulled away, I was shocked to see her tears. My entire life, Ma had cried many tears in front of me, but only when someone had hurt her physically or broken her heart. There would be many days in the years to come when I wished I could go back to that moment to comfort her. Instead I patted her shoulder and steered her gently to the car door.

It didn't take me long that first semester to see that, finally away from my mother and my family, I had an opportunity to totally redefine myself. No longer would I have to worry about being in a place where someone might call me a nigger, a half-breed with a Black mother, or just a poor-white-trash bastard. For the first time in my life, on that college campus, people would take me at face value.

I embraced that chance to become someone new, and around me were other seventeen- and eighteen-year-olds, many of whom were celebrating their own freedom from their lives back home. I noticed that, for the most part, they didn't spend much time talking about their families, so neither did I. Like them, I went to parties, drank a lot of beer, stayed up late, and skipped class. It wasn't long before my grades began to drop. During my rare calls home, I told my mother everything was fine. But it wasn't.

My grades weren't the only problem. While I was trying to shake off some of those Saturday- and Sunday-morning hangovers in my dorm room, I had time to think about one other way in which I wanted to fit in with the rest of the guys but, I was beginning to realize, I couldn't. There was something else different about me that couldn't be changed, no matter how hard I tried.

On a holiday break at home, the truth came spilling out in a way that neither Ma nor I expected. It began when she waved my semester grades in my face.

"What are you doing up there?" she shrieked. "I didn't send you all the way up to there to flunk out!"

I told her I was distracted, a little depressed. Ma, sensing there was more, followed me from room to room, demanding to know what I had to be depressed about. After an hour, her interrogation wore me down.

"I think . . . I don't know. Maybe, you know, I'm gay."

"Gay?" Ma said, planting her hands on her hips.

I shrank back, feeling as if I were six again. I wanted to jam my face into the cushions of her fancy new love seat and make it all go away. She poked and prodded at me, demanding to know what I meant by "gay." Unlike my siblings, I'd never really fought with my mother. Growing up, I'd always tried to be the good child. Yet I couldn't allow her to deny something that I knew for certain. I told myself Ma wouldn't be able to convince me otherwise, but on that day I was cornered. I wanted to just drop the subject and stop her from questioning me. In my family, I'd learned you could fight back with fists or with words that wounded.

"Well, maybe I'm just confused about what I am because I don't know my real father."

The logic made no sense, but it didn't matter. Ma suddenly grew quiet. She looked at me for a minute, then lowered her eyes. Then she shook a cigarette out of the pack.

"Pops is your father," she said as she inhaled, then coughed out the smoke.

I stared at her dumbfounded. Then I turned away, stormed off to my childhood bedroom, and slammed the door behind me. I lay on my bed and covered my head with a pillow like I'd done so many times as a child when I couldn't face the life outside that door. The idea that I had come from her and Pops was ludicrous, and we both knew it. Ma had changed some over the years, but her habit of denying the past and ignoring anything painful would never change. And some other things hadn't changed. I was back in the same room where I had run from Pops, dreamed of Ma remarrying, and then hidden away from Louie. I still had no father.

An hour passed, and Ma tapped on my door.

"Come talk to me," she said calmly.

I dragged myself to the living room. Ma sat in the corner of the couch, the same spot she occupied for years in that house, contemplating her life.

"Sit down."

She started a conversation that had been overdue for nearly two decades. It should have taken hours. It was over in less than two minutes.

"He was a traveling salesman," she said.

She fidgeted around on the couch.

"Well, where does he live?"

"I don't know. We only met a few times. He didn't live nearby."

"Did . . . he meet me?"

"No."

In my family, people learned to stare you in the face and lie. I could tell my mother was finally telling the truth. She couldn't look me in the eye.

Finally, all I could think of to ask was his name. If I search my memory, all I can remember is her telling me Bill, or Don, or Tom or Frank—a one-syllable name that sounded like it could only belong to some average white guy. I told myself it didn't matter. I walked back into the bedroom and quietly closed the door.

After two decades of silence and lies about part of my identity, Ma had finally told me the truth. In the moment it was all too much, yet still too little. The story sounded as if she had ripped it from the back page of one of the romance novels she kept on her nightstand. A white traveling salesman comes to a small town in 1966 and sleeps with a Black woman. He leaves her, never to be seen again. All that's left behind is their love child.

As I lay back on my bed, I looked at the door, wondering if my mother might return after a few hours, ready to share something more, but the door never opened, and we never talked about it again. Nor, to my knowledge, did she ever discuss it with anyone else.

My mother had already given so much to me—a dream of a better life and a chance to achieve it. It took time to understand that there were things I deserved that she could not or would not provide. One of those things was a public acknowledgment and acceptance that I was partly white. Another was that I was gay.

I could only take comfort in something else that she conferred on me, something that would be more valuable than money or the truth. It was her ability to shove away the most painful things in her past to make room for the things she imagined for her future.

CHAPTER 24

Sissy-fied

As a kid I loved listening to stories. I'd lie down on the grubby bedroom carpet that smelled like dirty sneakers as Mike read to me from his superhero comics. From him I learned that even ordinary people were capable of incredibly magical or evil things. Sometimes until you got to the end of the story, you could never be sure if they were the heroes or villains. But you could be sure they weren't always what they appeared to be.

The same was true of my family. The stories we told around kitchen tables, on porches, and later across bar tops, always had a bit of mystery: what heroes were really flawed and what victims might not be so innocent.

The story of Uncle Ray was one example of that. Ray was my mother's youngest brother and the member of her family she loved the most. From the time I first remember him, I could tell he was something special. First, he came from another world: the city. When he drove thirty miles to see us, it was always in the latest Lincoln Continental. When it rolled down our narrow gravel driveway, I would be the first to run out to see this big, dark, barrel-bellied man with a pimp Afro.

"There's Stevie," Uncle Ray would say, pulling himself out of his leather seats. "What you got in those pockets?"

I plucked them inside out, rabbit-ear style.

"Come here, boy, you need some walking-around money."

From his pockets he'd pull a wad of bills with a rubber band and peel off a few dollars. As a bonus I'd get some butterscotch candy and a bear hug. Out of all his nieces and nephews, he treated me best. Maybe it was because I looked different from the rest of the kids. Maybe it was because he sensed I was different too.

I thought Uncle Ray was good, one of the heroes. Sure, he drank gin-and-tonics like water, even while driving. I figured he could go to jail for doing that. But I didn't think so. He was too nice. Uncle Ray also seemed to be nice around his lady friends. He had a wife who divorced him before I was out of diapers. Then he had someone he called his woman, a tall thin lady named Thelma who had a gold tooth and always smelled like flowers. Together they gave me a small glimpse of what life might be like for people off our piss-poor hill. It apparently was an exotic place where people drove big new cars, wore heavy colognes, and could afford gold teeth. I thought my family would like her because she was Black and dressed fancy. But as soon as Uncle Ray turned up the radio in his Lincoln and began backing out of the driveway, I learned what they really thought.

Cathleen and I were in the next room playing with her dolls. I edged closer to the kitchen and peeked around the corner.

"Stuck-up bitch," my aunt declared.

"Raymond better look out before she try to fool him out his money," Ma concluded.

"Well, at least it's a woman this time," Aunt Bonnie half whispered. Then she led everyone including my mother in a loud chorus of cackles. She wiped the tears of laughter off her fat cheeks, then turned to Ma.

"What was the name of that old, sissified man he used to live with?" Bonnie asked. She waved a fat, limp hand back and forth and pursed her lips in imitation.

"*Ray! Ray, please don't leave. I love you.*"

Again she fell out laughing.

I cringed and looked at the dolls lying in Cathleen's room. I only knew that sissy-fied men, as we called them, liked girl things. I wasn't sure what it had to do with Ray.

But over the years, as the story was told and retold, I pieced together the account of how my uncle had lived with another man after first moving to the city as a young man. As my family told it, my grandmother, mother, and sister didn't like the looks of the roommate, so they showed up unannounced one morning to rescue my uncle. In the story, my female relatives were heroic for rescuing him and my uncle Ray was a victim, too naïve to understand what this other man really was.

As I grew up, I came to understand that no matter the story, if there were gay people involved, they were always going to be the villains.

There was the close cousin who was said to be a "bull dyke" and the unmarried farmer's son up the road thought to be an "old homo." Aunt Bonnie, who feuded for years with her husband, could think of no fouler thing to call him when angered than a "dumb-ass queer" or a "faggot." Then there were the kids at school who called people fags and the nuns who called gay people sinners.

Even as I began to secretly look up words like *homosexual* and *sodomite* in our battered old dictionary, to explain why I had a crush on my gym teacher, I told myself those nasty words didn't mean me. My skin might always make me different from the rest of my family, but I thought this feeling I felt on the inside might be something I could change.

Later, in high school, I batted away my grandmother's questions about whether there was a pretty gal I liked, and I told my siblings I was too busy studying to date. But inside I knew how I felt.

While I couldn't avoid the awful stories that my family told about gay people, there came a time when I realized they couldn't control every narrative in my head. One of those I heard from one of Grandma's cleaning clients. For years my grandmother had scrubbed the floors and toilets of a white woman who had grown too obese to clean her own home. On one Saturday, Grandma couldn't make it to Mrs. Bennett's home and begged my mother to go instead, so she wouldn't lose the business. My mother had helped clean houses as a little girl and hated the idea of doing that type of work again, even for a day, but Grandma badgered her, and Ma finally relented. I went along to keep her company.

I noticed that Mrs. Bennett was different from the other women my grandmother cleaned for. She talked to my mother, made her coffee, and asked her questions about her own family. After that day she began inviting my mother back just to talk, because she was lonely. On one of those trips, Mrs. Bennett began to cry and talk about her poor grandson. My ears pricked up when she said his name. It was the same as mine, Stephen.

She wrung her fleshy, liver-spotted hands.

"Oh, Virginia, he's such a nice boy, handsome and so smart. Now he says he likes other men. And he's going to pack up and move to New York City. I guess that's where all the homosexuals live now."

Ma patted her hands and nodded sympathetically.

"His father says if he leaves, that's it," Mrs. Bennett said between sniffles. Then she added, "I said, fine—just leave him the hell alone. But I'm not going to cut him off."

I understood something that day. In Mrs. Bennett's home, no one was going to call her grandson nasty names. And she wasn't asking anyone to go to New York City and rescue him.

Though I wasn't conscious of it then, the story of a Stephen who could somehow defy his family by going off to the biggest city in the world, just to be around other boys like him, seeped into me. In that story, Stephen didn't care what his family or other people might say back in our small town. He was off to New York. Besides, he wasn't ashamed of who he was. And he wasn't an old homo or a nasty queer or a dumb faggot.

He was just a nice boy.

And somewhere in my head, I knew he wasn't a victim. He was a hero.

CHAPTER 25

The Gaybies

Although I'd spent a lifetime hiding in plain sight, as a father I never had the option of passing as straight in public. Todd, the kids, and I would rarely be mistaken for something other than what we were. While people might see two women at the playground fussing over one set of kids and think they were sisters or best friends, for us it was hard to be seen as anything but a gay family.

Still, Todd and I noticed that some people avoided what was right in front of their eyes. They would come up with all sorts of mental math to make things add up. When we first moved to New Orleans, an elderly Latina passed our front yard every afternoon. As she walked by, she would stop and wave to the kids. On days when Todd was sitting on our front porch, she'd cluck "Hullo! Hullo!" to him. And when I had porch duty, we exchanged smiles and nods. It took about a month until she spotted all four us together in the front yard. Her normally wide-open face rearranged into a puzzled look.

"You the father?" she asked, looking from Todd toward the kids.

"No, no, they're both our kids," Todd explained, pointing to me and then to himself.

"Ohhhh!" she said. Her smiled returned to her face. "Brothers!"

Now I jumped in. I could see where this was going. "No, *partners*. We *live* together, you understand?"

She nodded enthusiastically and handed both kids a piece of

wrapped hard candy. As she got ready to push her folded shopping basket down the street, she tilted her head toward me and whispered conspiratorially, "So smart you are living together. Saves money."

Now Todd looked confused, but I'd watched just enough nineties TV shows starring John Stamos. This little old lady understood we weren't brothers, but she didn't recognize us as a couple, either. No, she'd done the math and seen that a couple of single men raising kids added up to one thing: a *Full House*.

By 2011 I was tired of other people trying to make sense of what they were seeing. Maybe for the first time in my life, I was ready to show all my true colors to the world. I was Black. I was white. And I was proud to be part of a rainbow family.

Though it had taken years, I'd grown increasingly comfortable telling people I was a "person of color." I liked the broad term. It didn't specify Black, brown, mixed race, or anything but white. It just hinted that there was the minutest bit of melanin lurking somewhere beneath my skin. But I'd never felt quite at ease wearing my gay identity publicly. Now I had to. It was my job.

When we moved to Washington, D.C., I became the communications director for a small but growing national organization that represents LGBTQ parents. The "gayby" boom of the late nineties was no longer just an emerging trend. Comedienne Rosie O'Donnell was the most famous gay parent in the country. Gay and lesbian parents stood alongside straight parents at an iconic national event, the White House Easter Egg Roll. In TV ads, on TV shows, and on Capitol Hill, modern families now had national visibility.

My new job was to help inform and inspire the public. Gay parents wanted people to know why adoption rights and more inclusive school environments were important issues. We also wanted people to see that we were a part of the rich fabric of American families. That meant putting our issues out in the world. In some cases, that meant putting my kids out in the spotlight.

Part of me relished the attention. I gave interviews to national reporters, posed for photos for a *Washington Post Magazine* spread, even returned to my old workplace at MSNBC, this time as a guest on one of their shows. And there were other perks. I met Rosie O'Donnell, *Glee*'s Jane Lynch, the cast of "Modern Family," and other Hollywood and Broadway celebs who helped raise money for the organization. I was even invited to an LGBTQ reception at the White House and shook President Barack Obama's hand.

While I was publicly discussing why "our families" were just as happy and healthy as other families, I wondered what people would think if they knew that wasn't the case in my own home. For that reason, I worked hard to maintain a positive image of my own modern family, especially in the public eye, and even more so during work events.

The biggest of these events happened every summer on the shores of Cape Cod. That's when several hundred gay families from across the country gathered in Provincetown. The organization that I worked for promoted it as a fun, inclusive, and safe space for gay families to vacation with each other. It was also a chance for our organization to raise money. Wealthy and accomplished parents with ties to Hollywood, Broadway, and the business world sat on our organization's board. I had to hobnob with these folks on Cape Cod for work. But when given the chance to bring my family, I jumped at it. It was a dream vacation for my daughters—a ticket to a world I once dreamed of as a kid.

As we stepped off the ferry that took us from Boston Harbor to Provincetown, the four of us already felt like fish out of water. Burly, bearded gay guys lumbered past us toward the ferry. Their annual Bear Week gathering was just ending. Going the opposite way were tanned, trim-figured gay dads and lesbians headed into town for Family Week. Mariah and Rachel stuck close to us and stared at everyone on the crowded boardwalk.

Todd and I told the kids this would be a chance to see more families like ours. We'd met a few gay families back in New Orleans, but the kids were younger then. Now they were looking in a mirror and seeing a "rainbow" of families—parents and kids in all shapes, sizes, colors, and configurations, some who looked just like us.

We took the kids by the hands and started to march them through the crowds. It was the largest gathering of gay families in America and surely our kids, especially Mariah, would feel at home here. But as the week wore on, I could see her studying the couples and kids, silently doing the math in her own head.

On one of the final nights of the week, we gathered at a picnic high atop Provincetown's Monument Hill. Below us the waters of Cape Cod were crystal blue, mirroring the sky above. Under a white tent, our organization had gathered families for a clambake fundraiser. Gay men wearing white linen shirts air-kissed lesbian moms wearing white linen dresses. Earlier that day I'd sifted through our luggage, looking at the faded polos and cargo shorts Todd had packed. I cocked an eyebrow at him.

"It's the beach, for God's sake," Todd said. "No one cares what we're wearing."

But a big part of me cared. Though I'd learned to move through the so-called white world, the little boy with uncombed hair, unbrushed teeth, and dirty clothes always felt judging eyes were on him. Now they'd be on my family.

As we walked beneath the big white tent, I nudged us into a corner away from almost everyone else. At nearby tables I heard parents chattering about good private schools, the best beach houses to rent on the Cape, or reviews of hot Broadway shows. I'd always known what kind of people financially supported our organization, but sitting here among them, I didn't feel awe at being in the company of these successful gay and lesbian parents. Instead I secretly felt like we didn't measure up.

After a while Todd scooted a few tables over to chat up some families. He couldn't care less about keeping up with the gay Joneses. He'd grown up always feeling comfortable and secure in his upper-middle-class skin. I'd grown up on the outside of this world, always wondering what it was like to fit in. Now I was ashamed to try. The kids felt out of place as well, but I couldn't figure out why. Around them that night they saw more gay families than they had in their lives.

"Why don't you go ask those kids to play?" I kept suggesting.

Instead they shrugged and edged away from the other children. They were like human magnets, repelling their counterparts.

After the organization's leader had spoken, urging everyone to discreetly fill out the donation cards on the table, parents gathered their playing kids and regrouped for family photos. A professional photographer posed them against the blue postcard backdrop of the water. White dads with a pair of blonde blue-eyed twins smiled for the camera. This was surely an egg donor family with good genes, I thought. Then there were kids who were near exact replicas of the moms behind them. Bio children. Finally there were some adoptive families—nearly all white parents and kids of color. Few and far between were Black and brown gay parents. They existed, out there in the world, though many avoided the public spotlight because of the cultural and religious pressures they felt. I knew most might not have the means to bring their kids to Cape Cod for a vacation.

When it came time for our family photo, I did my best to chase away the feeling that I didn't belong here. In my job each day, I told people that gay families were no different from theirs. We were all the same. But truthfully, I knew that not all families were created equal.

I worked for that organization, a worthy one, for a few more years, but the trip to Provincetown became the only time we took the kids to its summer gathering. I might have been willing to try to fit in again, but the decision was made by our kids. When I asked Rachel why she didn't want to go back, she gave me a preteen side-eye.

"Too many white people," she said.

It was shocking to hear. Rachel was just a shade darker than me— the color of a good summer tan. In some places she might pass for white, but clearly she had chosen to accept the skin she was in.

Even more shocking was Mariah's reaction.

"Rachel says you guys felt uncomfortable because there were too many white people there," I said a few days later. "What do you think?"

"That's not the problem," Mariah said, sucking her teeth. "Want to know what is?"

"What?"

"Too many gay people."

She headed down the hall but turned to offer me a quick smile.

"Nothing personal."

My heart sank.

CHAPTER 26

White Lies, Dark Secrets

My siblings and I often joked that if you didn't hear from one of us for a long time, it meant we were up to no good. It was particularly true for Rick and Mike. Out of sight meant in some kind of trouble.

Rick made no secret of the fact that he wanted nothing to do with our family and our small town. He divorced his second wife, this time leaving behind a daughter. He then moved to Rochester, where distant cousins told us he was using the same charm he inherited from Pops to score free drinks and fast dates around the city.

Mike stayed closer to home for a time. When he did check in with one of us, he never talked much about what was going on in his life. All we did know was that after high school there were a string of ex-girlfriends, each one younger looking and more ragged around the edges than the one before. Then there was a brief wife who stabbed him in the leg with a fork after an argument. My mother looked past his choice of companions and the fact he always smelled of beer and weed. To hear her tell it, he was a grown man now. He was working and paying his bills. But still she knew better than to believe any stories he told in his high-pitched, whining voice.

"What exactly are you up to, Mike?" she would ask. And when she did, she crossed her arms, stood in his path, and dared him to look away.

"Aww, Ma. I'm not doing anything," he would answer. Then he'd smile, showing the liar's gap between his two front teeth. "Honest."

This practiced innocence worked best for his childhood pranks. Mike's favorite trick was to loosen the tops of the salt and pepper shakers. Pops, always too drunk to remember the last time it had happened, lost several of his favorite meals to that one. Each time, he threatened to whip us all unless someone confessed. We never did, out of loyalty to one another or at least a shared hatred of Pops. Even though we told Mike we knew he was guilty, he never fessed up. I guess that was something he never learned to do.

When he was too old for pranks, Mike used a wide-eyed innocent look to cover his misdeeds with elaborate stories. One summer when he was sixteen, he came home and dropped his leather jacket on the living room floor before heading to the bathroom. When Ma picked it up and placed it on a chair, out dropped two joints.

"What the hell is this?" she demanded, and waved the pot in his face.

Mike feigned a look of confusion. He claimed the pot had mysteriously appeared in his pockets, as if by magic. Then he suddenly "remembered" that he'd loaned the jacket to a friend earlier in the day. Perhaps the pot belonged to this friend, he suggested, his eyes widening. Ma was relentless in her interrogation. She tried to poke holes in the story, and when Mike didn't budge, she threatened to take Mike and the joints down to the police station unless he gave up his nameless friend. I remember the rest of us kids sitting on the couch, ready for Mike's lies to finally catch up with him. It was better than *The Brady Bunch* which played in the background.

Finally Mike came up with a foolproof explanation. He'd left the jacket for his friend on a chair at school. It had been unattended, he said, so anyone could have placed the drugs in the pocket. Mike stood there, looking Ma straight in the eye. Ma stared back for a long time. When she dropped her hands from her hips, we knew Mike had escaped his punishment again.

Ma had a soft spot for Mike that we never quite understood. He'd been the baby of the family until I came along, and Ma was especially protective of him. She saw that Pops seemed to instill a special kind of fear in him, and so Ma tended to forgive his transgressions.

And it wasn't just Ma. Mike's baby face and affected proclamations of innocence made him seem more like a sweet rascal to some. In school, he sweet-talked teachers into overlooking late assignments. He'd convince his friends to trade him used dirt bikes and motorcycles in sweetheart deals. To me, his girlfriends seemed the most gullible. They jumped at the chance to do his laundry, cook his meals, and clean his apartments. On the surface, Mike seemed just a harmless huckster—an overgrown kid who could get by on a few little white lies and some help from his friends. But even his wildest stories wouldn't prove strong enough to hide his darkest secrets and sins.

In 1992 those painful truths all came out. By this time I had been on my own for almost a decade. When Ma called, her voice, normally steady, shook. I remember listening in shock as she told me a story that I couldn't have imagined possible. After years of deceiving his string of girlfriends, he'd finally been caught deceiving someone too young to ever question his credibility—the teen daughter of his latest live-in.

Within days of his arrest, Mike's mug shot appeared on local TV in Buffalo. Decades before, Ma had lived through shame each time Pop's name showed up in our small-town newspaper. This was far worse. Now her son was known across the entire region as an accused child molester.

For a while my family refused to believe the truth. Even as kids, if one of us was threatened by someone outside our family, we'd always come to one another's defense. Now we set aside our differences. For weeks we convened calls to discuss legal strategies and possible conspiracy theories.

"Look, this girl was white," Jim said. "Who's to say she didn't set Mike up for some reason. Of course, the police are going to believe her over a Black man."

We murmured in agreement. After all, this girlfriend had come from a troubled background. Despite our own questionable family history, we now were ready to slur her as poor white trash. I wondered aloud whether she might be trying to blackmail Mike and might drop the charges if we paid her off.

But as details of the allegations came out in the media, it became clear that the police had substantial physical evidence against Mike.

Denise was the first one of us to refuse to allow our family ties to get in the way of the truth.

"Bullshit," she said matter-of-factly. "He was caught messing with a kid. He's a grown man. Now, tell me how the hell we defend that?"

We couldn't. Slowly, my own series of long-distance calls to my mother to check on the status of his case tapered off. It was easy for me to forget about Mike. By this time I was living far away from my small town. Though I couldn't admit it at the time, I wanted to just focus on my own life and pretend that *family* had nothing to do with me. My mother, though, couldn't escape. She remained locked in place and relegated to her role as the suffering mother and the martyr of our family. She borrowed money from Grandma, took out a second mortgage for bail money, consulted with Mike's lawyers, and attended almost every court hearing. The case dragged on for more than two years before coming to trial. Ma remained steadfast in her support.

When the trial date finally arrived, Mike was confronted with the fact that he could spend decades in prison. So he copped a plea. At the time, he claimed it was to avoid forcing his victim to testify at trial. According to my mother, he spoke to the judge with tears in his eyes and blamed his behavior on his troubled childhood, an alcohol addiction, and anything else that might earn him a bit of mercy.

To this day I picture Ma sitting by herself in the courtroom, and I wonder if she questioned Mike's sincerity and whether he was telling the truth about his regrets. I thought I knew Mike well, and I was sure he would always lie through his teeth to get whatever he wanted.

As for the rest of my siblings, Mike's conviction represented another chapter in the dissolution of our family. From then on, Denise would say Mike was dead to her. Jim would begin to harbor some resentment toward Denise, accusing her of abandoning our brother during his greatest need. Rick showed little if any interest in Mike's troubles or the outcome, reaffirming that he had written us all off for good. It would be years before the five us ever came together. And even then, our time as a family would be short.

CHAPTER 27

There's No Place like Home

After Mike went to prison, my mother retreated into herself. In quiet moments, she admitted to us that she felt like she had failed Mike. As her youngest, I now shouldered an added pressure to not add to the heartache she suffered over how we had grown up and, in some cases, turned out.

In 1988, a few weeks before my college graduation ceremonies, I feared I would be the source of her next disappointment. After four years, I'd managed to lift most of my grades to something close to acceptable, but I sat there one May afternoon looking at the final grade sheet of my senior year. There amid the C's stood a stark F in Electrical Engineering. I was devastated. The class was a graduation requirement. An extra semester, to take the class over, was out of the question. I'd already maxed out the student loans. Plus, I had somewhere else to be that fall. There was a spot waiting for me in Ohio State University's graduate program in journalism. My friends had been stunned to learn that a poor engineering student had managed to transform mediocre grades into acceptance and full tuition to a top-level graduate school. What I never told them was that checking the diversity box on my grad school application probably made the difference.

Four years at a mostly white, affluent private university had given me a taste of how different life could be. Now I was about to throw it all away. I couldn't disappoint my mother. I couldn't head back to the country. I couldn't just slide back into the place where my family had been stuck for generations. Within days, I settled on a plan. I thought of all the times Aunt Bonnie and the rest of my family had shucked, jived, and talked white people into forgetting a bill or giving them something extra. I walked into my engineering professor's office two days before graduation. I wore my best khakis, a dress shirt, and an earnest look. As I sat on the edge of my chair and leaned in, I spun out my story. It was about an average student who had made one academic mistake. He had an otherwise clean, though unremarkable record. He was headed to graduate school, but just needed one small break.

I can't remember the professor's name or all that he said. All I can remember is how he looked into my eyes for a moment and then gave me a small understanding nod. He told me he'd make an exception and allow me to submit a paper over the summer to earn the required credits. I got to college by checking the boxes, gaining entry to the school and access to scholarships by declaring myself poor and Black. I was about to graduate by accepting a different kind of assistance—a sympathetic nod from one average white guy to another. I should have been ashamed and recognized it for what it was, the ultimate passing privilege, but I lied to myself. I told myself I was just doing what my grandmother and others in my family had taught me to do, playing to my audience.

At Ohio State, the journalism program played to my strengths. I loved writing. And the few A's on my undergrad transcript were the result of every writing elective I could find. Here my pathway was even clearer. After I passed the classes, I didn't have any final exams or thesis. All I had to do was take an oral exam. I'd proved to myself I had my family's gift. I could talk a good game. Standing before the all-white academic panel, I knew I had aced it.

Right out of journalism school, I talked myself into a television producing job at a local TV station in Columbus, Ohio. It was all about telling stories and playing to an audience. I had a lifetime of experience doing that, and so I was good at the job. For the next decade I would hopscotch across the country for a series of similar jobs at increasingly bigger TV stations. The years, jobs, and cities whizzed by in a blur—Columbus, Cincinnati, Pittsburgh, Detroit, Los Angeles, Tampa. In each place I rented a barely furnished apartment. A bed, TV, and sofa were all I needed. Home was just a place to sleep in between long hours at work. My friends were drinking buddies from work. They were quickly left behind when the next promotion, in another bigger TV market, came calling.

Each time I moved, Ma called to complain. "I don't understand why you don't stay in one place for a while, put down some roots."

At the time, I wasn't sure either. Much later in life I realized it was because no place felt like home. I'd watched my family plant roots on the hill and then my brothers and sister do it beyond. No matter where, bad things seemed to grow after a while. There was no need for me to stick around to see if it happened to me.

After a while Ma accepted my wandering. As someone who had spent her life seeking a better one through material things, she was comforted by the fact I was making a lot of money and moving up in the world. To her that was security. In city after city, job after job, she followed my progress. And I began making enough money to share the benefits of my new comfortable lifestyle with her. There were shopping trips in LA when I lived there, beach vacations near my apartment in Florida, and checks sent from every location in between. In later years, at Christmas, I bought her expensive gifts. In her way, she had tried to move us out of poverty when I was a kid. Now I felt I had to do the same for her.

What no one knew, not even Ma, was that there was another side to this cross-country climb up the career ladder. Every move was a chance for me to leave behind everything I didn't want to deal with. Unlike Ma, I wasn't limited to slapping a new coat of paint on a living room wall and changing out the furniture to give me new hope. I could just pack up my clothes and transport myself to an entirely new existence each time. As my income increased, I'd often sell off or simply leave what few furnishings I had and buy new when I arrived.

And in each location, I could choose how to present myself to the world. Most people didn't know my race or the story of how I'd been raised. Though I couldn't admit it at the time, "passing" meant I could go anywhere in my career and life.

There were times, though, I was reminded that choosing one side of my identity over another made a difference. During a job interview in St. Louis, the news executives gawked at me when I walked in the door. "Can you excuse us for just a moment?" they asked. There was a sudden phone call they had to make. Once I returned home from the interview, I learned they'd called the recruiter who recommended me to ask where their required minority candidate was: "I thought this guy was supposed to be black." In a bit of a huff, I told the recruiter to withdraw my application. She told me it didn't matter. After meeting me, the news executives now preferred *other* candidates.

After that, I realized that checking the diversity boxes would open doors, but once inside it made no difference. People tended to forget I had identified myself as Black. That forced me at times into awkward situations where I had to remind them, and myself. One such incident happened many years into my TV news career, when I landed a dream job in national cable news. I was invited one day to a corporate conference room at MSNBC where top executives—all white—were debating whether to book a controversial guest. A top-level producer casually tossed off the word "nigger." Later, in a separate meeting with Black and brown producers, I noticed he shyly said, "the N-word." It took me hours to work up the nerve to confront him, but when I did, he said he saw no difference in how he'd used the word in front of different audiences.

At that moment I reminded myself I worked at the most liberal, progressive cable channel in America, in the most liberal city in the country. But maybe it didn't matter. Maybe Grandma had been right. Maybe white people couldn't be trusted.

The secrecy about who I really was extended to other parts of my life. After I had tried to tell Ma that I was gay, she acted as if we'd never spoken about it. For years after, I felt I couldn't trust anyone else but Denise with the secret. Out of all my siblings, she had accepted me for who I was. The policy of "please God, don't ask; I sure as hell am not going to tell" also extended to most of my friends. By now I was far enough away from home that I didn't have to stand toe-to-toe with Ma. But I felt I did have to hide as I moved in and out of different communities and TV stations that had conservative views.

A childhood spent hiding what was going on at home had taught me how to conceal myself. After work, I slipped into dark gay bars and seedy dance clubs or trolled the back pages of cheap community newspapers for personal ads.

Drinking gave me the courage and held any shame in check. I convinced myself that it wasn't a problem. I told myself it was only my siblings who let their self-described self-medication get out of control. I thought I was better than that.

But saying it didn't make it so. By my late twenties I had racked up two DWIs, spent a night in the drunk tank, and passed out, blacked out, and thrown up more times than I could remember. I'd woken up with black eyes and busted lips and in beds alongside people I never remembered meeting. But I'd learned from Ma. That was just my business. Those were my secrets. Nobody in my family had to know.

On the outside, I showed only the successes to my family. At one point I lived in a waterfront condo, drove a red BMW convertible, ate out every night, and spent my money on two personal trainers who bulked me up to be muscular. My transformation had taken place. Into what, I wasn't yet sure.

In December of 1998 I flew home for the first time in years. I had been away for so long that the small town where I grew up didn't seem like my home anymore. But when Ma called, I was willing to come. She was getting older now, and she'd asked Denise, Jim, and me to make a rare appearance together at our house for Christmas. Pulling into the driveway, I noticed another year's worth of changes to Ma's little dollhouse. She had recently shifted her attention to the outside of the house. The extra money I was able to send home had helped her buy a little prefab garage to keep her new car out of the snowdrifts. There was now a small wraparound porch and a deck that swallowed up half of the tiny house.

I stepped through a new sliding glass door, now framed with fancy blinds.

"Ma, really?" I asked.

"You like? They're custom window *treatments.*"

She saw the look on my face and laughed hard until her smoker's cough overcame her. Ma had fought pneumonia that winter and was looking thinner. I wanted to get her out of the cold weather, so I picked out a special present that year. Later that night when I handed over her gift, an envelope, she got excited.

"A check?" she said, shaking the envelope.

Denise shook her head and laughed.

Jim rolled his eyes. "You never change, do you, Ma?" he asked.

"Nope!"

She tore open the envelope and waved it in the air. "A cruise!!"

Now Jim and Denise rolled their eyes at me. I was glad that Rick wasn't there to say what they may have been thinking. If he had been, he would have been right. Growing up, Ma did spoil me. I didn't want to know if it was because of the color of my skin or just because I was the baby. It didn't matter. Now I wanted to spoil her.

The cruise ticket was also a way of helping Ma get away from Grandma. A few years earlier, John had died. We all thought my grandmother could live on her own—she was only across the yard and just a holler away from my mother and aunt—but after she'd retired from scrubbing floors, she'd come to rely exclusively on John for everything. He cooked, picked up after her, and fetched even the smallest of items for her from a few feet away. This woman who had labored on her hands and knees her entire life now insisted that someone wait on her hand and foot. With John gone, she asked to move in with my mother. After all these years, it seemed as if Ma would never escape her.

"Jen-yah, I'm hawngry. Can you fix me something to eat?" Grandma would yell from her bedroom.

"What do you want, Mama? I can cook you some eggs, or do you want some rice and beans?"

"Naw, I'm tired of eggs, and those beans are nasty. What else you got?"

After all the times Grandma had made her beg for a loaf of bread, Ma was now a short-order cook. Ma just gritted her teeth, and so did I.

That spring, Ma didn't have to worry about Grandma, at least for a few days. She soaked up the life of luxury on her cruise through the Caribbean. In each port she shopped for new clothes and ate like a queen. She felt entitled to it all. I was happy that I'd given her a small taste of the life she'd always wanted. I told myself the time was coming when I could give my mother more of that life. In my head I imagined coming home the next Christmas to tell Ma she was going on a trip to Florida and never coming back. There she could finally be free of Grandma, her lasting regrets, and all the bad memories that still lingered in that little house.

CHAPTER 28

Shit Happens

I was raised on black magic and white magic. But in my family, we called it something different.

The women called the black magic "hoodoo." I'd never actually seen it, but to listen to our female cousins, you could find traces of it on the toilet seat. My mother's cousin Liz was the biggest believer. She and another relative once came to visit our house when I was 8. When the relative stepped away to use the bathroom, Liz waited until she was out of earshot to whisper to us.

"Now just be careful. You better get some Ajax on that toilet seat. You don't know if she's been in there, sprinkling hoodoo," she said.

All that week, if I had to go, I'd hover over the cold seat, afraid that hoodoo would get on my butt. I didn't know what it looked like. That film or dust on the seat might be hoodoo or just the leftover Ajax. No one told me why someone wanted to hoodoo our butts, but as far as I could tell, it was to bring us bad luck or send us to the hospital with cancer.

I didn't know whether to believe it or not. Cousin Liz did always seem to have bad luck surrounding her. Her mother, Grandma's sister Sadie, died suddenly. Liz feuded with one sister and had two more who everyone said weren't "right in the head." And then there was her dead sister, Pearl. Grown folks whispered about what happened to hear.

"How did Cousin Liz's sister Pearl die, Grandma?" I asked one day.

"She got poisoned."

"Poisoned? By who? Why?" I said, openmouthed.

"She was a doctor. She got poisoned by her husband. He was trying to get ahold of her money," Grandma said matter-of-factly.

I thought to myself in my head, hoodoo.

Our side of the family didn't dabble in hoodoo. We did take a stronger interest, though, in white magic—specifically fortune tellers. They were to be respected and feared. There was Mary Mickie, who was blind but saw the future. There was Mrs. Hale, who read tarot cards, and Mrs. Jenkins, who peered into tea leaves. A few times a year, Ma or Aunt Bonnie would drag Denise and me along when they went to see one of these women and get their "readings." The women, all white, seemed relatively normal to me. These weren't the kind who wore turbans, caftans, and lots of rings. And they didn't advertise with neon signs. Mostly they lived nearby in farmhouses up the road from us or in nice houses in town. Most of the women who did readings were older widows who supplemented their income baking wedding cakes or making homemade quilts out of frayed clothes. Just like their sewing and baking skills, they said their "gift" had been handed down over generations.

Mary Mickie was the exception. Struck blind by lightning as a child, she claimed to see the future. When Ma visited, I'd come along and sit beside her in a dark, dusty living room crammed with antique furniture.

"I'm getting a picture of you on a trip," she told my mother once. "Are you going to see someone soon?"

My mother searched her memory.

"Well, there's the trip to visit some out-of-town family," she said.

"Could be, could be," Mary said. "It's hard to tell."

Fifteen minutes and fifteen dollars later, we were out into the bright sunshine. Ma seemed lighter, with less to worry about. And I was excited. Who knew? Maybe we were going to England. The other ladies Ma visited also seemed to see things that Ma couldn't yet envision—money, new jobs, a change of luck.

"Okay, now sip from the left side of the cup. Drain it completely and then turn it over on the saucer," Mrs. Jenkins would say.

I'd sidle up between Ma and Bonnie and look at the black leaves clumped at the bottom of the cup. Looking inside, Mrs. Jenkins claimed she saw shapes—rings and hearts and stars. Riding home in the car, sometimes late at night, I would look at the moon following us. When, I wondered, would things change? Mrs. Jenkins had said, "Sometimes these things take time."

Some of the things they promised, and that Ma hoped for, did come true. She eventually earned more money. She did go on trips, and even to England. But was that fate or self-fulfilling prophecy? After all, I gave her that trip years later after I got a big bonus at work. She didn't find love as they predicted, but she did find companionship, at least for a time.

When Ma was at a stage where her dreams for the future were probably more modest, she may still have been looking for something out of life. Maybe that's what sent her to a reader just months before her diagnosis in 1999. Whatever she was looking for, the reader did not see it. She told my mother she saw only dark storm clouds all around. I wondered sometimes if those storm clouds followed my family, because a lot of bad things seemed to happen over the years.

"I swear, there must be a damn curse on this family," Grandma would say. She said it in a weary voice that made you believe she had lived long enough to have seen enough shit over the years. And having seen it all, only she could officially pronounce it a curse. But I didn't have to grow as old as Grandma to discover for myself that it wasn't really a curse, or hoodoo. While it was true that generations of poverty, poor education, and racism created some of the conditions for our failures, other times it was just our own damned fault.

Growing up, I could see proof every day in my own home. When my mother had money, she spent it on things that made her feel good. Her attitude was to buy now and pay the consequences later. So it wasn't a hex on our house when our furnace died and her car broke down in the same week. She hadn't spent money on the car in years, and she'd ignored the furnace for decades.

The same shortsightedness was true when it came to the maintenance of our bodies. Ma had spent her life drowning her worries in cigarettes and fatty foods. My siblings drowned their emotional demons in alcohol or drugs. Uncles and cousins gambled and drank away their jobs, while other relatives suffered health problems that could easily have been prevented. Even accounting for the fact that their poverty affected their access to medical and mental health care, they seemed to believe their fates were completely out of their control.

As a kid, Denise once told me that when bad things happen, some people will look for explanations anywhere they can find them—in storm clouds, at the bottom of teacups, or even on toilet seats. She taught me that sometimes there are no answers for the good things that elude us in life or the bad things that seem to follow us everywhere we go. Sometimes, she said, shit just happens. And in my family, I quickly learned, it probably always would.

CHAPTER 29

The Secret inside Her

As a child I was fascinated by the fact that my mother could look inside people.

"What did you see?" I would ask her.

In between sips of scalding black coffee and puffs on her cigarette, she'd give me a glimpse of her world at work.

"Just their trachea," she might say, or "A nasty gall bladder."

She then shrugged as if the things she saw were no more unusual than noticing someone's hair color. To her, work was a just a series of mundane operating room procedures. She'd done thousands of them, as a surgical scrub nurse. I was proud that my mother had such a job. It was the kind of role you normally saw on TV—nurses with sterile gowns, masks, and gloves peering over the shoulders of doctors and handing them sharp metallic instruments. Normally, to get such a position, you might have to go to college and then receive specialized training. But in the late 1960s and early 1970s you could learn the skills on the job, especially in a small-town hospital. After Ma had dropped out of high school, she spent decades working as a bedpan-cleaning orderly and then as a nurse's aide to try and work her way up, but as it turned out, her lack of formal education was the smallest barrier.

"Tell me again how you had to go to court, Ma?" I asked her, again and again. "And the part about the lawyer."

Ma would let out a tired grunt.

"Please!" I begged.

"I told you, they didn't have any Black nurses in the operating room."

"And they'd already trained a white lady to do the job, but not you, right?"

"Mmm-hmmm."

"So, you had to fight those bitches until they trained you!"

"Stephen!"

"What? That's what you said."

Ma laughed.

There was more to the story. My mother was the first and only Black operating nurse in our county. Because she hadn't gone to college, she wasn't paid like a professional. Nor was she always treated like one. She didn't like to talk about it, but it wasn't easy living in two worlds at work. The white nurses didn't take her seriously because she hadn't gone to college. Black workers at the hospital, who worked cleaning and cooking, thought she acted better than them. She swallowed the slights and sly slurs she heard from both sides, many days. For all her practiced good manners, she knew how the rest of the world saw her. They saw another single Black mother raising a houseful of dirty, funky kids. It didn't help that one of them, me, was a half-breed bastard.

Even though my mother didn't like to brag about her medical knowledge, everyone in our family treated her like the doctor on call.

"Jen-ya, would you take a look at this bump on me?" Aunt Bonnie would say. And then, as if saying it aloud would ward off bad luck, she'd whisper, "I hope it's not cancer."

Ma wasn't a doctor. She only handed them instruments. Still, everyone in our family assumed she could diagnose their ills. They'd pull aside a bra strap or hitch up their dress to show a bump or a bruise that didn't feel right. Ma didn't have much choice, sitting in her kitchen with Bonnie pushing a body part in her face.

"If you're that worried about it, why don't you go see the doctor?" Ma would ask her.

"Oh, you know I don't have that kind of money to keep running up to no doctor," Bonnie replied. "Oh, gee—do you think it's cancer?"

Ma reassured Aunt Bonnie it looked just like an ordinary lump of fat, but, unconvinced, my aunt would then go off to the doctor just to be sure. Though she often skipped out on paying the medical bills, she wanted to get her money's worth, so she might bring Cathleen along into the examining room. Even with a doctor, Bonnie would try to get a two-for-one.

"While we're here, can you just take a look at this lump on my daughter's neck?" I heard her ask a doctor once. "You don't think it's cancer, do you?"

I could picture the doctor rolling his eyes.

Grandma's mother had died of cancer when Grandma was a girl, and the fear that someone might get "the cancer" was spread to her daughters, who eventually infected the rest of us.

"What's this?" I said one day, rubbing something that seemed to be a swelling on the back of my head. Grandma happened to overhear me.

"Come here, let me see. What's that knot on your head? Jen-ya, come over here and feel this knot on this boy's head."

Ma should have known better, but she wasn't immune to this type of hysteria. Off to the doctor we went, where he soberly announced to Ma that it was part of my skull. There were other false alarms as well: I learned to panic if my ears ached, if my poop wouldn't come out, or if I saw stars when I rubbed my eyes too hard. You had to be careful. It could be cancer. If I was sick with worry, Ma would haul me off to the doctor for reassurance that I was just fine.

"I'm not sick!" I shouted triumphantly, after coming home from one of the trips to the doctor.

Jim flicked my ear, hard.

"No, you're just tender."

Triage became an important part of Ma's job—trying to figure out what could wait and what might kill us. Doctor visits were expensive, but

Ma's impulse was to panic and lean toward the "it can kill ya" category. This hysteria was likely caused by a diagnosis that she missed once, one that nearly killed Mike and Denise when they were in their early teens. Both wound up with strep throat. It started as just plain old coughing and a sore throat. That wasn't too unusual in that drafty house, which was built so cheaply that the single windowpanes rattled in the frames. Chronic colds and untreated flus were just the symptoms of being poor. It could wait.

When they got too sick to go to school, they were treated with plenty of tea with lemon and canned noodle soup. But Ma realized she waited too long when their strep throat became rheumatic fever and sent an infection throughout their entire bodies. I was five, old enough to remember the ambulance in our driveway coming first for Denise and then for Mike.

"Are they going to die?" I sniffled.

"Shut up," Jim said, but instead of cuffing me on the back of the head or flicking my ear, he let me climb up into his lap. "No one's going to die."

A few days later, Denise's heart began to fail. A Catholic priest gave her last rites. Back and forth, she and Mike hovered close to death several times before finally rallying. It was almost a year before they were back to normal.

When I was old enough to begin telling my own stories about our family's brushes with disaster or death, my tales started with the time Denise and Mike almost died of broken hearts.

With all the time my mother put into worrying about what could go wrong with one of us, there wasn't much left over to worry about herself. She'd smoked since she was sixteen. I can't remember a time when she really laughed out loud and didn't hack immediately after. She lived on a steady diet of two packs of Viceroy 100s and cup after cup of scalding black coffee. The caffeine and nicotine kept her going through twelve-hour shifts in the operating room. When she found time to eat, she ate for comfort and relief, just like the rest of us. Her favorite foods were fried in used bacon grease, baked with heaps of butter, and salted to death. As she got older and we weren't around for her to ask about our aches or pains, she finally started paying attention to the wear and tear on her own body. She started feeling the effects of the long hours, cigarettes, lack of sleep, and fatty foods. And she began seeing a doctor regularly.

During my weekly calls home, I began asking about her health. It was just one more thing she didn't want to talk about.

"What *did* he say?" I nagged Ma one week after she complained of lagging energy.

"Same old stuff about my blood sugar."

A few months later, it was her unhealthy cholesterol level, then later her high blood pressure. When her hacking got so bad, she cut back a bit on the cigarettes and, as a concession to the doctor, got yearly lung X-rays.

In May of 1999, two months after her return from the cruise I'd given her as a Christmas gift, she finally admitted that she'd been feeling sick for six months. She'd been losing weight rapidly all that winter and was unable to keep any food down. By June she realized she couldn't ignore the signs anymore and went for a checkup. It was stage 3 cancer of the pancreas. Ma had always taken care of us. After we left home, and although she had every reason to say no, she took care of my grandmother. In all those years, she'd rarely looked out for her own needs. I never understood why. And something else would always nag at me. My mother knew she had all the risk factors, and she was trained to recognize the warning signs, but cancer was the one possibility she didn't want to talk to anyone about.

It seemed it was the one thing she couldn't ever imagine seeing inside herself.

CHAPTER 30

Dead or in Jail

Prior to our mother's illness, my siblings and I had declared a truce of sorts. We'd keep our disputes from getting out of hand and wouldn't bother prying into old family secrets. We had an unspoken pact to stay away and keep out of each other's lives. The exception was if someone was dead, dying, or headed to jail.

Now Jim, Denise, and I prepared to reunite. We traveled from across the country back to our small town and up the little country road where we had grown up. As I came up the crest of the road, I noticed that John's fields had grown wild in the few years since his death. And now that Grandma lived with Ma, the screen door on her farmhouse swung back and forth in the wind. Otherwise, little had changed. The three houses still sat together, but alone and apart from everything else.

As I pulled into the yard, I saw that someone had dragged out a wobbly portable grill. Suddenly what was to have been a somber gathering became a family picnic. A few phone calls managed to drag my uncles in from the city, and old grudges were put aside so that even Bonnie and pop-eyed Shireen sat side by side trading gossip.

Perhaps the biggest surprise guest was Ma's first grandson, little Rickie. After Rick divorced his first wife, my nephew largely left the circle of our family. In all those years, Ma had never stopped missing him. The rest of us assumed that, even as an adult, he might be too ashamed of the Black side of the family to ever seek us out. But on that day, there little Rickie stood, tall, broad shouldered, fair skinned, and eager to see his people. He was joined by Rick's daughter from his second marriage, a light-tan-skinned young woman with beautiful blue eyes.

That afternoon they sprawled on the crabgrass in Ma's front yard alongside Denise's and Jim's grown children. We all sat under the shade of a maple tree Ma had planted after Jim's birth, nearly forty-five years before. She settled into a lawn chair, her kids and grandkids spread out on the ground around her.

Ma had always wanted to live like royalty. At least for that moment in time, no one was more important than her on that hill.

She was our queen.

But our family peace was fragile. That became clear a few weeks later when Rick materialized. He'd been living on the edge of our family for years, so none of us knew what to expect when he walked into the hospital room where Ma was being treated for complications from the first round of chemo and radiation.

As Rick stepped inside, we noticed he looked different. He acted edgy, and he looked much older. His once bright smile was yellowed with nicotine stains, and his eyes were bloodshot. Behind him he tugged a short brown woman who carried a Bible in her hand.

"Hello, everyone," he said. "This is my new wife, Tina."

"Allen has told me so much about you," she said with a beaming smile.

Denise shot me and Jim one of her looks. It warned us to keep our mouths shut, for now. We waited until Rick and our newest in-law walked out of earshot to Ma's bedside.

"Who the hell is Allen?" Jim whispered.

"More important, what the hell did he do with Rick?" I added.

"Damned if I know," Denise said.

Although we knew Allen was his middle name, he'd never been called by that name a day in his life. But we guessed that he decided he wanted a new name to go along with his new identity as a Christian family man. Even after all these years, he seemed like the same old Rick to me. He looked like he did when were kids, like he was afraid someone would steal his pork chop right off his plate. If there was any real difference, it was that he was more desperate.

I'd long ago decided I didn't have time for him. Ma, now, apparently didn't either. After he left the room, she beckoned to Denise, who leaned over the bed to hear her.

"But why, Ma?" Denise asked as she stood up.

Ma didn't answer. She had always kept her thoughts and secrets to herself. Now, even more, she felt she didn't have to explain herself. And that summer she turned still further inward. There were things I wanted to say and ask her. Was there really nothing more to tell me about my father? Did she love him? Did she love me—no matter who I was, or who I might be? But as the weeks went by, I couldn't bring myself to ask any of these questions. To me, it would signal to her and to me that we would be tying things up and saying goodbye. I just wasn't ready.

By September, Ma could hardly think straight, let alone say much of importance. Her gray-green eyes would flick open only a few minutes at a time because of the morphine. One night late in the month, we clustered around her hospital bed listening to her breathe in shallow pulls and surrenders. The nurse told us to be ready.

"It's okay, Ma," Denise said, stroking her sunken face. "We're here, and you can go if you're ready."

Ma stopped breathing. What seemed like a minute ebbed by. Then Ma suddenly gasped for air as if surfacing from underwater. She was back with us, for now. An ugly sob came out of my chest, surprising even me.

Denise pushed us all out of the room and then turned to Jim and me. "Mike," she said finally. "I think she's waiting for Mike."

Denise huffed and shook her head. After Mike had gone to prison, she vowed never to speak to him again, but now Ma was dying. She contacted the prison and inquired about a compassionate leave. A few days later Mike arrived. We heard his shackles first, clanking through the hospital hallway. Then, like the Ghost of Christmas Past, Mike appeared in the doorway, his hands and legs connected by chains. He was framed by two federal marshals. Mike lifted his hands toward us and offered a bashful grin.

"Oops!" he said, then laughed.

Amid all that had gone wrong and everything he had done wrong in his life, Mike still held on to his dark sense of humor. And even with Ma about to die, we shared it.

"Damn, Mike," I said. "Love that bling."

"Really?" Jim said, shaking his head.

The marshals unlocked Mike's hands and legs and withdrew to wait outside the door. Even without the leg chains, I noticed, Mike still shuffled.

"Ma, it's me," he said, crossing to her bed.

Ma's eyelids had been dragged down by the morphine. She fought to open them.

"I know," she whispered hoarsely.

Mike kissed Ma's hands.

"I want you to know," he said, "I'll meet you in heaven one day."

Looking at Denise and Jim, I knew we all wanted to get off a good line about that and laugh a little. For Ma, we held it together. Maybe she needed to believe she would see Mike in heaven. Maybe she still believed in his wide-eyed innocence.

After forty-five minutes the marshals eased into the room with the shackles ready.

"Well, guys, I guess this is it," Mike said.

Rick, Jim, and I gave him a quick hug. Denise grudgingly did the same.

"Denise," Mike said earnestly as he pulled away. "Ma always sent me care packages in prison. After she dies, do you think that's something you could do?"

We stood there, staring at him in disbelief. Jim was much older, heavier, and slower than he once was, but I thought if we weren't at Ma's bedside, he might have jumped Mike right then and there. And Denise and I would have piled on.

Jim stared through Mike, then signaled the marshals that we were done.

"Goodbye, Mike," said Jim. As soon as the hospital room door swung closed, Denise didn't hold back.

"Asshole," she said simply.

Ma was quiet, but the rest of us murmured in agreement.

Later that night, Ma at last seemed relieved. She stopped fighting the morphine and sank into an in-between world. As I sat watching her face grow peaceful, I accepted that the time had passed for me to say anything more to my mother. Even if I worked up the courage, it felt wrong to bring up things that might cause her pain.

Denise motioned for me to join her in the hallway.

"You should go home, now. It could be days or even a few more weeks," she explained. "Ma worked so hard to help you get started in life. She'd want you to get back to living it."

I started to cry. Denise pulled me into a hug. I heard her husky voice whisper in my ear.

"She loves you, baby brother. And yes—she knows you're gay. And it's okay with her."

Nearing the end of her life, Ma had finally been willing to trust Denise with at least one secret about her youngest son. Although she couldn't tell me herself, Ma accepted the part of me that was different. I'd like to believe that she wanted me to know I could finally be comfortable in my own skin.

Before she died, Ma had also shared with Denise another message for all her kids. She knew that, for years, she was the only uniting force in our family, the only one who could bring us together after all that had happened. Now she wanted us each to promise we would not let her death divide us. I was glad Ma had not told me her dying wish. Because it was a promise I didn't know if I could keep.

In early October of 1999, a few days after our mother's death, we returned for a final time to the tiny house where we had grown up. Jim sprawled across Ma's fancy new love seats. I watched him spread out like he did as a kid, taking up all the space that he thought he deserved as the oldest. Denise stood near the kitchen table, blowing cigarette smoke out of an open window past Ma's fancy new blinds. And I settled on the arm of a chair and looked around at the living room where so much had happened to us growing up. Jim was the first to break the silence.

"Shit," he said.

I thought I could imagine what he was feeling. Ma finally had built a real home for herself out of the shell of our past. Now she was gone before truly enjoying it. It was just sinking in for Jim. Denise flicked her butt out of the window. She moved around restlessly. With Ma gone, it seemed as if she fell into her default role of helping run the household.

"Steve should take the love seats and the tables. He's moving into a new apartment with no furniture," Denise declared. "The bedroom furniture should go to Goodwill."

Jim raised his eyebrow at Denise for a minute, evaluating whether he wanted to fight for control over what was left of our childhood. I tensed.

"Fine," he finally said, exhaling. "Just give me all the family photos."

Now I gaped at him, ready to argue.

"What? I'm the oldest. Don't you guys trust me?"

Denise gave me her look and I backed down. Within minutes we'd divided up a few more things, mostly things that would remind us of Ma. Then I saw Rick pull into the driveway.

"Here we go," I said.

Rick came in through the new sliding glass doors at the back of the house. He looked exhausted, and there were now bags rimming his bloodshot eyes, but he moved and talked like he was full of energy. His new wife trailed behind him.

"I suppose y'all didn't leave me anything," he announced, looking around.

Denise put her hands on her hips, like Ma often did, but Rick moved past her.

"What did you get?" He stood over me and jammed his finger in my direction.

Jim stood up between us and put his hand on Rick's shoulder. Rick shrugged it off.

"Easy there," Jim said. "Take whatever you want. Everything's going to get donated otherwise."

Rick didn't need to be told twice. I stood back as he began to muscle a floor-model color TV out the back door and into the open trunk of his car. Pretty soon the blender, a toaster, a cordless phone, and a microwave were all piled into the back seat.

"You do you, my brother," Denise muttered.

When they began to carry out pots, pans, and dishes, Jim passed me and Denise some beers. The three of us settled onto the love seats so we could watch this show. We were still drinking after Rick finished up by helping his wife bring a pile of Ma's clothes out to their car.

"Well, wasn't that something," Denise said just after the door shut behind him.

I looked around the room. Not much was left. Even Grandma had been hauled off across the yard to Aunt Bonnie's house earlier that summer, right after Ma was diagnosed. Bonnie didn't mind. My grandmother's Social Security check had gone along with her.

Finally Denise got up and moved toward the door.

"Well, it's been real, fellas," she said.

"Wait, is this it? Are we just gonna leave like this?" Jim asked. He threw up his hands in frustration.

"Are you serious?" Denise answered. "That's probably the last we'll see of Rick. Mike's in prison. And Stevie's moving to New York City. Come on, Jim. We just need to head our separate ways while we're still speaking to one another."

Denise gave me a kiss on the cheek and offered Jim a half wave. Then she was gone. I knew she was right. It was time to stop pretending we were any kind of family anymore. We had changed since we grew up together in that house. We'd come a long way, but watching Rick was an awful reminder of how far we still had to go.

CHAPTER 31

A Family of Choice

It would be ten years before any of us heard anything from Rick again. Through the family grapevine we found out his third marriage had fizzled. Later we learned the alcohol and drugs he'd used all his life had begun to take a toll on his body.

Finally, in 2010, my sister called. There was a part of me that wasn't surprised by what she said.

"Stevie, it's me, Denise," she announced over the phone. "Rick's liver is giving out. He's dying."

Jim, Denise, Mike, and I walked into his hospital room a few days later and gathered around his bed. Rick lay watching us as we awkwardly stood around him. The full head of hair, lean muscular build, and bright smile were gone. Now he reminded me of a cadaver. He had just turned fifty-four. I looked away from his decaying teeth and tried not to notice the taut gray face. None of us knew what to say to him, but Jim knew that, if nothing else, we shared a history and the same sense of dark humor.

"What's up, black boy?" Jim said. "You know, you look like shit."

Rick flipped him the bird.

"Yeah, well. I'm dying. What the hell is your excuse?"

Rick looked Mike up and down. Mike had been paroled from prison just a few years earlier and was living as a registered sex offender in a nearby town. Until now, we all had kept our distance from him.

"Look at who you dug up," Rick said. "They really let you go out in public now, Mike?"

Rick laughed, showing just what was left of his rotted front teeth.

"Damn!" Mike said with a smirk. "I guess some things never change."

And that included Rick.

"Steve, why don't you make yourself useful and get me some water," Rick ordered.

Jim elbowed me. I walked over to get the water pitcher to fill his glass. As soon as that task was done, Rick assigned another. He had Mike sweet-talk the nurse in the hall into bringing Rick another dinner plate. Then he set Denise to tidying the room. Finally, he turned to Jim and asked him to sneak him some cigarettes.

If we were another family, there were things we all could have said to Rick and to one another in what would be our final hours together, but with nothing to say, it was easier for us just to fall back into our childhood roles. Besides, anything we could have said would have been too much and far too late.

We all knew Rick had always put himself first in every relationship in his life. He'd wring everything out of people and then leave them. What was worse, he'd blame those he left behind for not giving him enough love. He'd done it to Ma. He'd done it to us. He'd done it to every friend he ever had, and he'd done it to his all ex-wives and children.

Now he had no one left to blame but himself. And that wouldn't happen.

That night in the hospital room, I looked at Rick and wondered whether I should even have come. I watched Jim, Denise, and Mike form a circle around Rick's bed. I hovered at the edge. No matter that we'd called ourselves full siblings, they would always have a connection without me—a result of having the same father and the same skin color. And given the age difference between us, they would have childhood memories, stories, and secrets that I could never share. Despite that, they were no closer as a family without me.

I came to accept that the five of us had never been close friends in childhood and might never be late in life. We had spent years trying to run away from one other. Maybe death truly was meant to be the only thing that could bring us together. And after fighting all our lives to get along, I was okay knowing that now it was time for us to concede defeat as a family. It was to be a decision that we were making not only for ourselves but also, perhaps, for our own children.

As Rick lay dying, I remembered the times we had tried and failed to make him feel as if he were a part of our family, and how he had instead pushed everyone away.

After his first marriage had broken down, Rick made a show of pretending that he felt some sort of emotional connection to his baby son. Little Rickie wasn't even out of diapers when Rick decided to leave his wife. One morning after she left for work, he loaded up all their furniture and belongings in a U-Haul. Seemingly as an afterthought, he took his son along too. To Rick, his son was another asset of the marriage, and he was determined to have possession of him. Later that day Rick arrived at our country hill with my towheaded nephew and a grocery bag of clothes and toys. He wanted to hide his son away. Rick should have entrusted him to our mother, but either out of spite or out of contempt, he took him next door to live with Aunt Bonnie.

"I need you to just watch him during the day while I work," Rick told her.

But long workdays often stretched into the night, and soon Rick was gone for days at a time. One rainy afternoon, before Rick returned from one of those long absences, little Rickie's mother arrived on my aunt's doorstep. From across the yard and through my bedroom window, I watched Aunt Bonnie's full bulk fill the front doorway. I could almost see her shake a large brown finger in Mary's face. Her booming voice was easy to hear.

"You can't come up in here," she said. "You better get your narrow white ass back down those steps."

Mary backed up, but her maternal instincts were apparently stronger than Aunt Bonnie's killer ones. As my aunt would later tell us, Mary appealed to her as a mother.

"I just want to hold him one more time," she told my aunt. "After that I'll go, and I won't come back."

Aunt Bonnie hesitated for a moment, but then waddled back, allowing Mary to follow her inside. The screen door closed behind them. I stepped away, but a few moments later I heard Aunt Bonnie scream across the yard.

"Help! Help! That bitch has got the baby!"

By the time I flew back to my bedroom window, I could see Mary sprinting for the car with my nephew in her arms. Bonnie's short fat legs were no match. Once Mary squealed away in her car, she was true to her word. She never came back. And for years, neither did little Rickie. My brother must have realized he would never win full custody of his son, but for years he didn't bother to even fight to visit him. His pet, his little white "dolly," his prized possession was gone. And it was time to move on.

Little Rickie did eventually live around the edges of our frayed family. His mother would be busy with a new husband and children and, for a time, left her firstborn behind. By the time my nephew was school age, he bounced from home to home, even staying with Denise and her family for weeks on end. But for the most part little Rickie, along with the rest of his father's children, was estranged from our family. Although it broke my mother's heart, his homecoming before she died restored a piece of it. When we saw this little boy grown into a man, we would still marvel at his straight hair, fair skin, and easy laughter.

Looking into his green eyes, I saw nothing of Rick in him, nor of my family, and for that I was secretly relieved.

Now I looked into the jaundiced eyes of my brother. He had four kids from three failed marriages. None had a relationship with him.

Perhaps it was his dying wish to claim a child solely as his own. Because as he lay there, he now had a deathbed confession. He announced to us that he had one more child, a girl. The real shock was that she was still a baby. There would be no final custody battle or arguments over child support. This time the mother wouldn't put up a fight. She'd given birth and walked out of the hospital, leaving behind the drug-addicted baby.

Rick knew his daughter faced a life in foster care. He looked at us and admitted he'd never felt a part of our family, let alone been able to sustain any of his own, but he wanted this little girl to have a chance in life. He wanted her raised by family. He left the request there as if it were no more than another errand to fetch him a glass of water.

Jim knew he couldn't manage to take this child in. He was still trying to rebuild his life and a relationship with his own adult daughter who had been raised by her mother. Denise, who had raised two girls, was now helping to raise her own grandchildren. Mike was out of the question. So that left me. I had a stable home, a solid income, and had already adopted twice before.

The voice in my head imagined my family asking me how I could not open my heart and home. This was family, after all, and as Black folks, this was what we'd done for generations—take care of our own.

Another voice, perhaps my own, whispered that maybe God was telling me to offer love to this baby since I'd never been able to give it to Rick. But I closed my ears to those voices and looked down at my feet so I could avoid Rick's gaze in that hospital room.

It's taken me years to realize that, had I spoken up in that moment, it would have been out of guilt for not loving my brother more and not out of love for his child.

A few weeks later Rick died. Before he did, he learned that once again one of his children would find refuge with our extended family. His daughter was taken in by my cousin Cathleen.

In the years since I'd left, I'd mostly lost touch with my first friend in life. After years spent cowering under the taunts and threats of her mother, Cathleen had finally found the bravery to leave. Like me, she too had gone off in search of a better life. She'd become a nurse, found a warm and loving husband, and borne three good-looking sons. She'd also found a deep religious faith, and it would preserve her when, a little more than year before Rick became ill, she lost her middle son in a tragic car accident. For a time she was bereft, and from afar our family worried that after everything she had endured in life, this might be the one thing Cathleen couldn't live through. But when she learned of this child in our family with no father, no mother, and no one to take her in, she opened her heart and home.

Although we never discussed it, my siblings and I were content to leave our niece's upbringing entirely to Cathleen. To this day, a decade after Rick passed, not one of us has met our niece. Nor do I think we ever will. I assuage whatever small guilt I should feel by asking myself what any of us could possibly tell her about the father she never knew.

She, Rickie, my niece Jamie, and the rest of my siblings' children are among a generation of children either born out of wedlock or separated from their parents by death or divorce. It didn't bother me that some of my siblings didn't step into their lives. Seeing how this generation flourished apart from our family, I felt grateful.

CHAPTER 32

The Wounds
That Won't Heal

After all the emotional and physical tumult in my family, I could only hope the new school year would bring a fresh start for my children. The family therapist had worked with us all summer, trying to help us put away the bad memories of the past year and replace them with new and better ones. That autumn, in 2016, we took her advice and tried to spend more time together as a family, planning activities that ranged from a simple family game night to a Halloween hayride. However, as fall turned to winter, there were reminders that our bonds as a family were still strained. By November, the regular regimen of middle school homework weighed on Mariah. A few years earlier, we'd been included in a *Washington Post Magazine* article about how parents—straight and gay—were rethinking their traditional roles at home to get the job of child-raising done. In the large photo spread, I'm shown sitting in the living room looking over their schoolwork while Todd cooks dinner. Scenes like this had become rare. A photographer who wandered into our home that fall would have snapped a photo of Mariah sitting in the middle of the living room floor with her homework crumpled up beside her and her face equally creased, sobbing, "I can't do it." Even simple chores like cleaning up her bedroom or clearing away her dishes seemed overwhelming. The easy laughter that filled our house weeks before had given way to door slams, tears, and angry declarations of "You don't understand me."

We knew Mariah had always been very sensitive. Small disappointments and setbacks loomed large in her head and sometimes drove her to outbursts. What we were coming to realize is that those actions were just a surrogate for the larger sorrow she felt in her heart.

One early December night, Todd stood at the kitchen counter prepping lunches for the next day. The kids were arguing with one another. In my memory, it was about another borrowed piece of clothing that wasn't returned. I could hear their voices rise, and I watched our two dogs go to their familiar hiding places—one under the table, the other under a bed. As I sat on the couch with my eyes closed, I tried to block the rising voices out. I tried to remember what the therapist had counseled me to do when I felt triggered. I wanted to will myself to just breathe, but I couldn't.

"It's not *fair*."

"Give it to me, *now*."

"*Don't touch me!*"

"Hey!" Todd called.

Suddenly two sets of hands tugged at my arm. I kept my eyes closed.

"*Tell her to stop!*"

Breathe, I said to myself.

"*Poppy, Poppy, Poppy, you're not doing anything!*"

In my head I was trapped inside another house, and there was no place to escape to. I couldn't hide from what was happening, and I couldn't make it stop. The noise, the shouts, the screams, the tears, the pounding footsteps kept following me. All I could do was shove off the arms pulling at me.

"*Let fucking go of me*," I screamed. "*Leave me alone!*"

I opened my eyes to see Rachel race to her room. She banged the door shut behind her. Mariah stood in front of me, those almond-shaped eyes blazing with hurt. I reached out my arms to her.

"I'm sorry. I didn't mean it. It's time for bed. Let me get you a piece of melatonin to help calm you down so you can get to sleep. Okay? I'm sorry."

She pulled away and ran past me and Todd.

"Mariah!"

I got up to follow. As I rounded the corner, I saw her pluck the small bottle out of the kitchen cabinet and dump the entire bottle of melatonin into her mouth. She stood there defiantly with the pills lying on her tongue. She looked too scared to swallow, yet too angry at me to spit them out.

"What are you doing?" As I reached for her, she backed away.

I thrust my hand in front of her face. Tears spilled down into my hand. Finally she leaned over and spat the half-dissolved white gob into my palm.

She leaned against my chest.

"I just want my mommy."

A few hours later, the doctor in the emergency room leaned over the bed where Mariah was lying wide awake.

"Your daughter doesn't seem to be lethargic or sluggish," she said. "Her pupils look fine. Her heart rate is good. I wouldn't worry about the melatonin, especially if she spat most of it out."

The doctor, a young Latina, shifted her soft brown eyes from me and Todd to Mariah.

"Look, sweetheart, your dads . . ."

Mariah slowly nodded.

"Your dads love you very much and would never want you to hurt yourself," she said. "Did you know what would happen if you swallowed all of that melatonin?"

Mariah shrugged.

The doctor sighed. She patted Mariah's arm and pulled Todd and me outside the curtained area. While Mariah hadn't planned to hurt herself, she warned that it was still dangerous because she hadn't thought through the consequences. She had to learn to regulate her own feelings in case someone wasn't there to stop her. The doctor advised it was best for Mariah to stay a few days for observation in the hospital's behavioral health center. It was a nice, polite, white-people word for the psych ward, I thought. Long ago I'd discovered that my grandma's angry badgering had once sent her estranged husband to the crazy hospital. Now I wondered if I'd done the same thing to my daughter.

That night I watched Mariah give me a sullen look as I turned to leave. She shuffled behind a locked door with a thick window set in the top. She would join a dozen or so other kids in the youth ward at the hospital for a few days of observation. She'd be home in less than a week with a clean bill of health. Healing her emotional childhood wounds would take much longer. Soon I was reminded that sometimes they never heal.

It was only a few weeks later that the phone rang.

"Stevie? It's me, Denise."

She identified herself as if I wouldn't recognize the croak in her voice after all these years. I braced myself for whatever bad news had accrued in our family since the last time we spoke.

"When's the last time you heard from Mike?"

Mike and I hadn't talked in ten years. Denise knew that, and she also knew why. I couldn't have him in my life anymore. None of us could. Her question meant that something had happened to change the status quo.

"I heard through the grapevine he's really sick now."

Long ago I'd learned Mike had hepatitis C. It had gone untreated for a while. His continued love of 40 ounces of Old Milwaukee a day hadn't helped.

"He still near Asheville?" I asked.

I pictured Mike living near the beach. Was he just drinking and smoking dope, living out his remaining years? Certainly he was also hiding out there, away from the rest of us and anyone who knew about his background.

Denise insisted I call Jim, thinking perhaps he might know.

In the years since we'd moved to Maryland, I'd probably spoken to Jim only half a dozen times, and he lived thirty minutes away in Baltimore. As the oldest, Jim had been the one to take charge. Now, talking to him on the phone, I heard a different side of him.

"Why the hell doesn't Denise try to call him?" he asked, sounding tired. "I'm just too old for all this bullshit."

Finally a bit of the old Jim resurfaced, the one who thought it was his role to tell us all what to do.

"I want you to call Mike right now and see what's going on."

I huffed into the cell phone. Of course, he and Denise could have just as easily called Mike themselves, but Denise had long ago refused to speak to Mike after what he'd done. And Jim seemed weary of all the years of fighting among us. In a family like ours, there was always the risk that a conversation might reopen old grudges and painful memories, not to mention our shared shame. So it fell to me, the one who had tried the hardest to leave them all behind, to reconnect them.

I guessed that maybe my role in the family had not changed so much over the years. They still saw me as the good boy—the one who could be counted on to follow the rules and try and keep the peace.

"All right," I said. "Let me see what I can find out."

As I hung up, I muttered to myself:

"Motherfuckers. Ain't this some shit."

It took several days to track down a working number for Mike. In the end, all I had to do was call Aunt Bonnie. The same family grapevine that was happy to sniff out something rotting on the vine could also be counted on to follow it back to its root.

When Mike picked up the phone, I recognized the same fawning tone he'd used as a kid when he wanted something.

"Steve!" he said. "I thought you all were just going to forget about me after all this time."

"Humph. What's this about, Mike?"

The skeptical tone sounded strange but familiar coming out of my mouth. I recognized it as the same one used by Ma when she was trying to reprimand one of her wayward kids. Mike repeated the same story that Jim and Denise had heard through various relatives, but there was more. Mike claimed the hepatitis C had severely damaged his liver and he couldn't wait for a transplant. He said his health was failing fast. I wanted to feel something, but I'd learned how badly Mike could manipulate people with his wild exaggerations and outright lies. He made himself sound helpless and harmless, when in fact he was anything but.

"What exactly is it that you need?"

I let the question hang there. Was he reaching out to us asking for money or maybe forgiveness for what he'd done?

"They tell me I'm going to die," he finally said. "And I really want to see you guys. You're the only family I've got. My own kids won't talk to me."

He paused, then added for effect, "And I know how badly you guys would feel if you didn't see me before I'd died. I didn't think that would be fair to you."

Same old Mike. Same old shit. As I hung up the phone, I turned around to see Rachel. She'd been hiding behind the chair, listening, as I had done as a kid.

"Who was that?" she asked.

The picture on the wall was the only evidence that my mother had five kids. For years I'd batted away their curiosity about Rick. He's dead, is all I would say. As for Mike—the chubby kid standing next to me in the picture—I'd just tell them "he lives far away" or "we're not close." They knew that my family was disconnected. Yet there had always been something unsaid about Mike. I steered Rachel over to the couch and sat down next to her.

"It was my brother Mike. He's sick and wants me to come to visit him."

She twisted her braid and thought for a minute.

"Wait. Are you talking to him now?"

"I guess. He's really sick. I think I should go see him."

She jumped up and ran down the hall to get Mariah. I could hear them talking in the bedroom.

"Poppy's brother, the one we don't know, Mike, called . . ."

Within seconds the two girls were circling me and peppering me with questions. Todd poked his head through the doorway of the kitchen and gave me an "it's time" look. A part of me had hoped Mike would remain just a name to my kids, and I hoped they would one day just remember him as that kid with a solemn face in that family portrait. But another part always feared the day would come when they would find out the truth about him.

I sat them down in front of me on the couch in the living room and thought about how to begin.

There's no easy way to tell your children that someone in your family, even a long-lost brother, is sick and dying, but it's much harder to tell them that he got sick in prison and that he was serving time for being a child molester.

For months Mike continued to call, pleading to see us all one last time before he died. During that time Denise, Jim, and I couldn't agree on what to do.

"I've got nothing to say to this joker. Let's send him a few hundred and be done with it," Denise said.

"His story doesn't add up," I said. "One day he's dying, the next day he says he's on a transplant list."

I knew what was behind our cynical reactions. So much had happened in our family over the years that we had all grown numb to whatever new family crisis or catastrophe might threaten to upend us. But there was more. Though I couldn't bring myself to admit it, I didn't want to do anything that might draw me back into the drama and dysfunction of our family. It had taken me years to escape it. I hoped that with time the issue might just somehow go away on its own. I could wait it out until Mike either died or stopped asking.

Maybe Jim had softened as he age, because he was the first of us to give in. He told me he felt obligated to try and grant Mike's wish to see us, but even his compassion had limits. He said if Mike wanted to see us that badly, we should buy him an airline ticket so he could fly north to see us.

"Besides, it'll be cheaper that way," Jim added.

I laughed, but I knew Jim was only half joking. He'd survived this far by holding himself at arm's length from our family, deciding when he'd step in to save someone and when he would leave them to flounder on their own. Although it was his own survival skill, I'd admired it, because once he had used it save my life.

CHAPTER 33

Blood Is Thicker

The partially wooded acres behind our home were Jim's kingdom. It was a place for him to smoke cigarettes, drink beer, and lord it over the rest of us. But we didn't mind. It was also the only place we could get away from whatever hell was happening in our house.

I was six, and my brothers said I was too little to go into the woods, but if Denise was busy after school and Ma was working late, they had to take me along. They hated that I slowed them down, but one late November, a quarter mile into those woods, I begged them to hurry up.

"Gotta pee bad," I said. "Can we go home?"

"Quit being so weak. We're too far. Go piss behind that tree," Rickie said.

He pulled a single cigarette from his back pocket. He glared at me, as if he were daring me to tell Ma.

"What if I get lost?"

"Mike, go walk him over to that tree," Jim ordered.

Mike rolled his eyes, but he took my hand and jerked me toward the tree. There I unzipped and watched my stream melt away the layer of ice covering the tree roots. I wasn't watching what I was doing. Pretty soon I was yelping again.

"I'm wet!"

I started to cry. In between the whimpers, I told them I couldn't walk with pee down the legs of my jeans. I tried to put on a brave face and choke back my tears, so they wouldn't tease me. I was afraid that Rick might call me a high-yella baby or that Mike might say I was acting like a little girl again. Only Jim showed some sympathy.

"Jee-zus Christ," Jim-Jim said. "Come on, I know a shortcut."

A few minutes later we broke through a dense stand of trees and into a clearing. Up ahead I could see a big, murky drainage pond. It wasn't the way we came in. Jim confidently said the shortest way to the other side and home was straight through. Mike sloshed in first, the freezing water soaking his pants. Rick flicked his cigarette into the water and followed. By the midpoint—the deepest part—the pond water lapped just below their hips. It was clear I wouldn't be able to make it on my own.

Jim-Jim already had the answer. He backed toward me, squatted, and allowed me to scramble up his back until my tiny arms were clasped around his neck and my tiny legs clenched his sides. Then he began to slog across. But just past the middle, he suddenly stopped, and we swayed for a second. I could hear a sucking noise as he tried to pry his tennis shoe from the bottom of the muddy pond. He grumbled "Jee-zus" again.

"Leave it," Mike called.

"Just make him walk," Rickie said, laughing.

"Noooooo," I screamed.

I snapped my legs back and forth, nearly tipping Jim-Jim over. Suddenly Jim-Jim shouted to Rick, who now stood watching us on the opposite bank.

"Catch him."

They both laughed like it was the brightest idea in the world. It would have been, had it worked. Rick came back into the water. He and Jim-Jim now stood about ten feet apart.

"Noooooo," I sobbed.

But Jim-Jim had decided. He reached back over his head, peeled me off his back, and held me under my armpits. Then he slowly counted to three and lobbed me like he was making a lateral pass of a football.

It happened so fast, I didn't have time to see if I ever got close to Rick's arms. All I remember is darkness and then being hauled up by the back of my pants as I coughed up dirty pond water. My whole body shook, from the cold and from the shock.

"Is he breathing?" I heard Jim-Jim say. Someone pounded me on the back, and I coughed up more water.

They could tell I was breathing by the chattering of my teeth.

"Look at that, his freaking lips are blue," Mike said. He thought it looked funny, so he laughed.

Jim-Jim quickly water-walked over to me and took me from Rick. After one look at my face, he pulled off my drenched coat until all I had on was my soaked T-shirt, which felt like it was already freezing. He took off his own jacket, wrapped me in it, and pulled me tight to his massive chest.

"Let's go!" Jim-Jim shouted, setting in motion a long, sustained drive toward the end of the field and our house. I could feel his heart thump through his chest and his body absorb the shock of each footstep pounding against the frozen ground. His grip on me was iron. By the time we got home, the heat of his body had eased my shaking.

There were times after that day when I wondered what my brothers really thought of me—especially Jim-Jim. I wondered about it every time he would shake his head and throw up his hands in surrender while trying to teach me how to fight or throw a football. He seemed to realize early on that I was never going to be the tough little brother he might have hoped for. As we grew, so did our differences and the perceptions of them in my head. But out of all my brothers, he was the one who was fiercely protective of me, no matter that I looked different. Long after he and my other brothers left in search of different lives, I took comfort in thinking back to that afternoon in the woods. I held on to the image of Jim-Jim raising me up, holding me tight, and bringing me home.

If I close my eyes even today, I can feel myself on his back. It's winter, I am five, and we are headed across the yard to Grandma's house through what seem like mountains of snow. I'm clutching his neck, and he, my giant robot, is making sure my feet stay dry. Suddenly I'm seven, perched on his shoulders and carrying his helmet after football practice. I look down at his white teammates, who stare at me funny. One glare from Jim-Jim and their smirks turn to smiles. And then I'm ten years old and riding shotgun in his muscle car as he races down country roads. As the car whips around a corner, I slide across the vinyl seat, coming to rest against his shoulder. Despite how different we were back then and how different we turned out to be, I never doubted that Jim loved me and that I could count on his strength whenever I needed it.

At first Jim always seemed strong enough to take on whatever came his way. His biggest obstacle in life was Pops. After that, he seemed to tackle any others easily. He was a standout high school football player and a fair enough student to get into college. There his knack for numbers attracted the attention of recruiters looking for more diverse bankers. Just a few years out of college, he had made it as far away from our family's little plot of land as anyone had ever been. He'd gotten married, bought a house, and started a solid career in banking. Ma's chest would swell with pride every time she pulled open the glass door and entered the air-conditioned lobby of the local branch where he worked. Jim would jump up to greet her at the door and usher her to one of the comfy leather chairs at his desk for special customer service.

His wife, a Boston-bred woman he met in college, was white. In the beginning she also took comfort in Jim's confidence and strength, but then Jim stumbled. Despite his good education and the expensive suits, he eventually couldn't hide the bad habits born of growing up inside our family. Within a few years of settling down, he was drinking like Pops and overspending like Ma. He was probably right when he argued that he wasn't a sloppy or violent drunk like Pops and made three times as much money as Ma, but the drinking and bad debts eventually caught up with him. He lost his job, his house, and his wife. Jim—the one who prided himself on being the man of the family—finally came to our mother and grandmother for money. I imagine that standing before Grandma, as he had watched Ma do for so many years, must have been humiliating. It looked that way to me.

"You's a damned fool," Grandma told him. "You got a good education and you gonna throw it all away?"

Jim hung his head. Then, like Ma, he held out his hand.

Watching Jim climb out of piss-poor poverty, and then seeing him slide back to our hill, would always stay with me. Maybe it meant there was something in our family blood, something that would make us always fall short.

"And if you git yoself in trouble again, don't come back begging to Grandmama ever again!"

The money Grandma grudgingly gave Jim, drawn from the stash she'd hidden around her home for decades, was enough for him to move to Baltimore, where he wanted to make a fresh start. Her parting message was clear: he was on his own now, and there was no coming back.

Jim wouldn't come back for years. When he did, it was generally for a funeral, and then only for a day or two. His pride never recovered from the fact that he had been the first to successfully leave, only to return in shame. But his loyalty to our family, especially his brothers and sister, never wavered. That's why he called me one day, with the same authority in his voice that I'd known as a kid.

"Look, I've been thinking about this. It's time for someone to finally go and see Mike," he said. "Denise is refusing to go, and to be honest, I'm not emotionally in a place where I can handle this right now."

I listened, waiting for him to order me to go, like I knew he wanted to. If he had, maybe I would have fought back for the first time and told him I was grown enough now to make my own choices.

But instead I just heard him sigh over the phone. Jim was sixty now, and for the first time he didn't sound as strong as he once had. I thought about all the times he'd been there for me when I needed that strength.

I sighed back at him. "Jee-zus Christ," I said. "Fine."

What I never told Jim is that, as much as I was doing this for him and possibly for Mike, I was also making this trip for my children. They were old enough now to realize that when you grow up, you can choose to leave your family behind, as I did. One day they might choose to do the same. But years from now, I wanted them to have this memory of me reconnecting with my family. I needed them to know life sometimes gives you a chance to find your way home.

CHAPTER 34

Sins of the Fathers

On the day I visited my dying brother Mike in 2017, I left just enough time to talk with him for a few hours before my scheduled return flight. I knew the limits of my patience and my compassion for him.

Old Fort, North Carolina, just east of Asheville, was exactly what I figured it would be: small and rural. From the window of my rental car, I saw mostly whites and a few Blacks going in and out of the 7-Eleven and Dollar General. Mike had to have known he'd fit in here. He'd grown up in a place like this—somewhere where an outsider could fit in if he just put his head down, did his job, and kept his mouth shut.

His home turned out to be a beat-up trailer at the crook of a country road several miles outside of town. When Mike came to the door, I barely recognized him. His normally big brown eyes were now yellowing and watery. He was stooped over and scuffed ahead of me in a pair of dirty slippers. He led me to a seat on his secondhand couch, clearing a tangled nest of blankets out of the way. As I sat down, I noticed that the trailer tilted a bit, as if it too was unsteady on its feet. A stack of medical bills, insurance forms, and disability claims covered the battered coffee table in front of us. Mike struggled to catch his breath, and I tried to slow mine.

"I'm glad you came," he finally said. "I'd really like to talk. There's a lot you should know about our childhood, Steve—things you might have been too young to figure out."

Mike paused and looked up toward the ceiling panels of the trailer. I couldn't tell if he was searching for the truth or a made-up story. All I knew is that when I spoke next, there was a lie on my own lips.

"Don't rush. I've got plenty of time," I said. "Let's just start by talking about how you are."

Mike shrugged and gave me a glimpse of his liar's gap. He was fifty-nine and looked much older. I spotted half a dozen portable oxygen tanks tucked behind a chair in the corner. Mike wasn't getting on a plane anywhere to visit the rest of our family, and in truth I probably wasn't coming back. Mike surely realized that too. He filled the time talking about his failing body. I could tell he was waiting until I was ready to hear what he really wanted to say.

"What did you want to tell me?" I asked.

Maybe for the first time in his life, the right words escaped him. Stopping frequently for sips of water and breath, he talked about our childhood. The darkly funny stories were the same ones we'd told around our Christmas tree when everyone had just enough to drink. Mike then talked about his own family—a son and daughter, now in their twenties. He regretted not seeing them since he'd been out of prison.

I kept looking across the trailer at the digital clock above the kitchen stove. There was something else Mike needed to say, and we were both short on time. He was struggling to tell me a secret that had been buried for years. It occurred to me that I had been trying to ignore it for just as long. I thought about what I'd come to learn regarding the nature of child sexual abuse—that abusers often report they were once victims themselves.

"Mike, I need to ask you something," I said. "We don't ever have to talk about this after today, okay?"

He took a sip of water and nodded.

"Did someone molest you, when you were growing up?"

Mike couldn't meet my eyes for a minute. From beneath the piles of paper on the coffee table, he pulled out a book and handed it to me.

"You should read this."

It was a collection of stories from inmates across the country. Mike told me he had submitted a story to the editor about the challenges of surviving behind bars while being a sex offender, one of the prison's most hated populations. Tucked toward the middle of a book was a Post-It note marking one page of his story.

"If you really want to know what went on in our house, look at this. Not now. Take it home."

I walked out the door an hour later carrying the book and a smiling photo of Mike as a much younger man. I overcame my shame at touching my brother and enveloped him in a hug.

"All right, man," I said, pulling away. "I talked to Jim and maybe we can fly you up to visit everyone at Christmas."

Mike's jaundiced eyes lit up with excitement. I stared into them, hoping to convince him of my story.

"Christmas! You promise? Okay, just don't forget me. Okay?"

"We won't."

I pulled away in the rental car and watched Mike stand at the trailer door, a blanket over his shoulders. I needed to catch my plane, but a few minutes down the road, I steered over to the side and took the book out to read what Mike had written.

> In the course of her . . . visits [to me in prison], my mother dropped a
> bombshell that I will carry for life. She told me . . . that my Dad repeatedly
> molested my sister. But there was more. He was molesting me, and to my
> horror, he was renting me out to four old men who picked me up once a
> week. She said that the only reason she had found out was that one day
> she put her car into the shop and stayed home sick. These men came to the
> door and said they were here to pick me up, and the truth came out when
> she confronted my dad. What little dignity I had left died on that day. To
> this day, though, I can't remember a thing.

I sat there staring at the words. I remembered Ma's sudden insistence when I was six or seven that I begin sleeping in Denise's room. She said it was to keep my sister from being lonely at night, but was it really to protect Neecie or even me from Pops and the leers of his drinking buddies? I thought about the shadow of fear that lay over our house and over Mike, long after Pops was gone. And I tried to imagine a terrified young mother who might try to bury shameful secrets, hoping her son was too young to remember. What horror must she have felt, decades later, when the sins of the father were visited upon her son?

Finally, I wondered about Mike. He had told a lot of wild stories in his life. Most of them he told to protect his fragile ego or repair his frayed reputation. Was this one of those tales, or was he finally telling the truth?

When I returned home, I called Jim to provide a full account of Mike's failing health and an assessment, in Jim's words, of "what the hell he was up to." Fully convinced now that Mike might not have much time to live, Jim sighed loudly into the phone.

"Shit," he said simply, and let the silence say all the thing he could not in that moment.

"There's one more thing," I added.

I read aloud from the book Mike had given me. I could hear Jim's breathing grow faster over the phone. When I stopped, he exploded.

"*What?* He claims that happened?"

"He says Ma told him this."

I paused for a moment, listening to Jim cuss and mutter to himself.

"Did you know?" I finally asked.

Jim claimed it was something he'd never heard—not from Ma or even from the other elders in my family who passed down the most painful chapters of our family history in whispers to one another.

"You believe him?" Jim asked in a tone that sounded like a challenge.

"I don't know, but he said it also happened to Denise."

"Do not bring any of this up to her, understand? There's no reason to open up any more shit right now. It's enough that Mike is dying."

Jim sounded desperate, and in that moment I thought he sounded a lot like Ma, hoping he could heal over a painful wound by just keeping it a secret. Out of all the terrible stories about our family, this was the worst. He didn't want it to be true. Neither did I. Yet I think we both knew it probably was. The sins of our past can never really be forgotten. But it's never too late to seek redemption. It's probably what led my mother to finally unburden her soul to Mike. And I believe it's why Mike shared the story with me—not to seek absolution for his actions, but perhaps to ask for some understanding of what made him the man he was.

I ignored Jim's warning and finally did tell Denise. She never admitted or denied that she'd also been abused. Yet the way she whispered to herself told me enough. I knew our family would never be able to forget or forgive all that we'd done to one another. But we had begun to acknowledge all that had happened. Perhaps in doing so, I thought, we might find some peace and have some compassion, at least for ourselves.

Despite Denise's reluctance to revisit those terrible memories of her childhood and her feelings toward Mike, she gave in and agreed she needed to see him one last time, so we told Mike that Denise, Jim, and I would travel together as a family to North Carolina after the holidays. But soon after the New Year, I awoke one morning to a series of pings on my phone. It was a group text, coming from Mike's phone number.

"Come now, there's not much time," it read.

I immediately called Mike's number, half suspecting he might be exaggerating the state of his health. But instead of Mike, a middle-aged woman answered. She sounded white to me.

"Hello, this is Barb."

"I'm sorry, I was calling my brother?" I asked.

"Oh," she exclaimed. "I've been trying to contact you. I found your name on Michael's cell phone. I'm his health proxy. We're here in the hospital."

Mike's liver and his kidneys had finally given out, and his lungs were filling up with fluid. There would be no chance for a transplant, and there might not be time to see him again.

"Do you wish to talk to him?" she asked.

Before I could answer, I heard the phone fumbling, then a ragged voice.

"Steve," he said. "They tell me I'm dying."

By the time I reached Denise, she was already in motion. She too had received the text and somehow had already tracked down Mike's adult son from one of his past relationships. She had booked them both tickets to North Carolina, and they were on the way to the airport. None of the family had ever met this young man before. Now Denise was bringing him on a plane to visit his dying father. Despite the deep grudge Denise held against Mike for what he had done, she was showing she had more balls than me, and probably more heart.

Jim and I soon spoke and arranged to book our own flights. I would arrive in the late afternoon and Jim later that evening. Hours later, as I sat in Charlotte's airport waiting for a connection, my phone rang. It was Denise, and she sounded out of breath.

"Stevie, it's me, Denise. We got here to the hospital twenty minutes ago. I sent Mike's son in first. When I walked in a few minutes ago, Mike had just died."

She sounded startled by what she said next. "I think he was holding on till someone in the family got here."

With Mike gone so suddenly, we were lost as to where we should go. Aside from us and Mike's son, there was no family to visit and comfort. So the next morning we made a pilgrimage to that weather-beaten trailer where I'd visited Mike just a few months before. As I parked the rental car, Mike's son unfolded himself out of the back seat. Jim had already christened Michael Jr. with a family nickname—Mike-Mike. He was handsome, early twenties, tall, with tan skin, straight hair, and light brown eyes. He looked more Latino to me than Black. On greeting him at the hotel the night before, I was at a loss for words. All I could think to do was tease him about his complexion.

"I didn't think our family made kids in your shade."

He laughed, letting me know he could appreciate our family's strange sense of humor, especially during the darkest moments. He seemed like a good kid. Now he was all we had left of Mike. Denise, especially, seemed protective of him.

"You're not alone anymore," she told him on the drive to the trailer. "We're here for you."

I looked at Denise in the passenger seat and wondered if she really believed that. It had taken our brother's death for us to reach out to our lost nephew. We were never the type of family to keep close ties, despite our years of history together. What would become of this boy we had just met?

Barb, the mysterious neighbor lady behind the text, stood on the small metal steps leading to Mike's trailer and waved us forward. She was neatly dressed, late fifties, with short blond hair gone mostly gray. As I got closer, I noticed the small gold cross around her neck.

Mike-Mike said what we were all thinking in that moment. "I'm confused. How did my dad know this white lady?"

"Beats the shit out of me," Denise said.

"Let's just get this over with," I mumbled. I nudged Mike-Mike ahead.

Barb eyed us all up and down, maybe trying to understand the connections between our multiflavored family. After we introduced ourselves, she explained that she lived in the next town over and had met Mike a few years earlier. She seemed to know quite a bit about Mike's last few years. But I guessed she didn't know much about his life before. She gave us a tight smile and swept her arms around the lopsided trailer.

"Okay, your job is to go through his belongings and take what you want," she said. "Though as you can see, Michael lived pretty simply. If you find any cash, disability checks, or bank statements, please give them to me. Michael asked me to handle his financial affairs and be the executor of his estate."

It was a statement that caused Jim to grunt and raise his eyebrows. I could tell Denise was biting her tongue. A part of me wanted to shake my finger at this white woman and accuse her of trying to fool us out Mike's money. I knew that was ridiculous. Mike had nothing, and there was no reason to believe Barb wasn't carrying out his wishes. I reminded myself that we weren't that kind of people anymore.

"And so how exactly did you and my dad meet?" Mike-Mike asked.

"Oh, he was doing day-labor work in town and he looked a little lost," Barb answered. "He said he had no family close by, so I brought him home for a home-cooked meal and just remained in touch. He helped do some work on my house."

Denise, for one, did not look impressed. Later she would tell me that the idea of this middle-class white lady "saving" our poor Black brother pissed her off.

"Well, all right then," Denise said. She pursed her lips at Barb, folded her arms, and peered around the trailer. It still looked as raggedy as when I last visited.

"We'll just step outside and let his son go through these things," Denise said.

For the next hour we paced around the rental car and stared down the country road that reminded us of where we'd grown up. Every few minutes, Barb stuck her head out of the trailer with some thrift store item.

"Do you all want this?"

Denise kept harrumphing. "This woman must think we are some hood-rats coming to argue over Mike's belongings and maybe look for money stashed under mattresses."

I laughed to myself. The truth was, we all were just a few years removed from acting like that.

We left the trailer not long after. Mike-Mike clutched a few childhood photos of himself with his dad. Later that night we met Barb back at a small-town funeral home for a final viewing of the body. Mike had asked to be cremated, so in the absence of a formal service, this would be the last chance for us to say our goodbyes.

As Barb shooed us into the viewing room, we saw that Mike lay un-

clothed, under a sheet marked funeral home laundry. The funeral director, a young white man in a poorly fitting suit, saw us exchange looks.

"Barb indicated he didn't want a formal service, so we didn't dress the
body."

Jim grimaced and shook his head in disbelief. "Damn." Later he
would say he felt ashamed for how we'd let Mike lie there without some
dignity.

My nephew walked up to his father's body and stood there a long
while. I looked away. When it was my turn, I stopped for a moment. I
didn't know what to say to Mike. Instead in my head I imagined what
I'd say to Denise and Jim when we sat down to drink later that night. I'd
gulp some of my cocktail, look over the rim of the glass, shake my head
slowly, and repeat the family prayer:

"What a goddamned shame."

Denise would respond, "Ain't that the truth."

As I walked toward the door of the viewing room, I knew I didn't feel
sorry for the way Mike's life had turned out. He had made some terrible
choices. All I could summon was sympathy for the little boy he once was.

I glanced back at my nephew, who lingered a few steps from the body.
I'd known he was out there for years, wanting his father and a family, but
before today I had barely given him a thought. A part of me had calculated that he meant nothing to me. He was no more than a half-breed,
a bastard, the son of a child-molesting drunk. It had never occurred to
me how much we had in common.

He nodded one final time over his father's body, turned, and joined
Jim, Denise, and me at the door.

"You guys are my only connection to my dad," Mike-Mike said.
"We're all going to stay in touch, right?"

"Of course," Denise said, hugging him tight. Jim reached over and
gave his shoulder blade a squeeze. I gently pushed past my family and
walked out into the damp January night. I wanted to tell Mike-Mike I'd
be there for him now, but I knew this was the kind of promise I might
not keep.

CHAPTER 35

Coming of Age

Though Todd and I had only had a commitment ceremony to recognize our relationship, for years we told the kids it was the same as being married. After all, we naively said, it was just a piece of paper. But after the 2016 election, Todd and I feared some of the rights we'd taken for granted might be rolled back. Formalizing our relationship and accepting the legal benefits that come along with marriage seemed important now. It might also help the kids see the challenges we faced as a gay family. In January, on Inauguration Day, we nudged them awake to tell them we had a surprise. We'd decided to be legally wed that morning. Sitting up in their beds, they both seemed more embarrassed than impressed.

"Why don't you come with us?" I said. "You could be our witnesses."

"Where?" Rachel asked.

"At the courthouse."

She shook her head and went back to sleep.

"Will other people be around?" Mariah asked.

When we told her yes, she rolled her eyes and waved us away. Apparently it was bad enough to be seen out in public with her gay parents. God forbid if people knew they were married.

Later that morning Todd and I stood in a hushed ceremony room off to the side of the busy clerk's office. It was 11:40 a.m. In a few minutes the next president of the United States would raise his hand to take the oath of office. Todd and I raised our hands and solemnly swore that the license application we'd just signed was true.

As Todd and I recited our own oaths, I realized that I'd spent a lifetime worrying about what other people thought of me—my family, my friends, and everyone around me. The one person who had always accepted me was standing beside me on this day. He'd never be ashamed of me, my past, or the family we were today. It was the kind of self-confidence I wanted to feel myself. And I prayed my kids would feel it one day too.

Six months later there was another ceremony that our daughter Mariah wanted no part of. It was something Todd had been looking forward to for years. Now that she was thirteen, it was time for her Bat Mitzvah, her ritual acceptance into the Jewish faith. Even though Todd felt it would weave her closer to his family and faith, Mariah continued to express doubts about whether she wanted to embrace this part of her identity. She'd grudgingly attended Hebrew classes to prepare for more than a year. Now as the day approached, she worried about what people would think of her being Black and Jewish.

"There are Black Jews all over the world," Todd told her. "If you grow up and decide you want to be something else, that's fine. But for now, you're a part of a Jewish family, and you need to go through with this."

Mariah wasn't the only one who needed convincing about this ceremony. The truth was, so did I. It was less about the ceremony than about the invitation list. Todd had insisted that I invite my family. I told him we were asking for trouble. My siblings and I were raised Catholic, but none of us went to church anymore. Bringing them to a synagogue—a place full of white Jewish people—would take a miracle. I knew that over the decades they'd grown more worldly and accepting of people who were different from them. Yet I still worried.

Then there was the issue of them just agreeing to be near one another. We'd been so accustomed to only coming together on rare occasions to mourn, it was hard to imagine how they might agree to reunite in celebration. But Todd put his foot down. His entire family was attending. He insisted it was time my family showed up to support our kids.

It had been two years since Todd and I nearly came to blows over our kids. In the old days, on our country hill, my family would have called the police. The kids might have been shuffled off to live with a relative. But there was no hill anymore, and the remnants of my family lay hundreds of miles away, not across the yard. I told them if they really wanted to help us stay together as a family, they just needed to show up.

When I called to invite Denise and Jim, I told them that things were better. We were in therapy now. I pictured Jim rolling his eyes over the phone, smirking at the word *therapy*. "White people crying on a couch," he might call it. Denise said she supported anything that might keep Todd, me, and the kids together.

In all the years since Ma passed, I had never been the one to call on family for help. I hadn't wanted to ask, because I was always the "good" one, the one who had his life together. Now I needed to bring one family together to keep another from falling apart. Denise picked up the phone and began calling the rest of our clan. Then she called me.

"We're coming, baby brother."

Todd's family arrived first. They'd traveled together from Florida. I watched as they strode across the hotel lobby, smiling, arm in arm. I swallowed a bit of what tasted like jealousy. My family would never be that close.

"Hello, sweetheart," Todd's mother said. She kissed me on the cheek and rubbed my back. "You ready? Need anything?"

I smiled politely and shook my head. After all these years, I knew I was still pretending to be someone else around them. Todd and I had agreed to spare them the full details of my upbringing when we first met. Telling them the full story now felt like it would be too much, too late. It was enough to just tell them that I was mixed race and had a rough childhood. I also held back from them because of my own self-judgment. Even after Ma's attempts to make her kids believe we could be better, I still carried a feeling that we were somehow inferior to other people.

Todd's mother glanced over at Mariah, who stood looking sullen and partly lost. "And how's my Mariah?" she asked.

"She's feeling anxious about tomorrow," I said.

"I am not!" Mariah shot back. Tears filled her eyes.

Todd's mother offered her a sympathetic hug. It took Mariah a moment to fully relax into it.

"She'll be fine, Mom," Todd said.

But truthfully, none of us was sure about that.

After months of preparation, thousands of dollars, and friends and family coming from across the country, there was no guarantee Mariah would go through with it. If she did, it would mean she'd be accepting one identity and, in her mind, denying another part of herself.

The morning of the Bat Mitzvah ceremony, I left for our synagogue to guarantee I would be there before my family. It was an inclusive congregation—the type of Reform community where the rabbi's own children were Black and adopted. But knowing my clan, it wouldn't matter that theirs weren't the only black and brown faces there. If they showed up and saw no one they recognized, they wouldn't think twice about turning around and leaving.

Denise arrived early, bringing her two grandsons. They had been in grade school the last time I saw them. Now I watched these handsome young Black men in their twenties, tall, educated, funny and polite, walk up to me.

"Hey, Uncle Stevie," Matthias called.

I let him pull me into an embrace. Growing up, we'd never been big on showing affection, but I supposed that this was who we were as a family now.

Denise beamed with pride. "Where's that brown baby girl?" Denise asked, looking around for Mariah. "Today's her day, and I want to make sure she shines. She is going through with it, right?"

"Yes, of course!" I said a bit defensively.

"Good. Those plane tickets were expensive," she said with a throaty laugh.

Denise stopped when she saw something in my eyes. I recalled the days she loomed over me, hands on hips, demanding to know the truth.

"What is it?" Denise asked.

"Neecie, this child—" I stopped.

"It will be fine. Today will be fine. And I believe in my heart, *everything* will be fine, okay?"

Minutes later Aunt Bonnie rolled in, her hefty frame now squeezed into a mobility scooter. It was more than a decade since we'd seen each other. After the deaths of my mother, grandmother, and uncles, she had become the last living link to our past. Painful as it had been, we had a shared history. And I was glad she was here to see how we all survived it.

I watched my aunt heave herself out of the scooter. Now divorced from Uncle Hunt, she leaned on the arm of her boyfriend of the last several years, a blue-collar guy in jeans and a white tank top. His name was Joe. And he was white. I trailed Joe as he maneuvered Bonnie's bulk through the door.

"Bonnie, watch your step here," he said, putting his hand gently on her back.

"Okay, sweetheart," she said, smiling up at him. "Don't forget to grab my bag, now."

Standing on the threshold of the synagogue, I marveled at the scene. Either Bonnie had fallen in love with a white man, or she was pulling off the best con of her life.

I turned back to the parking lot to look for any signs of Jim. He had a habit of backing out of the rare family events we held, at the last minute. Like all of us, I suppose, he was content to just know we were alive and out of trouble. When I moved to Washington, D.C., years ago, I moved only forty-five minutes away from his home in Baltimore. Yet we'd seen each other in person only three times. Todd routinely reminded me I was equally to blame.

I'd called Jim all week, and we'd exchanged texts that morning. "Don't worry," he messaged. "I'll be there." Although I'd grown to understand his need to keep his distance from our family and its history of drama, this time it would be different if he didn't show. I told him I needed him there to help me show Mariah that she was part of something—a family, a faith, and a community—that was bigger than all of us.

Denise came up behind me. "Jim says he's coming?" she asked, arching her eyebrow at me.

I shrugged, but before long I saw Jim duck into the receiving area, first giving the place a good once-over, as if he was making sure of all the exits. Then he spotted us and headed over.

"Didn't I tell you I'd be here?" he said, grinning.

He looked good. The huge muscle he used to carry in high school had long gone soft, and what little hair he still had was gray, but his voice was strong and his eyes clear. I grasped him in a hug. He tensed. This is what we do now, I said to him in my head.

As we gathered in the sanctuary, the afternoon sun began to slide through the skylights. It diffused through massive portions of tentlike fabric suspended from the ceiling. The design was intended to make the congregation feel as if they were wrapped in a traditional prayer shawl. I whispered to Todd that the setting was appropriate. My family certainly needed all the prayers they could get.

The rabbi motioned for Mariah to join him on the altar at the front of the sanctuary. Her medium-dark skin glowed against the pastel blue of her dress. She was nervous, I knew. She'd always hated being in front of strangers. I hoped she looked out to see the people who loved her, looking back. She gave me the smallest of nods. It filled my heart.

The service began to buzz by in a hum of Hebrew chants that were a mystery to me. I always joked to Todd that I was "Chewish"—Christian by birth, Jewish by marriage. Once again I was okay to exist somewhere in the murky middle of an identity. As for the girls, I was glad that I'd allowed Todd to declare their faith, although it was one more difference they would have to live with. I thought about the fact that, in some way, the ceremony represented another adoption. Out of love, Todd's family and this community of people had chosen Mariah to join them in this ancient and beautiful faith. On this day she was telling them as well that she had chosen them.

My Black, Jewish princess—I wondered what Ma would say if she were here today. I turned around to catch Jim's eye. He smirked. We both were thinking the same thing. Then I scanned the crowd for Denise. She nodded meaningfully to me, as if to say, after everything we've been through, after everything you've been through, just look where we are today.

I reached out and squeezed Todd's hand. John had rescued Grandma and her kids all those years ago in a time of crisis. I couldn't help but silently thank God for the man beside me and think of the road my life might have traveled without him. When I looked up, Todd was out of his seat and motioning for me. It was time for us to walk up the stairs to the bimah and take our place beside Mariah to offer her our blessings. The podium rose like a little hill above the entire sanctuary. I stood there for a moment and looked out at everyone gathered. There sat my past—the family I'd been born into. Despite their flaws and failings, they'd protected me, encouraged me and raised me into a man I was. Beside them sat our future—Todd's family and our friends who had taken me in, adopted me in a way, and were helping me become the man I ought to be. Black, white, Christian, Jewish, gay, straight, they sat side by side and accepted me, my husband, and our daughters for who we were. I also imagined Ma in that crowd, and Grandma and John. None of them were perfect, but they had loved me unconditionally and taught me to want more, or at least to make the most of what I had. Mike was in this room and Rick and Todd's brother Lee and his late father. All had difficult childhoods, and because of them I prayed that Mariah's first few years wouldn't define her entire life.

And finally Pops. Had he been alive, he would have swung through the back doors with a guitar in hand, having poached a bottle of Mogen David from the synagogue kitchen. At this moment I tried to not even judge his soul.

The rabbi had told Todd and me this was a moment to offer our blessings to Mariah. I felt like I owed the same to my family. I unfolded the paper in front of me and spoke.

If you think about it, there are not many times in a person's life when their family and friends come together for them, and in the presence of God. When they do, they are either united in grief or in love. I want my daughter to look around because this is one of those moments of love.

The love that is here for her today existed even before she was born. It was born out of grief. The last time my family gathered like this was for our mother's funeral. Her death changed us and changed me. It forced us to think about what kind of family we would be, without her. It also made me confront who I was going to be.

Three months after her death, I met Todd. Three years later, Mariah came into our lives. From that moment, I knew who I was going to be. I was going to be her father, and this was going to be our family.

I'd like to think my mother is here today—watching over me as I watch over you. She never held her. She never rocked her to sleep. She never kissed her. But the love she would have given to my daughter was held in my heart until she was born. Then I gave it to her.

My mother's love and the dreams she had for her family were passed on to me and my brothers and sister. All the people in this room, in one way or another, have been responsible for making sure the love and dreams of all those who have gone before us are given to our children.

Sometimes it may be hard for our children to see the good things that are passed on to them, the gifts they are given by their parents—love, hope, grit, resilience, and dreams of a better life.

But I would tell my daughter that on days like today, you can't miss the most important of these gifts. It's here right in front of your eyes. All in one room, all for you.

Mariah, our gift to you is our love and our belief in a better life for you.

My prayer for you is that your heart will be filled with both love and belief. Filled to overflowing. Just like it is for me, today.

I want you to hold those two things in your heart until it is your time to pass them on.

To your family

To those who are living

Or maybe someone who is dying
To a baby about to be born
Or someone who needs to feel reborn.
Pass them on
One day, to your own child
Let them know
Where that love and faith in the future first came from
And when you do,
Think of us.
Think of all who came before you.
Think of this day.
And remember
That you were loved.

By the end, Todd and I were in tears. I looked out to see Jim squeeze his eyes for a second. Denise arched that eyebrow at me. As we finished the ceremony, she walked up to me. Although I was a grown man, she jerked me by the jacket so she could look me straight in the eye as she did so many years ago.

"Well done, my brother," she said. "Well done."

A few hours later I watched the Bat Mitzvah party from the side of the social hall. Mariah moved effortlessly between my Black family, her Jewish relatives, and our friends, both gay and straight, accepting hugs and making small talk.

As she darted past, I folded her into my arms. I pulled her close, but only for a moment. She gently pulled away, letting me know I could only hold on to her for so long.

CHAPTER 36

All the Dirt

In 2018, a few months after the Bat Mitzvah, I sat at my kitchen table and called Aunt Bonnie. With Grandma, Ma, and all my uncles, as well as cousins near and far, dead and buried, she had become the keeper of our family history. That also made her the custodian of our family secrets. In the back of my mind I already knew what story I wanted her to finally spill out into the open. But first I knew I'd have to listen to her drag the names of family, friends, and foes through the dirt.

"And Stephen, let me tell you, that ole black bitch was something else," she cackled.

I laughed at the name-calling. I knew I shouldn't, but I reminded myself that with Ma gone, Aunt Bonnie had only a few of us left to talk to. When I ran out of responses and was tired of laughing, I grunted, just to let her know I was still there.

Bonnie had angered many people in our family over the years. They remembered the physical fights, the emotional blows, and her taste for what we called stirring up shit. Those things would never be forgiven or forgotten by some of us. But we deferred to my aunt out of, if not quite a respect for her, a respect for her endurance. She'd seen some shit and done some. We held a perverse sense of pride about her because everyone else drank, drugged, ate, or worked themselves to death. Bonnie was a survivor, and for that we had some mad appreciation.

After seeing her at the Bat Mitzvah, I knew I wasn't afraid of her anymore. Aunt Bonnie was too old, too overweight, and too lame to reach out and "snatch your ass" as she used to threaten. I should have felt anger at Bonnie for some of what she had done to my immediate family, let alone hers. I thought she had bullied my mother, humiliated her, and brought her to sobs. But Ma, at some point before she died, made one final trip across their shared side yard to have a talk with Bonnie.

"I want you to promise me that you will get along with my kids after I'm gone," Ma had said.

And Aunt Bonnie did. Since then, she had for the most part lived up to that promise and watched out for us.

Normally Denise had been the one to talk to her most frequently. Denise served as Bonnie's link to news about younger family members, while Bonnie acted as Denise's connection to the past. But it was seeing Bonnie at the Bat Mitzvah that reminded me of our own connection. We were both the youngest in our families. We were the ones who benefited from all the family wisdom that had come before and to whom all the history and secrets were passed. Perhaps that's why I reached out to her, just to talk.

I listened to Aunt Bonnie discussing all the dirt, past and present in our family.

I imagined her propped up on a couch inside her tidy home back on the hill. On a rare trip back there a few years earlier, I'd been astounded to see how her house had changed—perhaps as a reflection of how much she had. There were large vegetable gardens and multiple flower beds that her white partner, Joe, had planted around the property. There was also a new small porch where his children, who are white, and Bonnie's two children and grandkids, who are Black, could visit them. They kept the grass trimmed, paid their taxes, and flew the American flag in the front yard. Even in the middle of this deeply conservative majority-white farm community, I thought, this interracial couple didn't differ so much from their neighbors.

Now when I looked at the time, I realized two hours had gone by. I'd spent the time clucking my tongue and grunting in agreement at Bonnie's observations. I'd laughed at her name-calling and conceded that some members of our family were "no-good, conniving, light-fingered, money-stealing, hoodoo-practicing black bastards and bitches." There was nothing new about it. It was just a continuation of an ongoing conversation in our family: my shit smells better than your shit. It had been nurtured for generations over the phone and over kitchen tables.

With my ear getting numb from the cell phone pressed against it, I started to plot my escape. "Bonnie, I got to get my kids to bed," I told her, instead of what I wanted to say.

We still weren't the type of people to call family out to their faces. It would be easier to phone Denise later and then talk shit about Bonnie. But Bonnie ignored my request to be released from the conversation. I was annoyed, but I understood why. All her real and imagined villains were dead or dying. All she had left was the little land she was standing on and the little bit of dirt she could still dredge up from the past. Bonnie was, as Denise would say, the last Black person standing on that country hill, and all she had right now was my ear.

I lay back on the bed and let Bonnie's words wash over me, let her relive her past. I owed her that. Bonnie then talked about my grandmother and her husband and how they first came north as a young married couple.

"They fought like cats and dogs."

I pictured Grandma, her nostrils flaring when she was furious. Like mother, like daughter, I thought.

"Mama finally threw my father out of the house, because he was carrying on with a white woman, and they had that mixed-race baby, Chuckie."

My eyes flew open and I nearly dropped the phone.

"What?!"

"Oh *yaaas*, and you know it wasn't like it was now, back then. They would have killed you or put you in jail for sleeping with some white woman, let alone having a mixed baby. They hid that child for a few years. Then they put him up for adoption with some family up near Buffalo."

My mind reeled. Why was it so shocking? Because someone in my family had another baby out of wedlock?

Or was it because the baby was mixed race and had to be hidden away? When I pressed her, Bonnie told me that no one knew what became of her half-white and half-Black half brother. A picture once existed of him, at three, before he was adopted out, she said. She told me his "papers"—I'm unsure whether they were a birth certificate or adoption papers—were kept by Grandma in a locked blue suitcase in a closet for years. Bonnie knew because she used to sneak up there to read them. As she relayed all this to me, I thought back to myself digging through my mother's closet, decades ago. Ma always used to say, what goes around comes around. I sat there thinking that God was trying to tell me something in all this synchronicity. What it was, I had no idea.

"And that's why Mama took up with John, to get back at my father."

The facts overwhelmed me until later they fell into place. Grandma's husband cheated with a white woman. They had a mixed-race baby and hid the child away. My grandmother, angered at being betrayed, had her own affair with John. Her husband found out and beat my grandmother with a metal stool in a bus station. For that, he was arrested and thrown in a psychiatric hospital. My grandmother was freed from her husband but left alone to care for five kids until her lover, John, took them into his farmhouse which sat on a country road at the top of a hill.

I wondered silently why it took so long to hear how our family first came to that hill—a place where my grandmother sought safety and yet continued to battle her own inner demons. How might the lives of all her children and grandchildren have been different, had she not? And I thought about this half-Black, half-white child who was sent away from a life of abuse and trauma. Did Chuckie grow up scarred by the secret of his birth, or was he spared all our family pain? Bonnie couldn't answer that.

I waited until all the stories were spun out to ask the one question she might be able to answer. It was one I was scared to ask her my entire life—the identity of my father.

"Stephen, I truly do not know," she said with a sigh.

I jumped in, just to save her feelings and maybe my own. "It's okay. I guessed you probably didn't."

"I honestly don't understand why your mother would leave this Earth and not tell you. Every child deserves to know where they came from."

I tried to tell her it hadn't made a difference before and it wouldn't now. Then Bonnie interrupted.

"Let me tell you what I *do* know," she said in her conspiratorial whisper.

She told me this man would come to our house to meet my mother. It was an insurance salesman who lived in the next town over. Everyone wondered whether something was going on. He stopped visiting around the time Ma got pregnant.

"After that, that man packed up his family, put his house up for sale, and moved out of town." Bonnie gave half a cackle. "And nobody ever heard from that white man again."

Out of everyone in our family, only Bonnie would know if there was more to the story. I realized then that no amount of digging would uncover this family dirt. The answer had gone to the grave with Ma. Now I had to let the question in my heart die as well.

CHAPTER 37

The Truth Won't
Set You Free

For months I stared at the strange shadow on my forehead. For a while I told myself I was imagining something. When it began to change appearance, I made an appointment with the doctor. She peered closely at my hairline.

"I'm sorry, there's not much I can do at this stage."

She pointed the mirror back at me and traced the dark layers of skin noticeably creeping from my scalp to my face.

"It's melasma."

Time, sun, and heredity had caught up to me. The melanin beneath my skin was now shining through in unsightly patches. For a few months I furiously applied skin lightening creams and retinol to my face, hoping to erase it. One day the irony of what I was doing hit me, and I gave up.

Something else did grow inside me around my birthday that I couldn't live with: curiosity. Todd had long suggested I take advantage of the now popular over-the-counter DNA genetic tests, so I could just stop telling people I was "mixed." Even to me, that word sounded something like less than pure, mongrel, mutt. After I shared what Bonnie had told me about the mysterious salesman who was likely my father, Todd pressed me again.

The day I dropped an envelope into a battered postbox a few blocks from my house, I sat in the car and told myself to remember this moment. What came after might define me for the rest of my life. Several weeks later, I received that defining answer, one I'd been seeking since the age of five.

The 23andMe response jumped into my inbox at work. I feigned attention to an ongoing meeting but shifted the phone under the table to click the link and read the results. I shouldn't have been surprised by what was there, but still my heart pounded. Here was the validation of what I'd known all along and what I'd pulled out of the family in bits and pieces over the years. Of course I was not Pops's son, but it showed that I was someone's son, maybe the son of a wandering salesman. There was no doubt that this person who made half of me was white.

Many times throughout my life people have seen something in my features and asked, "What exactly are you?" My only reply was what I knew—mixed race, Black-and-white, a person of color, and sometimes biracial. Now, with confirmation of race and ethnicity, I say the same things. After all, how could I claim to be anyone else? But now I know I am my father's son—though I will never know him. There's a slim possibility that he might still be alive. If he had other children, they are surely out there. For a few months, I kidded myself that the DNA results could lead me to them or other relatives. With time and digging, I thought I might find that metaphorical genetic straw in the haystack. But I realized it wouldn't change anything.

Ma had told me as much about him as her soul or conscience allowed. She was telling the truth. My father was a traveling salesman, as she claimed. He traveled into her life for a moment and then moved on. If she knew any more, she kept it to herself, wanting to protect me from the truth. It's only now that I understand why. There was no other family out there for me. She and my siblings were all the family I had, and all that would matter.

It was around the same time that my younger daughter Rachel began looking for her tribe. Slightly darker than me and lighter than Mariah, she was what my grandmother would have called "red boned." Kids asked if she was Latino, Mediterranean, or even Filipino. The uncertainty about the race of her birth father left her without a complete answer. But when she walked out of her bedroom one morning in seventh grade, I realized she had begun to decide how she wanted to appear to the world. She wore faded jeans with stylish rips up both legs, revealing the light copper skin beneath. A swath of her stomach showed between the top of her pants and a Black Is Beautiful crop top. Large gold hoops hung from her earlobes. I noticed she had teased her loose, kinky curls out into an afro that now fanned around her face.

As she passed me in the hallway, I could hear the strains of Drake coming from her earbuds. He'd recently replaced Taylor Swift as her favorite artist.

"What's that about?" I asked, pointing to the book she'd been clutching like a Bible under her arm for the last several weeks. I read aloud the title: *The Hate U Give*.

For the next several minutes, her head bobbed and her brightly colored nails wagged in my face as she told me the novel's account of a Black girl caught between a white world at school and her Black family at home.

"Wow, what do you think about that?" I asked as I tried to tug her crop top a bit lower.

She swatted my hand away.

"Yo, that's so messed up."

We stood at the front door. Rachel slung her backpack over her shoulder and prepared to catch the bus. I gently put my arm around her shoulder.

"Rachel, I know it must be hard right now. Don't forget, I grew up not knowing who my dad was and not sure who I was either."

My daughter shrugged off my arm and laughed.

"Whatever. Poppy, I'm not confused. I'm know I'm Black."

Though she claimed to be comfortable with her own identity, the question of race seemed to be on her mind as the school year progressed. One night at the dinner table, she stifled a nervous giggle and then cleared her throat.

"Okay. Let me ask you a question. Is it *ever* okay for a white person to use the N-word?"

Mariah jumped in immediately.

"Did someone at school call you a nigger? Who was it?"

"Mariah!" I said sharply.

"What, it's not like Black people can't say it."

Todd peeked around the corner from the kitchen. "We don't say that word in this house, ever."

"Well, you can't. You're white," she shot back. "But I can if I want. Poppy can, and, well, I guess Rachel too."

Todd threw down a kitchen towel in exasperation and headed out onto the porch. Mariah's defense of the use of the N-word wasn't new. For months we'd tried to police songs on their iPhones and YouTube videos of artists who peppered their songs with that word, along with curses and homophobic language. But they were teens now, and we'd grown tired of putting our ears to their bedroom doors or scrolling through their playlists on their phones after they'd gone to bed. No matter what, though, we would hold the line on their using those words in front of us—or anyone else, for that matter.

The bigger issue, it now seemed, was how the kids were defining themselves in relation to others and the rest of the world. We'd been prepared by books, parenting blogs, therapists, and the occasional *New York Times* parenting article about the years-long search for identity that would kick off around age thirteen and last perhaps a decade. We knew the search would be even more emotionally charged for kids who had been adopted and who belonged to interracial families.

It's why, in part, we'd settled in this ethnically diverse and politically progressive community that attracted immigrants from Africa, the Caribbean, and Central America. Here yard signs began to sprout after the 2016 election proclaiming "Hate Has No Home Here" in English and multiple languages. But we'd begun to realize our kids were part of another community that was having an unexpected influence on their identity.

Later, as things cooled off after dinner, I pulled Rachel aside. "Sooo, what's the deal at school?"

"This white kid. He said the N-word. I mean, not once but multiple times. And his friends told us, 'Chill, he was just joking.' But now some of the Black kids said they're going to kick his butt if they hear it again. And then the Latino kids, well—wait, wait, should I say Hispanic or Latino? My teacher says . . ."

I'd become used to my daughter's rat-a-tat tales of middle school drama, and through them I was learning how race was a growing undercurrent. Roughly a third of the kids were white, another third were Black, and Hispanic and Asian kids made up the last third of the pie. In my mind's eye I imagined lunchroom tables filled with a rainbow of kids. As I dug deeper, I learned the tables at lunch looked more like a color spectrum with the room slowly changing shades as you moved from one side to the next. The diversity within the school's population had led to even more fracturing between the children.

"Wait. You're telling me the Ethiopian kids don't sit with the Black kids? Do the Latino kids who are new immigrants break up by country?"

My daughter gave me a patient look and began to give me what she called the "tea" on middle school lunchroom etiquette. There was even a detailed explanation of what tables the kids who proudly identified as gay, bi, trans, and pansexual gravitated to. When all the racial partitions and social segregations were fully explained, I took a deep breath and tried to sound nonchalant.

"And so, where do you sit?"

Rachel giggled nervously again and rolled her eyes. Her answer was clear. The conversation, for now, was over.

For more than two years I had kept my DNA results from my kids. I told myself the DNA profile was not secret or shameful, but it might raise uncomfortable questions for my daughters about their own birth parents, questions we couldn't completely answer. That changed one afternoon as the kids argued in the back seat over a hip-hop star's music.

"Not a fan," I chimed in.

"Are you even sure you're Black, Poppy?" Rachel said with a bit of attitude.

Mariah laughed.

I gritted my teeth and looked over at Todd, who shook his head. A few minutes later, I remembered the DNA test. Years before, my mother had hidden away my birth certificate in a locked box. Now the best answer I might ever have about my identity lay just behind a passcode on a website. I pulled out my iPhone and logged on to the site.

"Take a look at this," I said, and passed the phone into the back seat. The kids immediately began a tug-of-war.

"What is it? Stop hogging it. Let me see."

Todd rolled his eyes at me. "Couldn't this have waited until we got home?"

"It's fine," I murmured. Then I called over my shoulder, "It's a DNA test."

"Poppy, you're from Ireland?! Oh, look, it says he's from West Africa too."

"My ancestors were."

"Same thing."

"If you say so."

But it wasn't the same thing. The color wheel and percentage composition of my ancestry didn't answer the important question of who I really was. That was something I had to decide for myself after a lifetime of living.

That night I promised Rachel that when she was ready, I'd be willing to let her take her own DNA test and answer the questions swirling in her head. But I know that no matter what she discovers, it won't make a difference to her life until she's ready to look in the mirror and feel comfortable in her own skin.

CHAPTER 38

One Last Time

For a time, Mariah's Bat Mitzvah gave my siblings a sense of hope about our future. In the weeks after, Jim and Denise and I talked and texted more than we had in years. Denise summed up our feelings when she called me in early December.

"Stevie, you know, let's not wait again for something shitty to happen to see one another."

As a test of our renewed bonds, she proposed coming back to visit for Christmas. Todd had already made plans to travel to Florida to spend Hanukkah with his family. We'd previously agreed Rachel would go with him, to spend some one-on-one time with her grandma after ceding all the attention to Mariah at the Bat Mitzvah. That would leave me and Mariah at home, alone, with our own chance to bond.

Denise was now excited to join us. A few days after we spoke, Jim heard of our plans and, to my surprise, proposed that we visit him in Baltimore. His adult daughter planned to host a holiday party for her work friends, and now Jim wanted us to be present. Being the oldest, Jim didn't leave us much choice. We said yes.

Later that December, Mariah and I stood outside the security gate at Reagan International Airport searching the crowd for Denise. It didn't take long for us to spot the head of carefully weaved-in hair bobbing toward us. As she got closer, I braced myself to hear Denise's burning question, which had become familiar to me during our phone conversations for several weeks. She hugged, then kissed me, leaving the heavy scent of her perfume and airplane rum on my cheek.

"Are we sure we want to do this?" she said, out of breath. She wiped the sweat pouring from her forehead and sat down outside the gate to catch her breath.

"I told you, it'll be fine, it's a Christmas party. I mean, we survived the Bat Mitzvah, right?"

Denise harrumphed. "I'm just *saying*. I haven't seen Jim's daughter since she was a baby. She's a grown woman herself. Does *she* know what's she's in for? It's one thing to bring us all together out in public, in a church or a synagogue. We got to put on our best behavior. But to bring us jokers together in private? Just let someone have one too many and say something stupid. She doesn't want to see the real Majors showing their ass, now does she?"

Denise let out her full throaty laugh, then began coughing, like Ma used to.

Mariah giggled as Denise wrapped her arms around her tightly. How different things might be, I thought, had Denise been around for more of her childhood. But then I realized, all that mattered was that she was here now, for the both of us.

That December I had no idea how little time we would have left together. Denise had always delighted in describing herself as someone who "ate, smoked, drank, and cussed" like a sailor. From the time she was in high school, Denise was the life of any party. Unlike Pops and even her brothers, Denise was never a sloppy drinker. In fact, most of her drinking was done in private and alone. I'd become so accustomed to the heavily sweet scent of her favorite rum-and-Cokes that it was hard to distinguish the telltale signs of her alcohol consumption from the baby powder, perfume, Listerine, and breath mints she used to cloak herself in.

"I'm sorry, I make no apologies for the fact that I like to drink," Denise often said to her kids, grandkids, and me. "Now, if you find me in a gutter somewhere, someday, that's a different story. Well, let's just say if you can only save one brown woman that day, please let it be me!"

We'd laugh along with Neecie because how could you argue with someone so self-aware, self-confident, and self-deprecating? Besides, she'd been the large-and-in-charge presence in our family's life. It was hard to get a word in edgewise, let alone argue with her.

That was the case two months after her Christmas visit when she called.

"Stevie, it's me, Denise," she announced over the phone. "These jokers say I'm dying."

I remember walking out onto the tiny front porch of the house, once again to process something that seemed so out of my control. It was just eighteen months since Mike called. Now Denise. Her diagnosis was stage 3 COPD—chronic obstructive pulmonary disease—the disorder marked by progressive and irreversible restriction of airflow to the lungs. Though the smoking was causing it, doctors told her the decades of drinking had also taken their toll.

Denise sounded more matter-of-fact than scared as she ticked off contributing factors.

"High blood pressure, heart disease, cholesterol, lung and liver damage," she said. "It was just a matter of time before one of these things fucking got me."

I took a deep breath and opened my mouth to say something comforting. "Jee-zus Christ" is all that came out.

Denise had known something was wrong when she visited us just two months earlier. I'd later learn she'd been in and out of doctors' offices and emergency rooms for more than a year trying to figure out why she was fatigued, hacking, and losing breath and weight. She did her best to hide everything that December, moving around as if she were energized by the thought of bridging the past and present parts of our families. She gave special attention to Mariah. Together they baked cookies, wrapped gifts, cooked meals, and huddled their heads in what Denise called her "sistah to sistah" talks.

Just a few days before the planned holiday party, Denise and I sat on folding chairs inside a nearby nursing home. Mariah was part of a local choir. That holiday season, they'd planned to sing at nursing homes and homeless shelters. I'd long ago told Denise that Mariah had a talent for singing, but this was to be the first time she'd hear her niece perform.

Seeing us in the crowd of parents, Mariah scuffed her sneakers nervously against the tiled floor. Denise leaned over to me.

"What's wrong?" she asked in a stage whisper.

"The hell if I know."

A moment later the choir master's piano struck the opening chords of Mariah Carey's "Hero," and my daughter slowly moved closer to the microphone. My own chest tightened, so I could only imagine what she was feeling. She started to sing, softly.

I'd heard Mariah sing the song repeatedly in her room for weeks, but it wasn't until this moment that the lyrics meant anything. She sang of feeling alone in the world, searching for something, only to discover that the love she sought already existed within herself.

As the song concluded, Denise leaped to her feet, tears streaming down her face. A few songs later, the choir disbanded, and my sister bustled through the parked wheelchairs to find Mariah. As I came up behind her, I heard her hoarse voice.

"You have a gift. Don't you *ever* forget this moment, baby girl. Because I damned sure never will, you got that?"

Mariah melted into Denise's arms, closed her eyes, and nodded.

Months later, I sat next to Todd listening to a trio of gospel singers. Denise had requested them when she called me unexpectedly at work one day.

"I want them to sing at my funeral," she'd wheezed into the phone. "You promise me, okay?"

When I made that promise, I told Denise she was being overly dramatic. The COPD was serious, but the doctors had laid out a course of treatment.

"I may not be dying today, but damn straight I am dying," she said. "I don't want you to worry, because I am not afraid of going, baby brother. I'm only afraid of suffering."

At the time, I'd imagined the day would come when Jim and I

would gather at her bedside as we had with Ma and Rick. Before then, there would be time for me to talk about our fractured family and our long-overdue attempts to make it whole. But that last conversation never came. Instead I received a text from my niece one July afternoon. I read: *Have you heard from my mother today? She's not returning calls.*

A few hours later a New York State Trooper, sent to do a welfare check at her apartment, discovered her lying motionless on her sofa. She'd apparently lain down to rest at some point and died in her sleep. Denise was just a few weeks from celebrating her birthday. She would have been sixty-one.

As the trio brought the final song to a soulful close, I returned to the scene in front of me. The pastor of the church looked at me and nodded. I stood and walked to the front of the sanctuary to deliver the eulogy. Unlike at Mariah's Bat Mitzvah, I willed myself to just think about the living as I spoke. Looking out at the small group of mourners, I saw the two sole survivors of the hill, Jim and Aunt Bonnie. Here now, I knew we could no longer cause each other any pain. Maybe time and distance had healed some of the wounds.

As I scanned the rest of the crowd, I settled on Denise's two children and nearly grown grandkids. Although they'd deeply loved Denise, I knew they'd grown up chafing under her strong personality at times and had struggled to understand her need to use alcohol to chase away her demons. Still, just like Ma, Denise had done her best to launch them all into a better life than she had. Because of her, they had a firm foothold in the middle class.

Nearby sat Rick's son Rickie and Mike's son Mike-Mike. They and their children, along with Denise's brood, ranged in shade from light, bright, "we identify as white" to medium brown. Unlike me, they'd never allowed color to define them. Neither had they felt bound to let their parents solely determine who they grew up to be. Despite the fact my siblings had struggled with their addictions and the trauma of an abusive childhood, their children were striving for better lives.

As I spoke that day, I was reminded that I was born eleven years after

Jim and eleven years before Rickie, my mother's oldest grandchild. I am part of one generation still grappling with the past and part of another that often wants little to do with it.

In her last years, Denise had set out to make sure the sins of the fathers and mothers were not visited upon by their children. Now she was gone. And I felt that perhaps she was leaving that up to me now.

My kids did not attend the funeral. Todd and I decided that we wanted their last memory of their aunt Neecie to be the Bat Mitzvah and the final Christmas celebration. I remember Neecie sitting squeezed next to me and Jim on an expensive sofa in Jim's daughter Sarah's living room. We stared at the Christmas tree.

"That is one pretty tree," Denise said to no one that night.

Mariah wandered by. Jim eyed her plate, then cocked an eyebrow at her.

"There are some greens in there. Why don't you go get some? Put some meat on your bones."

Mariah wrinkled her nose. "I don't eat *greens*," she said. "But my dad makes me eat kale."

Jim's jaw dropped wide open. He arched sideways on the sofa across Denise so he could cuff me lightly on the back of the head.

"Kale? What the—? See, now that's some white people shit," he said conspiratorially to Denise.

Denise shushed him, nodding in the direction of a group of white guests in a nearby corner.

"Damn, Jim. We can't take you anywhere," she concluded. Then we all laughed.

It didn't matter that Jim's own daughter was biracial, as were Denise's kids. As I looked at my brother and sister trading good-natured barbs, I realized that only one of us had a child who was Black. That was me.

Maybe that is why, that night, it was important for Mariah to see that she was part of my family again—my unapologetically Black family. She might never see me as her Black parent or even her legitimate father, but I promised myself she would grow up at least knowing this: a family isn't something that is ever guaranteed or promised in life. It took a lifetime for me to accept my imperfect family, and I hoped my daughter would do the same. And there was one more thing I wanted her to see—the people in your family may serve as a mirror or modifier in your life, and if you're lucky, they might be a bit of both, like Denise was to me.

Well after I'd grown too old for her to tie my shoes or comb my hair, Denise still made sure I went somewhere in my life, if not by dragging me along, then by gently shoving me in the right direction. College, career, love, parenting—she had strong opinions and shared them whether I liked it or not. And when I had kids, she did the same type of nudging for them and for all the kids in the next generation. The poverty and trauma Denise and I had grown up in had indelibly left a mark on us and the rest of our siblings, but she didn't believe it should define us as a family or determine our future.

Labels, she thought, were important, especially the ones we place on ourselves. It took me a long time to understand why. Now I wonder, was I really raised dirt poor or just working class? Am I a bastard or just another child raised by a single mom? Today, am I Black, am I white, or am I just me?

My kids will have to answer those questions one day—deciding if they will forever be defined by what they lost in life, their birth family, or what they gained when we adopted them. Because in the end, none of us can choose the families we're born into, let alone the world we live in. All we can do is decide where we fit in.

Acknowledgments

This book, and any of my successes in life, would not have been possible without the love and support of my late mother and sister. I know they are looking down on me, as are my deceased brothers and extended family members who all helped shaped me in positive ways.

I recognize that my descriptions of their attitudes, or recollections of unsettling things they said or disturbing ways they sometimes behaved, might seem unkind. But I recounted them because they are true to the very best of my memory. And those memories do not diminish the love, affection, or at least the level of compassion I have for them. It should also be noted that these stories may in no way be construed as indicative of the experience of any Black or multiracial family other than mine.

I also want to acknowledge those of my family who are still living. I have changed some of their names in this memoir to protect their privacy. They have paid enough for the sins of the past. I believe that through their strength of character, they have helped make my entire family better people.

For those who wonder about our collective identity today, they should know my extended family is on a broader color spectrum—equally a family of light, bright, high yellows and tan to dark-skinned people. But for now, our racial identity remains rigid. Ask us, no matter our skin tone, and we will say we are proudly a Black family. In years to come, if you ask our grandchildren, who may be the offspring of a biracial or white parent, they may answer differently from one another. But we will still be family.

And then there is my family by marriage. Not only have they treated me as a surrogate son and brother, they also have raised a nice Jewish boy who, every day, enriches my life and the lives of our children.

Todd has helped me make peace with my imperfect past and my far from perfect present. He has helped me reconnect with my family and let go of any regrets for the times I let go of them and forgot where I came from. In doing so, I've discovered a way forward not only in the Black world or the white world, but somewhere in the middle. I am forever grateful to him for his unconditional love, his incredible patience, and his deep support of my writing.

I also need to acknowledge the wider "family" of people who, over the years, have nurtured my love of writing. These include my third-grade teacher, Ms. Horgan, and my seventh-grade teacher, Mrs. Lemon. It might have taken me a lifetime to finally become an author, but it wouldn't have happened without their support early in my life.

More recently, I'm grateful for early champions of this project like Debbie Holinstat and beta readers and editors including David Tabatsky, Ali Lawrence, Jim Parry, and Dale Erquiaga. My deep thanks to my agent, Gina Panettieri, and her team at Talcott Notch Literary, and to Bethany Snead and the staff of the University of Georgia Press for bringing this book to life.

Finally, and most importantly, I need to offer thanks to my children, for whom I am still trying to become the best human being possible. This family history, although sometimes difficult to read, is ultimately for them. I wish there were things I could erase from it, including any trauma they might have experienced as a result of my dealing with my own. I will never know what my daughters' lives would have been like elsewhere, with their own birth family or with another adoptive family. One day, I suppose, they can make that judgment. All I can promise them is this truth.

Despite the pain we have been through, I hope they will know they have been loved all along, through good times and bad. I hope that within this book they see the fractures that run beneath my family tree—and appreciate how the tree has splintered, flexed, and yet still grown to where it stands today. They have been grafted onto this tree and are now inextricably a part of it. For this, I'd like to believe we are all stronger.

Crux, the Georgia Series in Literary Nonfiction